The Maratha Senapatis

The Maratha Senapatis

Nidhi Srivastava

AGAM KALA PRAKASHAN
DELHI

First Published 2011

ISBN : 978-81-7320-117-2

Published by
Dr. Agam Prasad, M.A., Ph.D., Diploma in Museology
For **Agam Kala Prakashan**
34, Central Market, Ashok Vihar, Delhi-110 052.
Ph. : 27212195, 65688806-7
E-mail : agambooks@gmail.com, agambook@yahoo.com
Website : www.agamkala.com

Composed by
Elegant Printographics
319, IIIrd Floor, R. G. Complex,
Sector-14, Rohini, Delhi-110085

Printed at
Chawla Offset Printers
Delhi-110052.

Printed in India

To the cherished memory of

my mother,

Shrimati Santoshini Srivastava

Contents

Preface

The Marathas, an almost unknown political entity in the first half of the seventeenth century AD, suddenly rose to prominence under their great leader, Shivaji, around the middle of that century, and by the second decade of the eighteenth century, the Mughal emperor had granted them the right to realize *chauth* and *sardeshmukhi* of the six provinces of southern India, thus recognizing their *de facto* supremacy in the Deccan. Soon, the Maratha armies were active 'from Lahore to Murshidabad, from Delhi to Seringapatam'. But within less than two centuries of its establishment, the Maratha empire fell after offering a brief resistance of just fifteen weeks.

In its infancy, the Maratha state was a monarchy, governed by an enlightened aristocracy. Shivaji knew of the evils of the 'feudal structure'. The term, 'feudal structure' usually refers to the mediaeval European form of government based on the relation between the vassal and his superior, wherein the former was awarded holding of lands on condition of homage and service. In the context of the Marathas, the term has been used in the sense of the granting of land (*jaghir*) to high officials in *lieu* of salaries, and hereditary appointments to such posts. Shivaji tried his best to keep the Maratha state free of the evils of this 'feudal structure'. He was not in favour of granting land to his high officials in *lieu* of salary; also, he did not favour hereditary appointments. He believed that this was not compatible with the ideas of a strong monarchy that he envisaged. It has often been suggested that one of the main causes for the downfall of the Marathas was the reversion to the 'feudal structure' by the successors of Shivaji.

There are a number of books, written and published on the political history of the Marathas, while scholars like M G Ranade, J N Sarkar, G S Sardesai, S S Deo, D B Parasnis, V K Rajwade, and S N Sen have worked on the administrative system of the Marathas. The Select Bibliography appended to this monograph, at the end, will give an idea of the amount of work done on the subject. However, the works on the political history of the Marathas do not deal in any detail with the rôle of the *senapati* in Maratha polity, and the works on the administrative history of the Marathas do not deal in any detail with the rôle of the *senapati* in Maratha political history. Hence the present study, which has three main objectives :

1. To deal in some detail with the rôle of the *senapati* in Maratha history;
2. To see whether he had any rôle to play in Maratha polity—the army, *sena*, is one of the elements of the state, and the term 'polity', as used in this monograph, includes not only civil administration, but all the elements of the state; and
3. To examine the validity of the theory that the reversion to 'feudal structure' in the time of the successors of Shivaji led to the decline and fall of the Maratha empire, in the light of the decline in the status of the *senapati* in the post-Shivaji period, after lands came to be allotted to *senapatis* in *lieu* of salary, and the office became sort of hereditary.

The work is divided into five chapters. Chapter I is introductory in nature; after discussing the available sources, I have attempted a brief survey of the political history of the Deccan prior to the rise of the Marathas under Shivaji. In Chapters II, III, and IV, I have given an account of the activities of the Maratha *senapatis* under Shivaji, under Shambhuji and Rajaram, and under the successors of Rajaram, respectively. In order to appreciate the doings of the various Maratha commanders-in-chief, a brief but continuous narrative of the events in the history of the Marathas under these rulers, has been deemed desirable : those events, in which the commander-in-chief of the time played a prominent rôle, have been dealt with in some detail. The conclusions drawn from the study have been summarized in Chapter V.

Among the Maratha *senapatis*, Tukoji Chor Maratha, Mankoji Dahatonde, Netaji Palkar, Prataprao Gujar, and Hambirrao Mohite served under Shivaji. Hambirrao Mohite continued to serve under Shivaji's son and successor, Shambhuji, till the time of his death in December 1687. Khandoji (or Mahadaji) Nayak Pansambal, Santaji Ghorpade, and Dhanaji Jadhav served under Rajaram. Dhanaji Jadhav continued to serve under Shahu, and was followed by his son, Chandrasen Jadhav. When the latter went over to Nizam-ul-mulk, the position was given to Santaji Jadhav, Man Singh More, and Khanderao Dabhade, one after the other, in that order. The next *senapti* of Shahu was Trimbakrao Dabhade, who was defeated and killed by Bajirao at Dabhai in April 1731. Yashvantrao Dabhade was appointed to the post of *senapati*, and, after him, his son, Trimbakrao II Dabhade, succeeded him to that post; but, for all practical purposes, the duties of that office came to be discharged by the *peshva* himself. On 15 December 1749, Shahuji had to recognize the *peshva* as the head of all civil and military administration, and this marked the end of the significance of the rôle of the *senapati* in Maratha history and polity.

It is my pleasant duty to put on record my sincere, heartfelt thanks to all those, who have helped me in the preparation of this monograph, in one way or the other. First of all, I am forever beholden to my teacher, Professor P K Ghosh, Department of Mediaeval and Modern Indian History, University of Lucknow, and to Professor K K Thaplyal, formerly Head of the Department of Ancient Indian History and Archaeology, and Dean, Faculty of Arts, University of Lucknow, for being a constant source of inspiration, for always being there with a kind word of encouragement.

Professor Rashmi Pandey, Head of the Department of Mediaeval and Modern Indian History, University of Lucknow, took a keen interest in the progress of this work, and extended full cooperation of the Department. I take this opportunity to express my thanks to her.

For providing facilities of study, I thank the librarians and staff of the Tagore Library, University of Lucknow, Lucknow; UP State Archives, Lucknow; the State Museum, Lucknow; National Archives, New Delhi; and the Indian Institute of Research in Numismatic Studies, Anjneri, Nashik.

I gratefully acknowledge the financial support extended for the undertaking of this work by the Indian Council of Historical Research, New Delhi, in the form of a Post-doctoral Fellowship (2009-2011).

In the end, a big thankyou to my parents-in-law, Shrimati Pushplata Srivastava and Shri Priyonath Srivastava; my father, Shri Inder Prakash Srivastava; my husband, Dr Prashant Srivastava, Associate Professor of Ancient Indian History and Archaeology, University of Lucknow; and my daughters, Pratichi and Purvi, for being so accommodating; and to my sister, Ruchi, and her husband, Captain Piyush, for providing moral support.

19 April 2011. **Nidhi Srivastava**

Chapter I

Introduction

The Sources

Ample of source material is available for the Peshva period (1707-1802) of Maratha history. But there is a relative paucity of material for the period of Shivaji and his descendants (1660-1707).[1] Two main reasons have been suggested for this dearth :

1. Shivaji and his descendants/successors were so busy in the struggle against the Mughals that they had neither the time nor the resources to get historical records prepared; and
2. Around 1700, the Maratha capital and fort was occupied by the Mughals, and they destroyed the records preserved there.

Most of the work done on Maratha history is based primarily on the original sources available in Marathi, Sanskrit, Persian, English, French, Portuguese, and Dutch.

Marathi Sources

For the Marathi sources, B K Rajwade's *Marathyanchya Itihasachi Sadhane*, published in 22 volumes, is significant. But in this work, much attention has not been paid to chronology.

---

1 For details of the original sources available, see the Select Bibliography, below.

Some light on the history between the period 1618 to 1697 is shed by the *Jedhe Shakavali*. This was obtained by B G Tilak from the Jedhe *deshmukhs* of Kari near Bhor, whose ancestors sometimes sided with the Marathas and sometimes with the Mughals. Its edited version was published by D V Apte in *Shiva-charitra-pradipa*. Nine *bakhar* works give some information about the career of Shivaji. Of these, the most important is the *Sabhasad-bakhar* prepared by Krishnaji Ananta Sabhasad, an officer of the time of Rajaram. Chronology has not been adhered to in this text also. In the *bakhar* prepared by Malhar Ramrao Chitnis in 1810-1811, on the orders of Shahu the Younger (Aba Saheb), the sources have been ignored. *Shiva-digvijaya* is larger than these two *bakhars* in size. This is an anonymous work. According to J N Sarkar, it is based on that *bakhar*, which is not available in its original, but which is available in its Persian translation, *Tarikh-i-Shivaji*. Surendra Nath Sen has published parts of these three *bakhars* in their English translation in 1920. Another important work is the *Rajaram-charitam*, in Sanskrit. It was published by B S Bendre from Poona in 1931. G S Sardesai's work, *Rajaram*, is based on it.

Persian Sources

Among the Persian sources, *Ma'asir-i-Alamgiri*, *Akhbarat-i-Darbar-i-Maula*, and *Muntakhab-ul-Lubab-i-Muhammad Shahi* occupy a very important place. The first, *Ma'asir-i-Alamgiri* by Saqi Musta'ad Khan, gives the authoritative history of Aurangzeb between 1658 and 1707. Its author was the *munshi* of Inayat-ullah Khan, the *wazir* of Bahadur Shah, and this work was completed in 1710. It has been written like a modern gazetteer, and all important facts find a place in it. It gives ample of information about the southern campaigns of Aurangzeb. It has been translated into English by J N Sarkar in 1871 from the Asiatic Society of Bengal, and has been reprinted since then.

The *Akhbarat* give an account of the private and public acts and utterances of the Mughal emperor. It was written every day, and sometimes even twice a day. They are preserved in the library of the Royal Asiatic Society. Around 4000 *Akhbarat* are also available in the Rajasthan State Archives, Bikaner. But they are so far unpublished, and have been utilized on the basis of secondary sources.

The *Muntakhab-ul-Lubab-i-Muhammad Shahi* by Muhammad Hashim Khan (better known as Khafi Khan), gives the history of the Mughals from 1519 to the 14th year of the reign of Muhammad Shah. Khafi Khan served under Aurangzeb on several political and military posts. He has given a detailed account of the events of the reign of that Mughal emperor, including some facts which have been suppressed in the official versions. It was published in 1874 by the Asiatic Society of Bengal. Translations of some important excerpts related to the reign of Aurangzeb are also available in Elliot and Dowson's *History of India, as told by its Own Historians*, volume VII. Sarkar regards this work as very significant for the study of Aurangzeb's activities in the south.

Nuskha-i-Dilkasha of Bhimasena Burhanpuri gives an eye witness account of the Mughal activities in southern India. But the truly important and reliable account in this work begins from 1700. Its English translation by J N Sarkar was published in 1972 by the Government of Maharashtra.

For a political background, *Shiva-charitra-pradipa*, and *Shiva-charitra-sahitya* (13 volumes) in Marathi, and *Shiva-bharata* in Sanskrit, *Basatin-us-Salatin* of Muhammad Ibrahim Zubairi, *Tarikh-i-Firishta* of Muhammad Qasim Hindu Shah Firishta, *Tazkirat-i-Muluk* of Rafi-ud-Din Ibrahim Shirazi, *Muhammad-namah* of Muhammad Zahur, *Tarikh-i-Shivaji*, *Tarikh-i-Sultan Muhammad Qutbshah*, etc in Persian, deserve mention.

European Sources

It shall not be appropriate to give much credence to the political elements given in the accounts of European travellers. According to J N Sarkar, except for the events in which these European travellers themselves participated or witnessed, all their accounts are mainly based on the romours floating in the markets, and say so of the commoners. But the *English Factory Records* are quite reliable. Their originals are preserved in the India Office Library, but the records pertaining to the period 1659 to 1682 were published by B G Paranjpe as *English Records on Shivaji* in two volumes. The *Bombay Factory Records* are based on hearsay, but at Rajapur and Karwar, the English had employed agents to collect intelligence about the activities of the Marathas. The factual accounts given in the three *Factory Records* can be easily determined. Among the English sources, the *Madras Diary*, too, is helpful. The *Storia do Mogor* of Manucci has been edited and translated into four volumes by William Irvine. The *Memoires* of François Martin, an important source, has been translated into English by J N Sarkar in 1955, in his work, *The House of Shivaji*.

Evaluation of the Sources

It has been a common tendency among modern historians to doubt the authenticity of the original Marathi sources, especially the *bakhars* and the *Jedhe Shakavali*, and to largely ignore them as a source of Maratha history. Thus, these sources occupy the same position in Maratha history, as that occupied by the puranas as a source of ancient Indian history till some time back. But, just as the puranas have now been gradually recognized as a reliable source of ancient Indian history, these Marathi sources, too, are being studied with an open (and alert) mind to reconstruct the history of the Marathas. It is remarkable that renowned historians like J N Sarkar, have accepted the significance of the Marathi sources like the *Sabhasad-bakhar* as a source of Maratha history. The authenticity of the information supplied by the *Shiva-bharata* is vouched for by the fact that, while giving an account of the Battle of Bhatavadi, it mentions the names of 20 Muslim generals, and most of them are also mentioned in this context in a Persian work by Fazuni Astarabadi.[2]

The accounts given in the Persian, especially Mughal, sources, may be one sided : in these works, it is very common to praise the valour of the Mughals and look down upon the Marathas as cowardly and crooked. But the date and chronological sequence of events given in these works is quite reliable. This may be asserted in particular about the *Akhbarat*.

---

2 G S Sardesai, *New History of the Marathas*, I, p. 61, n. 10.

The European sources, too, are quite reliable, and generally free from bias, especially about those events in which the European powers were not directly involved.

In the present work, an attempt has been made to study all these sources factually, and present a new interpretation, as far as possible, so as to evaluate, in a balanced manner, the rôle of the *senapti* in Maratha history and polity.

Political Background

Before coming to the rôle of the *senapati* in Maratha history and polity, it would be worthwhile to cast a bird's eye view on the political background of southern India, so that the history of the Marathas may be placed in its true perspective, as the early history of the Bhonsles, before the advent of Shivaji, is entwined with the history of the Bahmani sultanate and its five successor sultanates, as also that of the Vijayanagara empire. Muslims entered the south with the southern campaigns of Alauddin Khilji against the Yadavas of Devagiri, in 1294. About a century earlier, these invaders had occupied almost the whole of northern India. The southern campaigns of Alauddin Khilji and his general, Malik Kafur, show that these invaders were not to be satisfied till they had conquered the southern India as well. The rulers of Devagiri tried to stem the tide, but proved unsuccessful. The Kakatiya kingdom of Warangal fell to Malik Kafur in 1309, and the Hoyasala kingdom of Dvarasamudra, in 1310. The general pushed further south, and overran the Chola and the Pandya kingdoms. Up to 1347, Maharashtra remained under the dominion of the Delhi *sultans*.

But some time earlier, an important event had occurred in southern India. Muhammad Tughlaq had led an expedition against Kampli on the Tungabhadra in 1327, which proved to be successful, and the *sultan* returned to Delhi with a large amount of booty and a number of prisoners. Among these prisoners were two brothers, Harihara and Bukka, who had served the ruler of Kampli as his ministers.[3] They were converted to Islam, and when, between 1330 and 1331, Kapayya Nayaka and

3 G S Sardesai, *New History of the Marathas*, I, pp. 33-34.

Somadevaraja raised banners of revolt in Warangal and Kampli, respectively, Muhammad Tughlaq sent these two brothers to quell the rebellion. But Madhava Vidyaranya, the Sankaracharya of the Sringeri Matha, and his two brothers, Sayanna and Bhojanatha, prevailed upon Harihara and Bukka to renounce Islam, enter the Hindu fold once again, and give up the cause of the Tughlaq *sultan*. The two brothers, Harihara and Bukka were crowned kings on 18 April 1336, and, thus, a new Hindu empire was founded—the Vijayanagara empire.[4] There is a view that this experiment of the Vijayanagara empire 'served as a source of power and inspiration to the genius of Shivaji', and led to the establishment of Maratha power in India.[5]

In 1347, the Bahmani sultanate was established by Hussain Zafar Khan, a trusted commandant of Muhammad Tughlaq, who had been dispatched by the *sultan* to suppress the rebellion in southern India, but who himself joined the rebels, and declared himself independent at Gulbarga.[6] The Bahmani *sultans* ruled over Maharashtra for about 150 years. However, owing to the weakness of the central authority, the provincial governors started acting like almost independent rulers within their provinces, and one after the other, five autonomous states came into existence—Ahmadnagar, Bijapur, Berar, Golkunda, and Bidar. This process of the disintegration of the Bahmani sultanate was initiated by Malik Ahmad Nizam-ul-Mulk, the governor of Junnar, who refused to obey the order of Qasim Barid, the prime minister of *Sultan* Mahmud Shah Bahmani (1482-1518), and established himself as an independent ruler at Ahmadnagar in 1490. The same year, Yusuf Adilshah, the governor of Bijapur, and Fath-ullah Imad-ul-Mulk, the governor of Berar, following in the footsteps of Nizam-ul-Mulk, declared themselves independent. In 1518, on the death of Mahmud Shah, Sultan Qutb-ul-Mulk, the governor of Telangana, also declared independence. Qasim Barid died in 1504. His son, Amir Barid, managed the affairs of the declining Bahmani sultanate for some

---

4 G S Sardesai, *New History of the Marathas*, I, pp. 34-35. For a brief history of the Vijayanagara empire, see K A Nilakanta Sastri, *A History of South India* (Madras, 1987), pp. 227-312.

5 G S Sardesai, *New History of the Marathas*, I, pp. 35.

6 G S Sardesai, *New History of the Marathas*, I, pp. 31, 36.

time. But in 1528, Qalim-ullah, the last Bahmani *sultan*, fled from Bidar to Bijapur, and from there to Ahmadnagar, where he breathed his last in 1538. Thus, Amir Barid came into possession of those parts of the Bahmani sultanate, which were ruled by the Bahmani *sultans* up to the time of Qalim-ullah. Amir Barid did not assume the title of *shah*, but his son and successor, Ali Barid, started ruling in 1542, after assuming the title of *shah*.

In Berar, the *khutba* was read for the first time in the name of Imad-ul-Mulk, in 1529.[7] In Bijapur, the title of *shah* was first assumed by the fourth ruler, Ibrahim Adilshah I (1553-1557), while in Golkunda, this title was formally assumed by the third ruler, Ibrahim Qutbshah (1550-1580). Although the earlier rulers of these dynasties had not assumed the royal title, in the absence of a Bahmani *sultan*, they were acting like independent rulers in their respective dominions for all practical purposes.

Thus, five independent sultanates came into existence in southern India—the Adilshahi sultanate of Bijapur, the Qutbshahi sultanate of Golkunda, the Nizamshahi sultanate of Ahmadnagar, the Baridshahi sultanate of Bidar, and the Imadshahi sultanate of Berar.[8] Of these, the Imadshahi sultanate of Berar proved to be short lived, and was conquered and annexed by Ahmadnagar in 1574. According to some scholars, Bijapur had conquered and annexed the Baridshahi sultanate of Bidar in 1609, but this date does not appear to be correct. *Ma'asir-i-Rahimi* informs us that in 1616, Bidar had helped Malik Ambar in his struggle against the Mughals.[9] According to *Basatin-us-Salatin*, Bijapur annexed Bidar in 1619,[10] and this date has been accepted by scholars like Hague[11] and J N

---

7 G Yazdani, *Bidar—Its History and Monuments*, p. 13.

8 For a brief history of these five sultanates, see J N Chaudhuri, Muslim Resistance to Mughal Imperialism, II : The Five Sultanates of the Deccan, in R C Majumdar, J N Chaudhuri, and S Chaudhuri (ed), *The Mughal Empire* (The History and Culture of the Indian People, VII), pp. 412ff. The following account of these sultanates is based primarily on it.

9 *Ma'asir-i-Rahimi*, II, 526.

10 *Basatin-us-Salatin*, 272.

11 W Hague, *Historical Landmarks of the Deccan*, pp. 18, 101.

Chaudhuri.[12] Of the remaining three sultanates, Golkunda, Bijapur, and Ahmadnagar, the last two played an important rôle in the history of India to the south of the river Narmada.

Ahmadnagar was situated in the southern Khandesh, to the north of Bijapur. Berar was located to the northeast of Ahmadnagar, and when Berar was occupied by Ahmadnagar, the northeastern boundary of Nizamshahi sultanate of Ahmadnagar touched the southeastern limits of Khandesh. Bidar was located to the east of Bijapur, and southeast of Ahmadnagar; its eastern boundary was almost the same as the western boundary of Golkunda. Thus, Bidar was surrounded by the three powerful sultanates of Bijapur, Ahmadnagar, and Golkunda.

The most important aspect of the history of southern India in this period was the continuous struggle for supremacy in southern India between Ahmadnagar, Bijapur, and Golkunda, once they had together brought about the end of the Vijayanagara empire. This had an adverse effect on the peace and prosperity of southern India. In this struggle, Berar and Bidar also played a rôle, in that they sided with this or the other sultanate at different times. At time, attempts were made to establish peace through matrimonial or friendly alliances, but these attempts did not meet with much success. For the first time in 1564, the *sultans* of Bijapur, Ahmadnagar, Golkunda, and Bidar entered into an alliance against the Vijayanagara empire, and this confederacy fought against the Vijayanagara empire in the battle of Talikota on 22 January 1565.[13] During the time of Malik Ambar, primarily as a result of his efforts, Ahmadnagar, Bijapur, and Golkunda formed a joint front against the Mughals, and were successful to an extent in checking the onslaught of the Mughals in southern India. Below is given a brief history of these sultanates as a backdrop against the Maratha history.

In 1490, Malik Ahmad, the governor of Junnar, declared independence. It is told about him that he was a son of Nizam-ul-

---

12 J N Chaudhuri, Muslim Resistance to Mughal Imperialism, II : The Five Sultanates of the Deccan, Chapter XIV, in R C Majumdar, J N Chaudhuri, and S Chaudhuri (ed), *The Mughul Empire* (The History and Culture of the Indian People, VII), p. 413.

13 P K Ghosh, The Battle of Talikota—1565, in K K Thaplyal and S N Misra (ed), *Select Battles in Indian History*, I, pp. 299-311.

Mulk Bhari, who was originally a brahmin of Vijayanagara. The Bahmani *sultan* imprisoned him, converted him to Islam, and gave him the name of Malik Hasan. He received education with Prince Muhammad. He was able and ambitious, obtained an influential position, and assumed the title of *nizam-ul-mulk*.[14] After his death, this title of *nizam-ul-mulk* was assumed by Malik Ahmad, and on this ground the dynasty came to be known as the Nizamshahi dynasty. He founded a city on the banks of the river Sina, and beautified it with magnificent buildings and gardens. This city was named Ahmadnagar, and became the capital of the Nizamshahi *sultans*. He never took the title of *shah*. Malik Ahmad was succeeded by Burhan Nizamshah I (1509-1553), Hussain Nizamshah I (1553-1565), Murtaza Nizamshah I (1565-1588), Hussain Nizamshah II (1588-1589), Isma'il Nizamshah II (1589-1591), Burhan Nizamshah II (1591-1595), Ibrahim Nizamshah (1595), and, after an interval, Hussain Nizamshah III (1630-1633). Political instability marked the history of Ahmadnagar during the period 1595 to 1630. Taking advantage of the struggle for succession between Chand Sultan, Ikhlas Khan, Abhang Khan, and Mian Manjhu, the Mughals attacked Ahmadnagar. Within one month of the murder of Chand Sultan in July 1600, the Mughals had conquered Ahmadnagar.[15] As a consequence of this victory, the Mughals gained control of the capital, Ahmadnagar, and its neighbouring territories. But on a greater part of the Nizamshahi sultanate, powerful Nizamshahi feudal lords, like Malik Ambar and Raju Dakkhini, continued to exercise sway as almost independent rulers. Malik Ambar was able to keep the Nizamshahi sultanate alive through his efforts. He declared the son of Shah Ali, a scion of the Nizamshahi dynasty, as *sultan* at Parenda, with the title of *Murtaza Shah Nizam-ul-Mulk*. But the actual power was vested in Malik Ambar as the *waqil-us-Saltanat* (regent). He was able to defy the Mughals during the reign of Murtaza Nizamshah II, between 1600 and 1630. In this struggle, the Maratha *jaghirdars* shifted their allegiance from Ahmadnagar to the Mughals. But Shahji

---

14 *Tarikh-i-Firishta*, II, 931.

15 *Akbar-namah* of Sheikh Faizi Sirhindi, see Elliot and Dowson, *History of India, as told by its Own Historians*, VI, p. 144; *Akbar-namah* of Abul Fazl, H Beveridge's translation, p. 1159.

Bhonsle always stood by the side of Malik Ambar.[16] After the death of Malik Ambar, his incapable son, Fath Khan, killed Murtaza II at the instigation of the Mughals, and declared his ten year old son, Hussain Nizamshah III, as the *sultan*. Later on, he somehow invited the wrath of Shahjahan, and had to seek shelter in the fort of Daulatabad, along with Hussain Nizamshah III. He then surrendered to the Mughals, but again succeeded in earning the anger of Shahjahan. The Mughal army besieged the fort of Daulatabad, and, after a siege of four months, captured the fort in 1633. Hussain Nizamshah III was taken captive, and sent as a prisoner to the fort of Gwalior.[17] Thus, the Nizamshahi sultanate of Ahmadnagar came to an end. In 1636, Shahji, with the help of Bijapur, made to attempt to declare a member of the royal Nizamshahi family as the *sultan*, but without success.

The Qutbshahi sultanate of Golkunda was established by Sultan Quli Qutb-ul-Mulk. He was a scion of a Turk family and was born at Hamadan in Iran. He reached India in his youth and took service as a bodyguard of the Bahmani *sultan*, Muhammad Shah III. He was an able person, soon rose to influential position, and was appointed governor of the eastern province of Telangana. He took advantage of the tottering fortunes of the Bahmani sultanate, and asserted his independence on the death of Muhammad Shah in 1518. But he never assumed the royal title of *shah*.[18] Although according to Firishta, he formally asserted his independence in 1512, some modern historians date this event to 1518. It is worth notice that Sultan is not his title, but a part of his name, and the title of *qutb-ul-mulk* was given to him by the Bahmani *sultan*.[19] He was a highly ambitious person, and made a successful bid to bring most of the Telugu regions

---

16 R V Nadkarni, *The Rise and Fall of the Maratha Empire*, p. 28.

17 Abdur Rashid, Shah Jahan, Chapter VII, in R C Majumdar, J N Chaudhuri, and S Chaudhuri (ed), *The Mughul Empire* (The History and Culture of the Indian People, VII), pp. 207-208.

18 Briggs, *Firishta*, III, 323; *Journal of the Hyderabad Archaeological Society*, 1918, p. 89; *Journal of Indian History*, 33, pp. 281-283; N Narayan Rao, Two Muhammadan Patrons of Telugu Literature in the Sixteenth Century, *Proceedings of the Indian History Congress*, 1945, pp. 159-162.

19 Briggs, *Firishta*, III, 321-322, 339-345.

under his sway. In September 1543, when he was 98 years old, his son, Jamshid, had him assassinated.[20]

Jamshid Qutb Khan (1543-1550) proved to be an able ruler. In 1543, he sided with Ahmadnagar against Bijapur. By 1548, he had raised the power and prestige of Golkunda to the extent that both Bijapur and Ahmadnagar vied with each other to gain his support against the other. Besides, he played an important rôle in the release of Ali Barid from the captivity of Ibrahim Adilshah I. On his death, his minor son, Subhan Quli was raised to the throne. But soon, his younger brother, Ibrahim, who had fled to Vijayanagara during his lifetime, returned to Golkunda and occupied the Qutbshahi throne from 1550 to 1580. He was the first Qutbshahi ruler to assume the title of *shah*. He attacked the Vijayanagara empire, and captured a considerable part of it.[21] Golkunda enjoyed peace during his reign, and Telangana became a famous market like Egypt.[22] He patronized Telugu literature, and appointed Hindus to high administrative positions.[23] Ibrahim was succeeded by his son, Muhammad Quli Qutbshah (1580-1612). In 1586, he married his sister, Mallika Jaman, to Ibrahim Adilshah I, and this led to friendly relations between Golkunda and Bijapur. Shah Abbas, the Safavid ruler of Iran, sent his envoy, Agujlu Sultan, to Golkunda.[24] In 1611, the British East India Company founded a factory at Masulipattanam, an important port town of the Qutbshahi sultanate. Muhammad Quli transferred his capital from Golkunda to Haidarabad, where he founded a magnificent city. On his death, he was succeeded by his nephew and son-in-law, Muhammad Qutbshah (1612-1626). He formed an alliance of the south Indian kingdoms against the

---

20 Briggs, *Firishta*, III, 232-324, 377.

21 N Narayan Rao, Two Muhammadan Patrons of Telugu Literature in the Sixteenth Century, *Proceedings of the Indian History Congress*, 1945, pp. 159-162.

22 Briggs, *Firishta*, III, 446.

23 *Islamic Culture*, 1957, pp. 130-131, 246; N Narayan Rao, Two Muhammadan Patrons of Telugu Literature in the Sixteenth Century, *Proceedings of the Indian History Congress*, 1945, pp. 296-298.

24 H K Sherwani, Political and Military Aspects of the Reign of Muhammad Quli Qutbshah, *Journal of Indian History*, April 1962.

Mughals. *Tarikh-i-Muhammad Qutbshah*, the famous work on the history of the *sultan*s of Golkunda, was completed in the fifth year of his reign. When he died, his 12 year old son, Abdullah Qutbshah became the *sultan*. During his long reign of 46 years, his mother, Hayat Bakhsh Begum, and after her, his son-in-law, Sayyid Ahmad, had to look after the administration of the sultanate till February 1667.[25] In 1636, Abdullah accepted the suzerainty of Shahjahan. In 1656, Aurangzeb, as the viceroy of his father in the Deccan, besieged Golkunda, but had to raise the siege due to the efforts of Dara Shikoh and Jahanara. Abdullah died in 1672, and his third son-in-law, Abul Hasan assumed kingship from 1672 to 1687. During most of his reign, he was under the influence of his prime ministers, initially Sayyid Muzaffar, and then Surya Prakash Rao (Madanna). There was political confusion in Golkunda.[26] In 1677, Abul Hasan established friendly relations with Shivaji. He offered military help to Bijapur against the Mughals in 1685. Angered by all these activities of Abul Hasan, Aurangzeb dispatched his son, Shah Alam, to invade Haidarabad in 1685. In this endeavour, he was helped by Mir Muhammad Ibrahim, the general of Golkunda. Haidarabad was occupied by the Mughals.[27] Abul Hasan had to seek shelter in the fort of Golkunda. After some time, there was a truce between Golkunda and the Mughals. But in February 1687, Aurangzeb besieged the fort of Golkunda, where Abul Hasan was residing. After a siege of seven and a half months, he was ultimately able to breach the fort with the help of Sardar Khan, a high officer of Golkunda.[28] Abul Hasan was taken captive to Daulatabad, and Golkunda was annexed to the Mughal empire.

The Adilshahi sultanate of Bijapur was founded by Yusuf Adil Khan. According to Firishta, he was the son of *Sultan* Murad II of Turkey. On ascending the throne, his elder brother ordered the killing of the remaining brothers. Yusuf somehow escaped, and fled to Iran, and was sold as a 17 year old slave to

---

25 J N Sarkar, *History of Aurangzib*, IV, p. 395.
26 J N Sarkar, *History of Aurangzib*, IV, p. 400.
27 *Khafi Khan*, II, p. 306.
28 *Khafi Khan*, II, p. 361.

Mahmud Gavan, a minister in the Bahmani sultanate.[29] His abilities were recognized, and he was appointed the governor of Bijapur. When the central authority in the Bahmani sultanate weakened, he took advantage of the situation, and declared independence in 1490. Due to his religious policy, he had to face the combined onslaught of Malik Ahmad of Ahmadnagar, Mahmud Shah, the Bahmani *sultan*, and Quli Qutb-ul-Mulk, the governor of Telangana.[30] In 1510, the Portuguese governor, Albuquerque occupied Goa, but Yusuf soon conquered it. He died in October 1510, and was succeeded by Isma'il Adilshah (1510-1534) and Mallu Adilshah (1534-1535). Mallu proved to be an incapable ruler, and he was replaced by his younger brother, Ibrahim, who became the first ruler of his dynasty to assume the title of *shah*. He died in 1557, and was succeeded by Ali Adilshah I (1557-1580), Ibrahim Adilshah II (1580-1627), Muhammad Adilshah (1627-1656), and Ali Adilshah II (1656-1672), respectively. Ibrahim Adilshah II had ascended the throne at the age of nine, and during his minority, Chand Sultan, the widow of Ali Adilshah I and daughter of Hussain Nizamshah I, played an important rôle. Ibrahim II had cordial relations with Malik Ambar, and the two together were able to stem the tide of Mughal expansion in the south.[31]

Sikandar Adilshah (1672-1686) was the last Adilshahi ruler of Bijapur. He was a minor, and during his reign, the royal power was exercised by his *wazirs*. J N Sarkar writes that from 1672 to 1686, the history of Bijapur is actually the history of its *wazirs*.[32] The condition of Bijapur declined due to the policies of these *wazirs*, namely Khawas Khan, Bahlol Khan, Mas'ud, and Aka Khusro. The Mughals took advantage of this situation, and started occupying the Bijapuri territories. In May 1684, they captured Mangalvadi and Sangola. The *sultan* of Golkunda and Shambhuji tried to help Bijapur against the Mughals. In April

---

29 Briggs, *Firishta*, III, 4-8.

30 Briggs, *Firishta*, III, pp. 22-29.

31 J N Chaudhuri, Muslim Resistance to Mughal Imperialism, II : The Five Sultanates of the Deccan, Chapter XIV, in R C Majumdar, J N Chaudhuri, and S Chaudhuri (ed), *The Mughul Empire* (The History and Culture of the Indian People, VII), pp. 437ff.

32 J N Sarkar, *History of Aurangzib*, IV, p. 158.

1685, the Mughals laid siege to the fort of Bijapur, but could not gain any success even after a siege of 15 months. In 1586, Aurangzeb himself reached Rasulpur, to the west of the fort, and this disheartened the people of Bijapur. In September 1686, Sikandar Adilshah surrendered before the Mughal emperor.[33] He was taken captive, and assigned an annual pension of one lac of rupees. He breathed his last in April 1700, at the age of 32. Thus, the Mughals established their sway over the sultanate of Bijapur.

The Imadshahi sultanate of Berar was established by Fath-ullah Imad-ul-Mulk. He was originally a Hindu from Karnataka, who had been taken captive by the Bahmani army, and converted to Islam. He was appointed as a bodyguard of Khan Jahan, the governor of Berar. But later on, he himself rose to the position of the governor of this northern province of the Bahmani sultanate. He took advantage of the weakness of the central authority, and declared independence in 1490.[34] On his death in 1504, he was succeeded by his son, Alauddin Imadshah (1504-1530) as the ruler of Berar. His reign saw a protracted struggle between the Imadshahi sultanate of Berar and the Nizamshahi sultanate of Ahmadnagar, in which Berar had ultimately to suffer defeat.[35]

The next ruler was his eldest son, Darya Imadshah (1530-1562), during whose reign there was relative peace and prosperity in the kingdom. When he died in 1562, he was succeeded by his minor son, Burhan Imadshah. His regent, the minister Tufal Khan, confined him to the fort of Narnal, and he himself exercised royal powers. In 1566, Adilshah and Nizamshah launched a combined attack on Berar. But Tufal Khan pleased Adilshah with a cash gift and presentation of 50 elephants. Nizamshah found himself alone, and retreated to Ahmadnagar. But shortly afterwards, Murtaza I invaded Berar, and Tufal Khan fled to the fort of Narnal. Murtaza I occupied the fort in April 1574. Burhan Imadshah and Tufal Khan were taken

---

33 *Ma'asir-i-Alamgiri* (Sarkar's translation), p. 171; Bhimasena, *Dilkasha*, pp. 202-203; *Basatin-us-Salatin*, p. 540.

34 Briggs, *Firishta*, III, pp. 485-486; *Cambridge History of India*, III, p. 398.

35 *Cambridge History of India*, III, pp. 435-436.

to Ahmadnagar, where they breathed their last in captivity. Thus fell the Imadshahi sultanate of Berar.[36]

Mahmud Shah, the Bahmani *sultan*, who ruled from 1482 to 1518, proved to be a worthless ruler. His *wazir*, Qasim Barid, took advantage of this situation, and consolidated his position in the administration of the Bahmani sultanate. He was originally a Turk, who had arrived in the Bahmani sultanate during his childhood, and entered the services of Muhammad Shah III. He gradually rose to the position of a *wazir* through sheer dint of his abilities. When he died in 1504, his son, Amir Barid, succeeded him as *wazir*. Mahmud Shah died in 1518, and four of his successors proved to be mere pawns in the hands of Amir Barid. Of these successors of Muhammad Shah, the last, Kalimullah, tried to assert himself with the help of Babur. But his efforts did not succeed, and he had to take shelter in Bidar in 1528. He died in 1538. When he fled to Bidar, Amir Barid started acting as an independent ruler for all practical purposes, although he never formally declared independence or assumed the title of *shah*.

Amir Barid was a very clever person.[37] He had a conflict with Isma'il Adilshah of Bijapur in 1529-1530, and had to surrender the fort of Bidar to the Adilshah.[38] But when he assisted Isma'il Adilshah in conquering Raichur and Mudgal in 1530, Bidar was returned to him, on the condition that he would hand over Kalyani and Kandahar to Bijapur. He did not fulfill this condition, and had to suffer defeat near Naldurg, at the hands of Isma'il Adilshah. He died suddenly in 1542. His son and successor, Ali Barid, ruled up to 1580. He was the first ruler of Bidar to assume the title of *shah*. In 1564, he, together with the *sultans* of Ahmadnagar, Bijapur and Golkunda, defeated Vijayanagara empire in the battle of Talikota. He was succeeded by his son, Ibrahim Baridshah, and Qasim Baridshah II. As a result of the success in the battle of Talikota, the sultanates of Ahmadnagar, Bijapur, and Golkunda became very powerful, and smaller kingdoms like Bidar started dwindling in size. When Qasim Baridshah II died in 1591, he was succeeded by his minor son, who was removed from the throne by a relation, Amir

---

36 Briggs, *Firishta*, III, pp. 254-255.

37 G Yazdani, *Bidar—Its History and Monuments*, p. 13.

38 Briggs, *Firishta*, III, pp. 57-64.

Barid. This Amir Barid himself became the *sultan* as Amir Baridshah II, and ruled till 1601, when he was himself replaced by Mirza Ali Barid as *sultan*. The next ruler, Amir Baridshah III, who ascended the throne in 1609, was the last Baridshahi *sultan* of Bidar. He fought with Ahmadnagar, Bijapur, and Golkunda, against the Mughals, up to 1616. In 1619, Ibrahim Adilshah II conquered Bidar, and annexed it to the Adilshahi sultanate of Bijapur. Amir Baridshah III was brought to Bijapur, where he was kept 'under observation'.[39]

Thus, the rule of the Imadshahi sultanate of Berar came to an end in 1574, that of the Baridshahi sultanate of Bidar in 1619, of the Nizamshahi sultanate of Ahmadnagar in 1633, of the Adilshahi sultanate of Bijapur in 1686, and of the Qutbshahi sultanate of Golkunda in 1687. But a new power had risen in Maharashtra; Aurangzeb was destined to struggle with this power constantly, and still remained unsuccessful in his Deccan campaigns.[40]

The Deccan, particularly Maharashtra, remained a centre of Hindu culture, right from the time of the Sātavāhanas, till the decline of the Yādavas of Devagiri in 1311. But there was decline in this culture during the period of the Bahmani sultanate, and its five successor sultanates. In the sixteenth century, it saw an upsurge in the Vijayanagara empire. Vijayanagara had to suffer defeat in the battle of Talikota, but Venkata II, who ruled between 1584 and 1614, was able to reassert the power of Vijayanagara. However, by 1650, the power of the rulers of Vijayanagara had weakened. The Hindu resistance to Islamic imperialism had become directionless in the absence of a leader of national stature. This vacuum was sought to be filled in the middle of the seventeenth century by Shivaji, the son of Shahji Bhonsle and his Jadhav wife, Jijabai, and a follower of the famous Saint Ramdas.[41]

---

39 *Basatin-us-Salatin*, pp. 272-273; G Yazdani, *Bidar—Its History and Monuments*, p. 14.

40 J N Sarkar, *Studies in Mughal India*, pp. 50-51.

41 J C Grant Duff, *History of the Mahrattas*, I, pp. 69-72.

A number of Maratha families were employed in the service of one of the three Muslim sultanates of southern India.[42] For instances, the Ghorpades of Mudhol served under the Adilshahi sultanate of Bijapur. The Mores, to the west of Satara, were in the employ of the same sultanate. The powerful Jadhavs of Sindhkhed, near Daulatabad, were in the service of the Nizamshahi sultanate of Ahmadnagar. These Jadhavs are believed to be descendants of the Yadavas of Devagiri.[43] The Bhonsle family, to which Shivaji belonged, was in the service of these Jadhavs, and, thus, indirectly served the Nizamshahi sultanate of Ahmadnagar.

The Bhonsles claim descent from Poros, the famous ruler of northwestern India, who opposed Alexander and impressed him due to his bravery, and from the Sisodia Ranas of Udaipur.[44] According to a tradition, supported by copies of some Persian *firmans* in the possession of the Mudhol royal family, when Alauddin Khilji captured Chittor in 1303, Sajjan Singh or Sujan Singh, a scion of the ruling family of Udaipur, went to the south in search of employment. His fifth descendant was one Ugrasena, who had two sons, Karna Singh and Shubha Krishna. Karna Singh's son, Bhima Singh, entered the service of the Bahmani *sultan*, and received the *jaghir* of 84 villages at Mudhol. Shubha Krishna's descendants became known as Bhonsles.[45]

The origin of the name Bhonsle is obscure. There is a suggestion that it might be a corruption of the dynastic name, Hoyasala, the ruling family of Dvarasamudra, though doubts have been expressed about it.[46] The name Bhonsle has also been

---

42 J C Grant Duff, *History of the Mahrattas*, I, pp. 65ff.

43 J C Grant Duff, *History of the Mahrattas*, I, pp. 68-69.

44 See David Kincaied, *Shivaji, the Founder of the Maratha Empire*, p. 25; G S Sardesai, *New History of the Marathas*, I, pp. 51-52.

45 G S Sardesai, *New History of the Marathas*, I, p. 52; however, writers, like Orme and David Kincaied, have expressed doubt regarding the authenticity of this tradition. See David Kincaied, *Shivaji, the Founder of the Maratha Empire*, p. 25.

46 G S Sardesai, *New History of the Marathas*, I, p. 52, n. 2.

traced to Bhosavat in Udaipur, a fief to which Sajjan Singh or Sujan Singh belonged.[47]

Shubha Krishna's grandson, Babaji Bhonsle, lived in the latter half of the sixteenth century. He had two sons, Maloji and Vithoji, both the brothers devoted to each other. Maloji married Dipabai, the sister of Jagpal Rao Nayak Nimbalkar, the *deshmukh* of Phaltan and a prominent courtier in the Nizamshahi sultanate,[48] and this matrimonial alliance enhanced the prestige of the Bhonsle family. The Bhonsles had purchased the position of *patil* (headman) of Verul (modern Ellora) and some other villages in the vicinity of Daulatabad, and rendered military service to Ahmadnagar. Maloji entered the service of Lukhji Jadhav, who had a large *jaghir* from the Nizamshahi *sultan* for the maintenance of 10,000 horsemen under the sultanate of Ahmadnagar.[49] He then became a *shiladar* in the service of Murtaza Nizamshah in 1577, due to the influence of Lukhji Jadhav over the *sultan* of Ahmadnagar, and soon made a mark for himself.[50] Lukhji Jadhav's casual remark, on the occasion of *holi*, that Maloji's son, Shahji, and his own daughter, Jijabai, made a striking couple, ultimately led, not only to the marriage of the two in 1605, but also to Maloji prevailing upon the Nizamshahi *sultan* to grant him a small *jaghir*, comprising the regions of Poona and Supa.[51] Jijabai gave birth to six sons, of whom only Shambhuji and Shivaji survived.[52] Shivaji was born on 6 April 1627,[53] in the fort of Shivner near Junnar, to which

---

47 David Kincaied, *Shivaji, the Founder of the Maratha Empire*, p. 25.

48 David Kincaied, *Shivaji, the Founder of the Maratha Empire*, p. 27.

49 J C Grant Duff, *History of the Mahrattas*, I, pp. 68-69; G S Sardesai, *New History of the Marathas*, I, p. 53.

50 G S Sardesai, *New History of the Marathas*, I, pp. 52-53.

51 G S Sardesai, *New History of the Marathas*, I, pp. 58-59; see David Kincaied, *Shivaji, the Founder of the Maratha Empire*, p. 28-30.

52 Paramananda Kavindra, *Shiva-bharata*, 8-23.

53 This is the generally accepted date for Shivaji's birth. See G S Sardesai, Shivaji, Chapter IX, in R C Majumdar, J N Chaudhuri, and S Chaudhuri (ed), *The Mughul Empire* (The History and Culture of the Indian People, VII), p. 248. For other dates,

Jijabai had retired after a battle between her husband and her father.[54]

The Bhonsles played a prominent rôle in the struggle of the Nizamshahi sultanate against the Mughals between 1608 and 1636. But Lukhji Jadhav switched over his allegiance to the Mughals, and this provided the Bhonsles with an opportunity to show their loyalty to Malik Ambar. However, it had an adverse effect on the marriage of Shahji and Jijabai—Shahji starting neglecting her,[55] and married a second wife, Tukabai, from the Mohite family of Supa.[56]

On the death of Maloji Bhonsle, Shahji succeeded to his position and *jaghir*, his younger brother, Sharifji, proving a loyal *confidante*. Shahji played a significant rôle in the subsequent history of the Deccan, and is noted especially for his defense of the Nizamshahi sultanate from Mughal designs.

Shahjahan left for northern India in 1622, and for a period of over five years, was engaged in a bitter struggle for succession. This provided Malik Ambar and Shahji with an opportunity to fortify their position in the Deccan. Then Shahjahan revolted against his father. Jahangir feared that he might join forces with Malik Ambar. Hence, he ordered Prince Parviz to march against Malik Ambar. But the guerilla tactics of Malik Ambar triumphed over the combined forces of the Mughals and the Adilshahi sultanate, who suffered a crushing defeat in the Battle of Bhatavadi in November 1624. In this battle, Shahji exhibited

---

suggested by various scholars, see J N Sarkar, *Shivaji and His Times*, p. 18, and n.

54 G S Sardesai, Shivaji, Chapter IX, in R C Majumdar, J N Chaudhuri, and S Chaudhuri (ed), *The Mughul Empire* (The History and Culture of the Indian People, VII), p. 248.

55 G S Sardesai, *New History of the Marathas*, I, p. 59. There is a suggestion that Shahji never loved Jijabai, but was forced into this 'loveless' matrimony by 'a sudden childish impulse, and his father's quick ambition'. See David Kincaied, *Shivaji, the Founder of the Maratha Empire*, p. 48.

56 She gave birth to Vyankoji or Ekoji, the founder of the kingdom of Thanjavur. See G S Sardesai, Shivaji, Chapter IX, in R C Majumdar, J N Chaudhuri, and S Chaudhuri (ed), *The Mughul Empire* (The History and Culture of the Indian People, VII), p. 248.

such military brilliance,[57] that Malik Ambar became jealous of him, and the Maratha had to quit the service of the Nizamshahi sultanate and enter the service of the Adilshahi sultanate.[58]

Shahjahan ascended the Mughal throne on 4 February 1628, and almost immediately, he undertook to subjugate the Deccan. Khan Jahan Lodhi, the Mughal viceroy in the Deccan, had revolted and sought asylum with the Nizamshah. The Nizamshah recalled Shahji to his service. However, the *sultan* suspected that Lukhji Jadhav, the father-in-law of Shahji, was conspiring against him with Shahjahan. He invited the Jadhav chief, along with his family, to Daulatabad for consultations, and treacherously killed him and most of his family members. This act rendered the position of Shahji at Ahmadnagar, rather untenable, and he also feared for his life. So, he deserted the Nizamshah, and, from November 1630 to March 1632, served as a *mansabdar* under the Mughals.[59]

In the meantime, Murtaza Nizamshah II was imprisoned by his minister, Fath Khan, and was subsequently murdered in March 1631. Fath Khan submitted to Shahjahan.[60] But the Mughal emperor, bereaved by the death of his favourite wife, Mumtaz Mahal, had to leave the Deccan for Agra to bury her, before he could make proper arrangement for the permanent attachment of Ahmadnagar.[61] The fort of Daulatabad was captured by Mahabat Khan on 17 June 1633.[62]

Shahji took advantage of this opportunity, and he made a bold bid to re-establish the power of the Nizamshah. He made the inaccessible fort of Pemgiri or Bhimgadh, the new capital of Ahmadnagar, and, in September 1633, raised a young scion of the Nizamshahi family to the throne, administering the sultanate on his behalf.[63] But his position soon became untenable.

---

57 Paramananda Kavindra, *Shiva-bharata*, Chapter 4.

58 G S Sardesai, *New History of the Marathas*, I, pp. 60-61.

59 G S Sardesai, *New History of the Marathas*, I, pp. 61-65; See J C Grant Duff, *History of the Mahrattas*, I, pp. 78-80.

60 J C Grant Duff, *History of the Mahrattas*, I, p. 85.

61 G S Sardesai, *New History of the Marathas*, I, p. 65.

62 G S Sardesai, *New History of the Marathas*, I, p. 66.

63 Khafi Khan, *vide* J C Grant Duff, *History of the Mahrattas*, I, p. 87.

Shahjahan returned to the Deccan in 1636, and forced the *sultans* of Bijapur and Golkunda to desert the cause of Shahji and the Nizamshah. The Adilshah, however, prevailed upon the Mughal emperor to leave for Agra, and leave the task of taming Shahji to him. The Adilshah soon captured the forts held by Shahji, and forced him to seek shelter in the mountains of Kondhana and Torna. After the rainy season, Shahji retreated to the fort of Mahuli. But the Mughals besieged him, and forced him to enter into a treaty. Making 'the best of a bad bargain', Shahji agreed to hand over the fort of Mahuli and the Nizamshah to the Mughals. In return, he was allowed to serve under the Adilshahi sultanate, and was also allotted a *jaghir* in the former Nizamshahi territories to the south of the Godavari.[64] The Adilshah gave Shahji the command of 12,000 horsemen.[65] Shahji also managed to retain his *jaghir* of Poona, which was left to his wife Jijabai and her guardian, Dadaji Konddev.[66] Jijabai resided there, in a palatial house called *Lalmahal*, with her son, Shivaji, for about ten years, while the elder son, Shambhuji, lived with Shahji in the service of Bijapur. It was only later, that Jijabai and Shivaji shifted to the new fort of Rajgadh, and then to Raigadh, which was to become the capital of Shivaji.[67]

In view of the increasing Mughal acitivities in the Deccan, the *sultans* of Bijapur and Golkunda decided to conquer Karnataka and divide the territories, which formerly belonged to the Vijayanagara empire, among themselves. This resulted in three expeditions to those regions, in which Shahji took part under the command of Ranadulla Khan.[68] In the course of the first expedition, Ikkeri was captured in 1637. The second expedition resulted in the capture of Bangalore in 1638, by

---

64 See *Jedhe Karina*, in *Shiva-charitra-pradipa*, p. 39; also G S Sardesai (ed), *Shivaji Souvenir*, pp. 115-116; J C Grant Duff, *History of the Mahrattas*, I, pp. 87-92, 94.

65 *Shiva-charitra-pradipa*, p. 70.

66 J C Grant Duff, *History of the Mahrattas*, I, p. 93; G S Sardesai, *New History of the Marathas*, I, pp. 66-71.

67 See G S Sardesai, Shivaji, Chapter IX, in R C Majumdar, J N Chaudhuri, and S Chaudhuri (ed), *The Mughul Empire* (The History and Culture of the Indian People, VII), pp. 248-249.

68 See J C Grant Duff, *History of the Mahrattas*, I, p. 94.

Shahji. The third expedition, in 1639-1640, was also a successful one, and Ranadulla Khan was able to capture Basavapattan, and reduce several places like Tumkur, Balapur, and Vellore. He returned to Bijapur with a booty of four crore of *huns*.[69]

Shahji established himself at Bangalore, and started acting like an independent ruler for all practical purposes. He transplanted several Maratha families to Karnataka, and entrusted them with civil and military work, training them as hereditary officials loyal to him. He, however, remained loyal to Bijapur, paying his dues to the Adilshah, and giving him no cause for complaint. It has been remarked that the people of Karnataka 'looked upon Shahji's rule as almost a providential continuation of the old Vijayanagar tradition carried on in its essential spirit by a Hindu leader.'[70] Between 1640 and 1643, his wife, Jijabai, son Shivaji, and the latter's wife, Saibai, visited him at Bangalore, and also stopped at Bijapur for a time during their return voyage to Poona.[71]

However, in 1643, Ranadulla Khan, who was Shahji's friend and patron at the Adilshahi court at Bijapur, died. Around this time, there was a revolt against Muslim rule in Karnataka, in which Srirang Rai of Vijayanagara and Shivappa Nayak of Bednur played an important rôle. Muhammad Shah dispatched Mustafa Khan to lead an expedition against the rebels in Karnataka. This Mustafa Khan harboured a suspicion that Shahji was sympathetic to the cause of the Hindu rebels, and it was reported to the *sultan* that he was conspiring with Srirang Rai. This suspicion was strengthened by the activities of Shivaji, the son of Shahji, who had captured Singhgadh in Maharashtra, and practically asserted his independence at Poona. The Adilshah sent an expedition against Srirang Rai in 1646, and Vellore was captured by Mustafa Khan. But the loyalty of Shahji remained in doubt, and Bangalore and Singhgadh were regarded as two dangerous spots for the sultanate of Bijapur.[72]

---

69 J N Sarkar, *The House of Shivaji*, p. 27.

70 G S Sardesai, *New History of the Marathas*, I, pp. 75-79, on p. 79.

71 G S Sardesai, *New History of the Marathas*, I, p. 80. A detailed account of this visit has been given by David Kincaied, *Shivaji, the Founder of the Maratha Empire*, pp. 48-55. See below, Chapter II.

72 G S Sardesai, *New History of the Marathas*, I, pp. 81-83.

To settle the matters,[73] an expedition, under the command of Mustafa Khan, was dispatched in 1648, and it reached Jinji. There was some misunderstanding between Mustafa Khan and Shahji, in the course of which, the latter threatened to withdraw with his forces, if he was not paid immediately for his expenses. At the instigation of Mustafa Khan,[74] Baji Ghorpade of Mudhol, who was serving under Bijapur, raided the residence of Shahji, and arrested him on 25 July 1648.[75] After the fall of Jinji in December 1648, Shahji was taken captive to Bijapur in 1649, at the instructions of Muhammad Adilshah.[76] However, Shahji's two sons continued to strongly hold on to the two centres of Maratha power—Shambhuji at Bangalore, and Shivaji at Singhgadh. Paramananda informs us that the attempts of the Adilshah to capture these two strongholds were rendered unsuccessful by the two brave sons of Shahji.[77]

Shivaji was able to secure the release of Shahji through the intervention of Murad Bakhsh, the representative of the Mughal emperor in the Deccan.[78] Shahji agreed to surrender Singhgadh and Bangalore to Bijapur, and to continue to serve the Adilshah as before. After his release from the ten month confinement,[79] on 16 May 1649, he returned to Karnataka, and made Kanakagiri

---

73 J N Sarkar (*Shivaji and his Times*, pp. 37-39), however, says that this expedition against Shahji was dispatched to teach him a lesson for his insubordination, and had nothing to do with Shivaji's activities in the *jaghir* of Poona. *Cf* C V Vaidya, *Shivaji, the Founder of the Maratha Swarajya*, p. 59.

74 According to J C Grant Duff (*History of the Mahrattas*, I, p. 113), Baji Ghorpade was secretly ordered by the *sultan* himself to arrest Shahji.

75 For the rôle Baji Ghorpade played in the arrest of Shahji, Shivaji wrecked vengeance on Mudhol in 1661, razed it to the ground, and is reported to have ordered a general massacre there. See R V Nadkarni, *The Rise and Fall of the Maratha Empire*, p. 54, and n. 35.

76 G S Sardesai, *New History of the Marathas*, I, pp. 83-84.

77 Paramananda Kavindra, *Shiva-bharata*, Chapters 13 and 14.

78 J C Grant Duff, *History of the Mahrattas*, I, pp. 113-114; David Kincaied, *Shivaji, the Founder of the Maratha Empire*, pp. 82-88.

79 J C Grant Duff (*History of the Mahrattas*, I, p. 114) gives the period of confinement of Shahji at Bijapur as four years.

his new headquarters, where he was joined by his son, Shambhuji.[80]

Shahji was sympathetic to the endeavours of Shivaji to set up an independent Maratha kingdom in Maharashtra. But he did not involve himself in the enterprise, and remained loyal to the Adilshahi *sultan* till the end. In 1662, he even tried to bring about reconciliation between Shivaji and the Adilshah, in which attempt he was successful, and Shivaji promised not to antagonize Bijapur through any of his activities, provided that Bijapur gave him no provocation.[81] He, however, in the company of Shivaji, toured extensively between Nasik and Belgam in search for a suitable place for the capital of the future Maratha kingdom, and selected the plateau of Rairi, near Mahad, for the purpose. Here was constructed the fort, which became famous as Raigadh.[82]

In 1663, Ali Adilshah led an expedition against Bankapur, and sent urgent summons to Shahji to join him. However, he arrested the Maratha leader, kept him confined for two days, and then sent him against the Nayak of Bednur. When Shahji was returning to Bangalore after a successful expedition, he halted at Basavapattan on the Tungabhadra, where he fell down while hunting, and died instantly on 23 January 1664.[83]

It has been observed that Shahji continued, as it were, the tradition of the Vijayanagara empire. He has been regarded as 'the real inspirer of Shivaji in creating the Maratha Swarajya'.[84]

---

80 G S Sardesai, *New History of the Marathas*, I, pp. 85-86. J C Grant Duff (*History of the Mahrattas*, I, p. 116) says that Shambhuji died while taking Kanakagiri.

81 See *Shiva-digvijaya*, p. 330.

82 G S Sardesai, *New History of the Marathas*, I, pp. 88-89.

83 G S Sardesai, *New History of the Marathas*, I, pp. 89-90; see J C Grant Duff, *History of the Mahrattas*, I, p. 160.

84 G S Sardesai, *New History of the Marathas*, I, p. 90.

Chapter II

Senapatis under Shivaji

Shivaji was served by at least five[1] commanders-in-chief (*sarnobat*, later, *senapati*)—Tukoji Chor Maratha (about whom, not much is known),[2] Mankoji Dahatonde (an equally ephemeral figure as his predecessor)[3], Netaji Palkar,[4] Kadtoji Gujar (who was given the title of *Prataprao* on his elevation to the position of *sarnobat*),[5] and Hansaji Mohite (who was given the title of *Hambirrao* on his elevation to the position of *sarnobat*).[6] All accounts of the military activities of Shivaji reveal that, most of the time, he himself led his forces from the front, entrusting to

---

1 The number of Shivaji's *senapatis* may be six. V G Dighe and S N Qanungo, Administrative and Military System of the Marathas, Chapter XVII, in R C Majumdar and V G Dighe (ed), *The Maratha Supremacy* (The History and Culture of the Indian People, VIII), p. 538, also speak of one Noor Beg, who was appointed by Shivaji as *sarnobat* on the death of Dadaji Konddev in 1647.

2 Sabhasad (*Sabhasad-bakhar*, p. 8, *vide* S N Sen, *Administrative System of the Marathas*, p. 42) mentions Tukoji Chor Maratha as the first *sarnobat*, serving under Shivaji. But the circumstances of his replacement by Mankoji Dahatonde, sometime around 1659, are not known. See also S N Sen, *The Military System of the Marathas*, p. 12.

3 *Sabhasad-bakhar*, p. 9.

4 *Sabhasad-bakhar*, p. 11; *91 Qalmi Bakhar*, pp. 76-77.

5 *Sabhasad-bakhar*, p. 59.

6 *Sabhasad-bakhar*, p. 79. It was Hambirrao Mohite, who was the *senapati* at the time of the coronation of Shivaji. See *Chitnis-bakhar*, p. 162.

his commanders (and even the commander-in-chief, when he had appointed one), such tasks as suited the schemes devised by him. It was only on some rare occasions, usually when he was busy elsewhere, that he despatched expeditions led by his commander-in-chief of the time. In order to appreciate the doings of his various commanders-in-chief, a brief but continuous narrative of the events in the life of Shivaji has been deemed desirable : those events, in which his commander-in-chief of the time played a prominent rôle, have been dealt with in some detail.

Shivaji was born on 06 April 1627,[7] in the fort of Shivner near Junnar, to which his mother, Jijabai, had retired after a battle between her husband, Shahji Bhonsle, and her father, Lukhji Jadhav.[8] The relations between Jijabai and Shahji had become strained, perhaps following the marriage of Shahji

---

7 This is the generally accepted date for Shivaji's birth, on the basis of the information provided by the Maratha *bakhars*. See G S Sardesai, Shivaji, Chapter IX, in R C Majumdar, J N Chaudhuri, and S Chaudhuri (ed), *The Mughul Empire* (The History and Culture of the Indian People, VII), p. 248; R V Nadkarni, *The Rise and Fall of the Maratha Empire*, p. 41, and n. 2. There is no unanimity among scholars over the issue of the date of birth of Shivaji, primarily because contemporary records are not much helpful in this regard. Thus, J C Grant Duff (*History of the Mahrattas*, I, p. 95) and Rawlinson (*Shivaji, the Maratha*, p. 28) would place his birth in the month of May 1627. For a discussion on the dates suggested by various scholars, see V K Rajwade and B G Tilak, *Shiva-charitra-pradipa*; G S Sardesai (ed), *Shivaji Souvenir*, Marathi section, Chapter 5. J N Sarkar (*Shivaji and His Times*, p. 18, and n) prefers 10 April 1627. G S Sardesai (*New History of the Marathas*, I, p. 93) also refers to some sources, giving 19 February 1630 as the date of Shivaji's birth.

8 G S Sardesai, Shivaji, Chapter IX, in R C Majumdar, J N Chaudhuri, and S Chaudhuri (ed), *The Mughul Empire* (The History and Culture of the Indian People, VII), p. 248. According to R V Nadkarni (*The Rise and Fall of the Maratha Empire*, p. 41), Jijabai had been left in the fort by Shahji himself, while he was on the run, being pursued by Lukhji Jadhav. J N Sarkar, *Shivaji and His Times*, p. 19.

with Tukabai of the Mohite family of Supa around 1630.[9] After his accession to the Mughal throne, Shahjahan came to the Deccan, and, fearing for his life, Shahji fled.[10] Jijabai and Shivaji, in the care of Naro Trimal Hanumante and Gomaji Nayak Pansambal,[11] wandered about from place to place for well nigh nine years.[12] In 1633, Jijabai was even captured by the Mughal forces,[13] but she somehow managed to save her son from captivity; the Mughals released her only after a huge fine was paid to the emperor.[14] In 1636, peace was concluded between Shahjahan and Shahji. The Bhonsle chief delegated the care of his first wife and the younger child, Shivaji, to Dadaji Konddev, who had also been entrusted with the task of managing the paternal *jaghir* of Poona.[15] At last, Jijabai and her son could settle down in a palatial house called *Lalmahal*, at Poona, for

---

9 G S Sardesai, *Marathi Riyasat*, I, p. 159; J C Grant Duff, *History of the Mahrattas*, I, pp. 95-96; C A Kinkaid and D B Parasnis, *A History of the Maratha People*, I, pp. 16, 18, 20; M G Ranade, *Rise of the Maratha Power*, p. 62; J N Sarkar, *Shivaji and His Times*, p. 19; etc. J C Grant Duff (*History of the Mahrattas*, I, p. 95) goes so far as to assert that, after the second marriage of Shahji, Jijabai had repaired to her relatives, with whom she lived till 1633, does not seem to be convincing. See R V Nadkarni, *The Rise and Fall of the Maratha Empire*, p. 42, n. 5. But scholars like N S Takakhav and Keluskar (*Life of Shivaji Maharaj*, p. 66) and C V Vaidya (*Shivaji, the Founder of the Maratha Swarajya*, p. 40) are against the view that there was any discord between Shahji and Jijabai.

10 See R V Nadkarni, *The Rise and Fall of the Maratha Empire*, p. 41.

11 G S Sardesai, *New History of the Marathas*, I, p. 93.

12 J N Sarkar, *History of Aurangzib*, IV, p. 23.

13 David Kincaied, *Shivaji, the Founder of the Maratha Empire*, p. 34.

14 J C Grant Duff (*History of the Mahrattas*, I, p. 95), however, says that she was able to secure her release, probably by pleading that she was a neglected wife. See also R V Nadkarni, *The Rise and Fall of the Maratha Empire*, p. 42. But *contra* David Kincaied (*Shivaji, the Founder of the Maratha Empire*, p. 37), who says that Jijabai managed to escape from the fortress, where she was being kept a prisoner.

15 J N Sarkar, *History of Aurangzib*, IV, p. 24; also *Shivaji and His Times*, p. 19.

about ten years,[16] while the elder son, Shambhuji, lived with Shahji in the service of Bijapur.[17] It was only later on, on 07 March 1647, that Jijabai and Shivaji shifted to the new fort of Rajgadh, and, much more later, in 1666, finally to Raigadh,[18] which was to become the capital of Shivaji.[19]

Thus, Shivaji grew up under the tutelage of his mother and his guardian, Dadaji Konddev. 'Proud of her Kshatriya extraction, with vivid memories of her royal ancestors of Devagiri and their splendour, chastened by years of suffering even since her marriage and now practically deserted by her husband, this spirited lady [Jijabai] developed in her son a spirit of defiance and self-assertion....'[20] M G Ranade remarks : 'If ever great men owed their greatness to the inspiration of their mothers, the influence of Jijabai was a factor of prime importance in the making of Shivaji's career and the chief source of his strength.'[21] Marathi sources are ambiguous regarding Shivaji's education.[22] Shivaji is believed to have learnt reading, writing, arithmetic,[23] and, through recitations and storytelling

---

16 G S Sardesai, *New History of the Marathas*, I, p. 94.

17 J N Sarkar, *Shivaji and His Times*, p. 22.

18 G S Sardesai, *New History of the Marathas*, I, p. 94.

19 See G S Sardesai, Shivaji, Chapter IX, in R C Majumdar, J N Chaudhuri, and S Chaudhuri (ed), *The Mughul Empire* (The History and Culture of the Indian People, VII), pp. 248-249.

20 G S Sardesai, Shivaji, Chapter IX, in R C Majumdar, J N Chaudhuri, and S Chaudhuri (ed), *The Mughul Empire* (The History and Culture of the Indian People, VII), p. 249.

21 M G Ranade, *Rise of the Maratha Power*, p. 63. No wonder, Shivaji's love for Jijabai bordered almost on 'an adoration for a deity'. See J N Sarkar, *History of Aurangzib*, IV, p. 24; also *Shivaji and His Times*, p. 20.

22 Sabhasad does not volunteer any information in this regard. Chitnis refers to Shivaji as 'very learned', which has been regarded as 'vague'. The account of Shivaji's learning in *Shiva-digvijaya* seems to be highly exaggerated. See R V Nadkarni, *The Rise and Fall of the Maratha Empire*, pp. 48-49.

23 V K Rajwade, *Saraswati Mandir* (Marathi magazine), V(5); G S Sardesai, *History of Modern India*, I(2), pp. 163, 165; G S Sardesai, Shivaji, Chapter IX, in R C Majumdar, J N Chaudhuri, and S Chaudhuri (ed), *The Mughul Empire* (The History and

sessions, the Hindu scriptures, particularly the epics—the *Ramayana* and the *Mahabharata*;[24] not only did he draw inspiration, but also learnt lessons of the 'arts of government and war', from the exploits of Rama and the Pandava heroes.[25] Some scholars would, however, have us believe that the founder of the Maratha empire was an illiterate, who could hardly write his own name.[26] Even if that had been the case, '[t]he want of book-learning, therefore, did not leave his mind a dull and sterile soil, nor impair his efficiency as a man of action in a world that was mediaeval'.[27]

Dadaji Konddev, originally a brahmana *kulkarni* of Malthan within the *jaghir* of Poona,[28] was an able administrator,[29] with an inborn skill for managing the national resources, and a strict disciplinarian. The *jaghir* of Poona, the management of which he had been entrusted with by Shahji, was in a very sorry state of affairs.[30] The region had only recently been taken over by the Adilshahi sultanate, and no concrete effort had been made by Bijapur towards administering the region efficiently; even the defence of the region, was much neglected.[31] No wonder, J N Sarkar calls it a virtual 'No Man's Land'.[32] It had also suffered successively at the hands of the Bijapuris, Mughals, and Shahji

---

Culture of the Indian People, VII), p. 249; N S Takakhav and Keluskar, *Life of Shivaji Maharaj*, p. 76.

24 R V Nadkarni, *The Rise and Fall of the Maratha Empire*, pp. 44-45.

25 J N Sarkar, *Shivaji and His Times*, p. 25; J N Sarkar, *History of Aurangzib*, IV, p. 24; R V Nadkarni, *The Rise and Fall of the Maratha Empire*, pp. 44-45.

26 J C Grant Duff, *History of the Mahrattas*, I, p. 99; Elphinstone, *History of India*, p. 603; J N Sarkar, *Shivaji and His Times*, pp. 25, 389; J N Sarkar, *History of Aurangzib*, IV, p. 24.

27 J N Sarkar, *History of Aurangzib*, IV, pp. 24-25; J N Sarkar, *Shivaji and His Times*, p. 27.

28 V K Rajwade, *Marathyanchya Itihasachi Sadhane*, XVIII, p. 19.

29 M G Ranade (*Rise of the Maratha Power*, p. 64) calls him 'a masterhand in the art of civil government'.

30 J N Sarkar, *Shivaji and His Times*, p. 23; G S Sardesai, *New History of the Marathas*, I, pp. 98ff.

31 J C Grant Duff, *History of the Mahrattas*, I, p. 109.

32 J N Sarkar, *Shivaji and His Times*, p. 23.

himself, as a result of their warlike activities, and at the hands of 'robber chiefs' like Moro Tandev Honap.[33] The famine of 1630-1631, and the abundance of wolves and other wild beasts, had taken their toll on the local population, and hampered cultivation. As such, it is hardly surprising to learn that, initially, Dadaji Konddev could realize only a part of the revenue due to the Bhonsle chief.[34] But he soon started the process of correcting the situation by carrying out several administrative and revenue reforms, clearing the area of wild beasts, and encouraging agriculture.[35]

Dadaji Konddev started grooming Shivaji as a future king. He made provisions for the training of Shivaji in the martial arts, who soon became 'a good archer and marksman, skilled in the use of the spear, and of the various swords and daggers common in the Deccan'.[36] He gathered around Shivaji, a strong and devoted group of friends, like Yesaji Kank, Baji Pasalkar, Tanaji Malasure, and others, who were to help him in his future endeavours.[37] As a part of the practical training of Shivaji in the art of governance, Dadaji Konddev made his charge accompany him while he went on tours of inspection of the *jaghir*. Together with Shivaji, he administered quick and impartial justice,[38] and took measures to ensure the safety and prosperity of the subjects.[39] The paternal Bhonsle *jaghir* of the Mavals, which extended from Junnar to Wai towards the west of Poona, provided Shivaji with an ideal place and plenty of opportunity for adventure and experiments, and, in the course of his

---

33 J N Sarkar, *Shivaji and His Times*, p. 23.

34 J N Sarkar, *Shivaji and His Times*, p. 24; R V Nadkarni, *The Rise and Fall of the Maratha Empire*, pp. 46-47.

35 See David Kincaied, *Shivaji, the Founder of the Maratha Empire*, pp. 59-60.

36 J C Grant Duff, *History of the Mahrattas*, I, pp. 99-100.

37 J N Sarkar, *Shivaji and His Times*, p. 28; R V Nadkarni, *The Rise and Fall of the Maratha Empire*, p. 49.

38 G S Sardesai, *New History of the Marathas*, I, p. 100.

39 G S Sardesai, Shivaji, Chapter IX, in R C Majumdar, J N Chaudhuri, and S Chaudhuri (ed), *The Mughul Empire* (The History and Culture of the Indian People, VII), pp. 250-251. See also R V Nadkarni, *The Rise and Fall of the Maratha Empire*, p. 52.

extensive wanderings in the company of his devoted followers, he soon became well acquainted with 'secret paths, recesses and strongholds of the long Sahyadri range of the Deccan plateau'.[40] And this acquaintance proved to be a great advantage to him in his future career.[41]

For some time, administrative orders were being issued in the *jaghir* of Poona in the name of Shivaji as Shahji's representative.[42] With the blessings of his mother and the able guidance of his tutor,[43] Shivaji soon put together a 'compact, well-knit geographical unit of a small *swarajya*', 'in which law and order prevailed, duties of officials were clearly defined, justice quickly rendered, honest work well rewarded and where life and wealth were perfectly secure'.[44]

These activities of Shivaji and his guardian earned them the suspicion of the *sultan* at Bijapur, and this adversely effected the position of Shahji in the Adilshahi court. When the *sultan* took Shahji to task, the Bhonsle chief invited Shivaji, Jijabai, and Dadaji Konddev to Bangalore, under the pretext of meeting Saibai Nimbalkar, the newly married wife of Shivaji. Shahji's family stayed in Bangalore for about two to three years, that is from 1640 to 1642 or 1643.[45] But he was unable to elicit any

---

40 *Cf* R V Nadkarni, *The Rise and Fall of the Maratha Empire*, p. 49.

41 J N Sarkar, *Shivaji and His Times*, p. 31.

42 J N Sarkar, *History of Aurangzib*, IV, p. 27.

43 There is a view that Dadaji Konddev was not a man possessed of 'bold ambitions' or 'lofty ideals', and was not in favour of Shivaji's plan for the assertion of independence; all he desired for his ward was 'a position of wealth and power' under the *sultan* of Bijapur. It was only in his last days that 'the old man yielded and blessed Shivaji'. See M G Ranade, *Rise of the Maratha Power*, p. 66; J C Grant Duff, *History of the Mahrattas*, I, p. 104; J N Sarkar, *History of Aurangzib*, IV, p. 26; R V Nadkarni, *The Rise and Fall of the Maratha Empire*, pp. 49-51.

44 G S Sardesai, Shivaji, Chapter IX, in R C Majumdar, J N Chaudhuri, and S Chaudhuri (ed), *The Mughul Empire* (The History and Culture of the Indian People, VII), p. 252.

45 These are the usually accepted dates for the visit of Jijabai and Shivaji to Shahji at Bangalore. See J N Sarkar, *Shivaji and His Times*, p. 399; G S Sardesai, *New History of the Marathas*, I, pp. 80, 101. However, at one place (Shivaji, Chapter IX, in R C

commitment, from either his son or his wife, that they would, in future, refrain from any activity, which would be frowned upon by the authorities of Bijapur; in fact, Jijabai spent almost the whole of her two year stay in Bangalore in undertaking tours of pilgrimage to the sacred shrines.[46] When the Adilshahi *sultan* saw that no such assurance was forthcoming from Shahji and his family, he ordered the Bhonsle chief and his family to visit him at Bijapur. But trouble broke out once Shahji and his son were there, when Shivaji refused to bow before the *sultan* in the court.[47] Then, there was an incident between Shivaji and a butcher he found slaughtering a cow,[48] and Shivaji had to leave Bijapur in haste to avoid capture and possible imprisonment.[49]

Thereafter, Shahji made an outwards show of his inability to control the actions of his son, thus washing his hands of any responsibility for him.[50] That the endeavours of Shivaji were, however, secretly blessed by his father, is known from the despatch of elephants, soldiers, flags and royal insignia, and treasury, by Shahji from Bangalore for the use of Shivaji.[51] He also sent some of his able officials, like Shyamrao Nilakanth Peshva, Sonopant Dabir, and others, to assist Shivaji in

---

Majumdar, J N Chaudhuri, and S Chaudhuri (ed), *The Mughul Empire* (The History and Culture of the Indian People, VII), p. 253), G S Sardesai gives the dates as 1642-1644.

46 G S Sardesai, Shivaji, Chapter IX, in R C Majumdar, J N Chaudhuri, and S Chaudhuri (ed), *The Mughul Empire* (The History and Culture of the Indian People, VII), p. 253.

47 David Kincaied, *Shivaji, the Founder of the Maratha Empire*, p. 51.

48 Rawlinson, *Shivaji, the Maratha*, p. 29; David Kincaied, *Shivaji, the Founder of the Maratha Empire*, pp. 54-55.

49 G S Sardesai, Shivaji, Chapter IX, in R C Majumdar, J N Chaudhuri, and S Chaudhuri (ed), *The Mughul Empire* (The History and Culture of the Indian People, VII), p. 253.

50 See J C Grant Duff, *History of the Mahrattas*, I, p. 113; G S Sardesai, *New History of the Marathas*, I, p. 130. See also J N Sarkar, *House of Shivaji*, p. 87, for the Adilshahi authorities accepting his plea, that he was unable to exercise any authority over Shivaji.

51 Paramananda Kavindra, *Shiva-bharata*, 10. 25-27. See G S Sardesai, *New History of the Marathas*, I, p. 102.

Maharashtra.[52] Shivaji, himself, was also not without resources; the revenue from the Maval *jaghir*, now being ably administered over the past years, was sufficient to enable him to undertake the maintenance of his forts and recruit soldiers. With the help of his followers, particularly the *deshmukh*, Kanhoji Jedhe, of Kari,[53] he succeeded in occupying all the twelve forts of the Maval region, some of them through bribery.[54] These included the strongholds of Singhgadh and Rohida. Three of his brave officers, Yesaji Kank, Tanaji Malasure, and Baji Pasalkar, occupied the fort of Torna in 1646.[55] It is reported that, from the wealth he discovered while conducting repairs to the defence walls of the fort of Torna around 1646,[56] Shivaji also constructed a new fort, which was named Rajgadh.[57] These activities of Shivaji again won him the ire of the Adilshahi *sultan*, but a paralytic stroke prevented him from taking any concrete action against Shivaji for nearly ten years (from 1646 to 1656).[58]

Dadaji Konddev died on 07 March 1647,[59] but this did not dishearten Shivaji, who continued to work towards establishing an independent Maratha state. He assumed the *de facto* charge of

---

52 J N Sarkar, *Shivaji and His Times*, p. 34.

53 See G S Sardesai, *New History of the Marathas*, I, p. 106. It has been suggested that Shahji had asked Kanhoji Jedhe to help Shivaji in his endeavours.

54 For example, Singhgadh. See R V Nadkarni, *The Rise and Fall of the Maratha Empire*, p. 53.

55 J N Sarkar, *History of Aurangzib*, IV, p. 27. *Cf* J C Grant Duff, *History of the Mahrattas*, I, p. 102), who says that Shivaji 'induced' its *qiledar* to hand over the fort to him.

56 J C Grant Duff, *History of the Mahrattas*, I, p. 103; G S Sardesai, *New History of the Marathas*, I, p. 105; R V Nadkarni, *The Rise and Fall of the Maratha Empire*, pp. 52-53. According to J N Sarkar (*History of Aurangzib*, IV, p. 27), wealth seized at Torna by the Marathas amounted to two lac of rupees.

57 J N Sarkar, *History of Aurangzib*, IV, pp. 27-28.

58 G S Sardesai, Shivaji, Chapter IX, in R C Majumdar, J N Chaudhuri, and S Chaudhuri (ed), *The Mughul Empire* (The History and Culture of the Indian People, VII), pp. 254-255; also J N Sarkar, *History of Aurangzib*, IV, p. 27; R V Nadkarni, *The Rise and Fall of the Maratha Empire*, p. 52.

59 J N Sarkar, *Shivaji and His Times*, p. 32.

the *jaghir* of Poona in the name of his father.[60] He captured the fort of Chakan in the north,[61] and renamed it Sangramdurg.[62] During the Divali celebrations of 1648, he persuaded Nilopant Sarnayak, the guardian of the fort of Purandar in the east, to make over his charge to Shivaji.[63] He was also able to wrest the market town of Supa, to the southeast of Poona, by easily defeating Shambhuji Mohite,[64] the brother of his stepmother, Tukabai.[65] He took ample measures to secure his new acquisitions.[66] Meanwhile, as seen above,[67] Shahji was imprisoned by Baji Ghorpade of Mudhol, on the instructions of the Adilshahi *sultan*, and Shivaji had to give up Singhgadh in order to secure the release of his father, who was being held a prisoner at Bijapur.[68]

From 1648 onwards, Shivaji started affixing a new seal on all official papers, which read : 'This seal of Shiva, son of Shah, shines forth for the welfare of the people and is meant to command increasing respect from the universe like the first phase of the moon'.[69] Papers also started bearing Shivaji's title

---

60 J C Grant Duff, *History of the Mahrattas*, I, p. 104; J N Sarkar, *History of Aurangzib*, IV, p. 28.

61 J N Sarkar, *History of Aurangzib*, IV, p. 28.

62 G S Sardesai, *New History of the Marathas*, I, pp. 109-110.

63 J N Sarkar, *Shivaji and His Times*, pp. 39-41.

64 The name given by J C Grant Duff (*History of the Mahrattas*, I, p. 105) and R V Nadkarni (*The Rise and Fall of the Maratha Empire*, p. 53) is Baji Mohite.

65 G S Sardesai, *New History of the Marathas*, I, p. 110.

66 G S Sardesai, Shivaji, Chapter IX, in R C Majumdar, J N Chaudhuri, and S Chaudhuri (ed), *The Mughul Empire* (The History and Culture of the Indian People, VII), p. 255.

67 See Chapter I.

68 Paramananda Kavindra, *Shiva-bharata*, 16. 45. See G S Sardesai, *New History of the Marathas*, I, p. 108; J N Sarkar, *History of Aurangzib*, IV, pp. 28-30; G S Sardesai, Shivaji, Chapter IX, in R C Majumdar, J N Chaudhuri, and S Chaudhuri (ed), *The Mughul Empire* (The History and Culture of the Indian People, VII), p. 256.

69 G S Sardesai, Shivaji, Chapter IX, in R C Majumdar, J N Chaudhuri, and S Chaudhuri (ed), *The Mughul Empire* (The

of *chhatrapati* and the seals of his ministers.[70] This has been taken as evidence to show that, about this time, Shivaji was ruling over 'a small cohesive independent State with ministers and officials charged with definite duties'.[71] Towards the close of the fifth decade of the seventeenth century, we see Shivaji 'watching and crouching like the wily tiger of his own mountain valleys, until he had stolen into a situation from whence he could at once spring on his prey'.[72] Although the first phase of *svarajya* was completed sometime around 1653,[73] the formal coronation of Shivaji was to take place much later.

The More *deshmukhs* of Javli in the Mahabaleshvar range owed allegiance to the Adilshahi *sultan* of Bijapur, and were a source of constant irritation to Shivaji.[74] The *bakhars* would also have us believe that the Mores had refused Jijabai's proposal of a marriage alliance between the Bhonsles and the Mores.[75] All the efforts of Shivaji at reconciliation with the Mores proved futile.[76] When the More chief, who bore the hereditary title of *chandrarao*, allowed Baji Shamraj passage through Javli to invade Shivaji's *jaghir* of Poona, Shivaji retaliated by attacking Javli towards the beginning of 1656, killing Hanumantrao More, and capturing the More stronghold on 26 January 1656.[77] In this

---

History and Culture of the Indian People, VII), p. 255. *Cf* G S Sardesai, *New History of the Marathas*, I, p. 111.

70 G S Sardesai, *New History of the Marathas*, I, pp. 111-112.

71 G S Sardesai, Shivaji, Chapter IX, in R C Majumdar, J N Chaudhuri, and S Chaudhuri (ed), *The Mughul Empire* (The History and Culture of the Indian People, VII), p. 255.

72 J C Grant Duff, *History of the Mahrattas*, I, p. 107.

73 G S Sardesai, *New History of the Marathas*, I, p. 113.

74 J N Sarkar, *Shivaji and His Times*, pp. 41-42; G S Sardesai, *New History of the Marathas*, I, pp. 117ff.

75 Jijabai had proposed that Balaji More marry one of his three daughters to Shivaji, but the More refused on the grounds that the Bhonsles were socially inferior to the Mores. *Contra* C V Vaidya, *Shivaji, the Founder of the Maratha Swarajya*, p. 67, who does not believe in the historicity of the account.

76 J C Grant Duff, *History of the Mahrattas*, I, p. 116; G S Sardesai, *New History of the Marathas*, I, p. 118.

77 15 January 1656, according to J N Sarkar, *History of Aurangzib*, IV, p. 31.

endeavour, two of his officers, namely Raghunath Ballal Korde and Shambhuji Kavji, played an important rôle.[78] Shivaji tried unsuccessfully to negotiate with those members of the More family, who had taken to flight in the face of Shivaji's invasion. In May 1656, Shivaji killed three more members of the More family, namely Yashvantrao and his sons, Krishnaji and Baji.[79] Prataprao More escaped to Bijapur, where he took shelter with the Adilshahi *sultan*. Shivaji constructed the fort of Pratapgadh near Mahabaleshvar to secure his new conquest.[80] He occupied all the territories of the Mores, capturing, in April 1656, Raigadh, which was later to be his capital.[81] The punishment meted out to the More family by Shivaji established the Bhonsles as the foremost Maratha family, and none dared challenge their might.

On 04 November 1656, Muhammad Adilshah died. When Prince Aurangzeb was making preparations to invade Bijapur, Shivaji, in March 1657, entered into an understanding with him, offering his services to the Mughals, on the condition that he be confirmed in his possessions in Maharashtra.[82] He made an outward show of helping the Mughals against Bijapur, but,

---

78 Raghunath Ballal Korde is said to have treacherously stabbed Chandrarao to death, and grievously injured his brother, Suryarao. J C Grant Duff, *History of the Mahrattas*, I, p. 117; J N Sarkar, *History of Aurangzib*, IV, p. 31; also *Shivaji and His Times*, p. 42. But *contra* C V Vaidya, *Shivaji, the Founder of the Maratha Swarajya*, pp. 65-69, who holds that the Mores were killed in a fair fight.

79 For details, see J N Sarkar, *History of Aurangzib*, IV, pp. 30-32; J N Sarkar, *Shivaji and his Times*, pp. 41-45; C A Kinkaid and D B Parasnis, *A History of the Maratha People*, I, pp. 29-33; R V Nadkarni, *The Rise and Fall of the Maratha Empire*, p. 55-56; etc.

80 G S Sardesai, *New History of the Marathas*, I, p. 120; also G S Sardesai, Shivaji, Chapter IX, in R C Majumdar, J N Chaudhuri, and S Chaudhuri (ed), *The Mughul Empire* (The History and Culture of the Indian People, VII), pp. 256-257.

81 J N Sarkar, *History of Aurangzib*, IV, p. 32.

82 J C Grant Duff, *History of the Mahrattas*, I, p. 128; J N Sarkar, *History of Aurangzib*, IV, p. 34; *Shivaji and His Times*, p. 49; G S Sardesai, *New History of the Marathas*, I, p. 127; R V Nadkarni, *The Rise and Fall of the Maratha Empire*, p. 56.

taking advantage of the withdrawal of the Mughal forces from Bijapur, the Marathas raided Junnar on the night of 30 April 1657,[83] and Ahmadnagar around the same time.[84] In both these ventures, which proved to be singularly fruitful in terms of booty,[85] Shivaji was helped by two of his officers, Minaji Bhonsle and Kashi.[86] Shivaji repaired to his country due to the military actions of officers like Multafat Khan, Rao Karna, Shayista Khan, and Nasiri Khan, and the arrival of monsoons.[87] When the *sultan* of Bijapur made peace with the Mughals, Shivaji, early in 1658, thought it wise to ask for the forgiveness of Aurangzeb,[88] which the Mughal prince was obliged to grant, given the political circumstances of the time, though his military officers and other subordinates were urged to remain vigilant gainst the activities of Shivaji.[89]

After the occupation of Javli, Shivaji first plundered the large amount of money being sent from Kalyan to Bijapur,[90] and subsequently despatched Abaji Sondev against Kalyan, which was captured in October 1657.[91] The family of the governor, an Arab named Maulana Ahmad, was taken captive, but was

---

83 J N Sarkar, *History of Aurangzib*, IV, p. 35; *Shivaji and His Times*, p. 50.

84 J N Sarkar, *History of Aurangzib*, IV, p. 37; David Kincaied, *Shivaji, the Founder of the Maratha Empire*, p. 109; G S Sardesai, *New History of the Marathas*, I, pp. 122, 127.

85 From Junnar alone, Shivaji is reported to have gained three lac of *huns* in cash, and 200 horses. J N Sarkar, *History of Aurangzib*, IV, p. 35. Also J N Sarkar, *Shivaji and His Times*, p. 50.

86 J N Sarkar, *History of Aurangzib*, IV, p. 34ff; *Shivaji and His Times*, pp. 49-50.

87 J N Sarkar, *Shivaji and His Times*, pp. 50-52.

88 G S Sardesai, *New History of the Marathas*, I, p. 127.

89 J N Sarkar, *History of Aurangzib*, IV, pp. 39-41; *Shivaji and His Times*, pp. 53-54; G S Sardesai, *New History of the Marathas*, I, p. 127.

90 J C Grant Duff, *History of the Mahrattas*, I, p. 111; *The Leading Nobles of Bijapur*, p. 55.

91 *Cf* David Kincaied, *Shivaji, the Founder of the Maratha Empire*, p. 80, where the year of this event is wrongly given as 1648.

released later on.[92] Thereafter, the Marathas also occupied Bhivandi on 24 October 1657, and Mahuli on 08 January 1658. These successes made Shivaji master of most of northern Konkan.[93] He toured the Konkan coast, and made plans for the construction of forts for the naval defence of the region.[94] Shivaji now had 10,000 horsemen with Mankoji Dahatonde, and, on his passing away, Netaji Palkar as *sarnobat*,[95] and 10,000 Mavali infantry with Yesaji Kank as commander.[96]

Alerted by the activities of Shivaji, Badi Sahiba, the widow of Muhammad Adilshah, sent Abdullah Bhatari *alias* Afzal Khan, a trusted officer, to put an end to the Maratha menace. The Bijapuri officer left for Maharashtra in September 1659, and, wrecking havoc on the way, reached Wai, where he pitched his camp.[97] 'Pretending friendship' with the Maratha,[98] he sent his

---

92 G S Sardesai, *New History of the Marathas*, I, pp. 122ff; also G S Sardesai, Shivaji, Chapter IX, in R C Majumdar, J N Chaudhuri, and S Chaudhuri (ed), *The Mughul Empire* (The History and Culture of the Indian People, VII), p. 257. The officers of Shivaji tried to present the daughter-in-law of the governor to their master. But Shivaji showed proper respect to the lady, and sent her home under his own protection. G S Sardesai, *New History of the Marathas*, I, pp. 123-124. R V Nadkarni (*The Rise and Fall of the Maratha Empire*, p. 54) would place this event before the capture of Shahji by Baji Ghorpade.

93 J N Sarkar, *History of Aurangzib*, IV, pp. 41-42; *Shivaji and His Times*, pp. 54-55; G S Sardesai, *New History of the Marathas*, I, pp. 128ff.

94 G S Sardesai, Shivaji, Chapter IX, in R C Majumdar, J N Chaudhuri, and S Chaudhuri (ed), *The Mughul Empire* (The History and Culture of the Indian People, VII), p. 257.

95 *Sabhasad-bakhar*, p. 9. See also G S Sardesai, *New History of the Marathas*, I, p. 125.

96 *Sabhasad-bakhar*, p. 11. See also J N Sarkar, *History of Aurangzib*, IV, p. 43; *Shivaji and His Times*, p. 57.

97 G S Sardesai, *New History of the Marathas*, I, pp. 131-132.

98 *Factory Record, Rajapur, 10 December 1659*, *vide* J N Sarkar, *History of Aurangzib*, IV, p. 45 and n; also J N Sarkar, *Shivaji and His Times*, p. 59 and n.

envoy, Krishnaji Bhaskar,[99] and invited Shivaji for a meeting, on 10 November 1659, below the fort of Pratapgadh, where the Maratha chief was residing at the time.[100] He planned to smother Shivaji by holding him in a powerful embrace. But Shivaji arrived fully prepared for any kind of treachery. When Afzal Khan took him into a tight personal grip,[101] and tried to stab him,[102] Shivaji ripped open his bowels with a tiger claw.[103] Shortly afterwards, Shambhuji Kavji killed and decapitated Afzal Khan.[104] Maratha soldiers, led by Moropant Trimbak Pingle, Netaji Palkar,[105] and others, attacked the Bijapuri army, which was routed.[106] Shivaji put the severed head on display on the top of the fort.[107] An immense booty, including 65 elephants,

---

99 See G S Sardesai, *New History of the Marathas*, I, pp. 132-134. But J C Grant Duff (*History of the Mahrattas*, I, pp. 134ff, on p. 134) gives the name as Pantoji Gopinath.

100 J N Sarkar, *History of Aurangzib*, IV, pp. 44-47. *Cf* J N Sarkar, *Shivaji and His Times*, p. 62.

101 David Kincaied, *Shivaji, the Founder of the Maratha Empire*, p. 123.

102 G S Sardesai, *New History of the Marathas*, I, p. 136.

103 *Cf* Khafi Khan (II. 117), who says that both Afzal Khan and Shivaji came to the meeting unarmed. But *contra* J N Sarkar, *History of Aurangzib*, IV, p. 48n.

104 J N Sarkar, *History of Aurangzib*, IV, pp. 49-50; *Shivaji and His Times*, pp. 67-68.

105 The two Maratha officials, who were active in the Konkan and the Ghats, respectively, had been ordered by Shivaji to proceed towards Pratapgadh, before he went to meet Afzal Khan. See J N Sarkar, *Shivaji and His Times*, p. 65.

106 J N Sarkar, *History of Aurangzib*, IV, p. 50; *Shivaji and His Times*, pp. 68-69.

107 G S Sardesai, *New History of the Marathas*, I, p. 136. See also J N Sarkar, *Shivaji and His Times*, pp. 58-72; J C Grant Duff, *History of the Mahrattas*, I, pp. 134-140; C A Kinkaid and D B Parasnis, *A History of the Maratha People*, 1, pp. 37-41; N S Takakhav and Keluskar, *Life of Shivaji Maharaj*, pp. 151-175; Rawlinson, *Shivaji, the Maratha*, pp. 47-55; M G Ranade, *Rise of the Maratha Power*, pp. 95-99; C V Vaidya, *Shivaji, the Founder of the Maratha Swarajya*, pp. 88-104; G S Sardesai, Shivaji, Chapter IX, in R C Majumdar, J N Chaudhuri, and S Chaudhuri (ed), *The Mughul Empire* (The History and Culture of the Indian People,

4,000 horses, 1,200 camels, 10 lacs of rupees, and other treasures fell into the hands of the Maratha.[108] The hold of Bijapur over the region was, thus, weakened,[109] and Shivaji followed up this success by extensive conquests in southern Konkan in the period from December 1659 and February 1660.[110]

Shivaji divided his army into three parts. He entrusted the security of his possessions in the Poona region to one part, and despatched the second part to guard against the Savants of Savantvadi and the Siddis of Janjira. He himself led the third part of his army towards the south, and captured Panhala, Vishalgadh, Rangana, and Pavangadh.[111] The Marathas reached as far as the vicinity of Bijapur, and indulged in plunder.[112] However, they were forced to withdraw in face of the army of Siddi Jauhar, an Abyssinian general, who had been given the title of *Salabat Khan* by the Adilshahi *sultan*, Ali Adilshah II, and sent to repulse the Maratha attack.[113] Shivaji was besieged in the fort of Panhala on 02 March 1660.[114]

The death of Shahjahan was followed by a struggle for succession between his sons, in which Aurangzeb emerged victorious, and he declared himself emperor on 21 July 1658. He appointed his maternal uncle, Shayista Khan, as his viceroy in the Deccan, and instructed him to take stern action against Shivaji.[115] The Mughal viceroy arrived at Aurangabad in January 1660, soon captured most of the territories of Shivaji, including Poona on 09 May 1660,[116] and Chakan to the north on 15 August 1660.[117] Returning to Poona, he took over the *Lalmahal* of

---

VII), pp. 258-259. J N Sarkar (*Shivaji and His Times*, p. 68n), however, says that the head was buried beneath a tower in the southeast of the lower fort.

108 J N Sarkar, *History of Aurangzib*, IV, pp. 50-51.

109 *Cf* G S Sardesai, *New History of the Marathas*, I, p. 137.

110 J N Sarkar, *History of Aurangzib*, IV, p. 51.

111 G S Sardesai, *New History of the Marathas*, I, p. 138; R V Nadkarni, *The Rise and Fall of the Maratha Empire*, p. 58.

112 G S Sardesai, *New History of the Marathas*, I, p. 138.

113 R V Nadkarni, *The Rise and Fall of the Maratha Empire*, p. 58.

114 J N Sarkar, *History of Aurangzib*, IV, p. 52.

115 See J C Grant Duff, *History of the Mahrattas*, I, pp. 154ff.

116 G S Sardesai, *New History of the Marathas*, I, p. 139.

117 J N Sarkar, *History of Aurangzib*, IV, p. 53.

Shivaji as his residence, and forced Shivaji to live like a fugitive for about three years.[118]

Shivaji had to spend around six months in the fort of Panhala, which was besieged by Siddi Jauhar and his 15,000 soldiers.[119] Although Netaji Palkar harassed the besieging forces from outside the fort, while Kadtoji Gujar (later, Prataprao Gujar) conducted the defence of the fort from the inside, the position of Shivaji was fast becoming untenable.[120] So precarious was the position, that, according to Paramananda Kavindra,[121] Jijabai took Netaji Palkar to task for not doing his utmost to relieve the siege of Panhala. Shivaji made a show of negotiating peace with the enemy,[122] but escaped from the fort in the night of 13 July 1660, taking advantage of rain and darkness.[123] Fazal Muhammad Khan, the son of the slain Afzal Khan, at the head of some Bijapuri horsemen, pursued Shivaji, and caught up with the Marathas some six miles from Vishalgadh. Baji Prabhu and 700 of his soldiers sacrificed their lives, defending their master,[124] and Shivaji was able to reach the safety of Vishalgadh.[125]

In this venture, the Adilshahi *sultan* of Bijapur, was helped by the Savant of Savantvadi, the Ghorpades of Mudhol, and others, who had made common cause against Shivaji. Court feuds, however, rendered the Adilshahi *sultan* ineffective. He doubted the loyalty of Siddi Jauhar, driving his able general to

---

118 J N Sarkar, *History of Aurangzib*, IV, pp. 52-60; *Shivaji and His Times*, pp. 78ff; G S Sardesai, *New History of the Marathas*, I, p. 149; also G S Sardesai, Shivaji, Chapter IX, in R C Majumdar, J N Chaudhuri, and S Chaudhuri (ed), *The Mughul Empire* (The History and Culture of the Indian People, VII), p. 259.

119 J N Sarkar, *History of Aurangzib*, IV, p. 52; *Shivaji and His Times*, p. 76.

120 G S Sardesai, *New History of the Marathas*, I, p. 138.

121 *Vide* G S Sardesai, *New History of the Marathas*, I, p. 139.

122 J N Sarkar, *History of Aurangzib*, IV, p. 53.

123 G S Sardesai, *New History of the Marathas*, I, p. 140.

124 David Kincaied, *Shivaji, the Founder of the Maratha Empire*, pp. 127-128; G S Sardesai, *New History of the Marathas*, I, p. 140.

125 J N Sarkar, *History of Aurangzib*, IV, p. 53; J N Sarkar, *Shivaji and His Times*, pp. 76-78; R V Nadkarni, *The Rise and Fall of the Maratha Empire*, pp. 58-59.

rebellion.[126] Shivaji later on subjugated Savantvadi,[127] and also came to an understanding with the Portuguese.[128]

Early in 1661, Shivaji gained a decisive victory over the Mughal general, Kar Talb Khan, near Umbarkhind in the Konkan. He cut off all the Mughal avenues of advance and retreat, and forced Kar Talb Khan to surrender all the property in his camp to the Marathas in exchange for permission to retreat.[129] Shivaji then divided his army into two parts. One part was placed under the charge of Netaji Palkar, and despatched against the Mughals,[130] Shivaji himself, at the head of the other part, invaded the Bijapuri territories in the Konkan. Soon, he reoccupied Kalyan, although he lost it in May 1661 to the Mughals, who remained masters of the region for the next nine years.[131] However, towards the south of Kalyan, Shivaji was successful in occupying all the regions along the west coast, from Danda Rajpuri to Kharepatan.[132]

The year 1662, as also the first three months of the next year, were not so fruitful for the Marathas. In 1662, Shivaji had a conflict with Namdar Khan at Mira Dongar in the Konkan,[133] but his attempts to plunder the prosperous city of Pen were rendered unsuccessful by the Mughal forces stationed there.[134] The Marathas could not gain any notable success against the Mughals throughout the year 1662 and early 1663. In fact, in March 1663, Netaji Palkar, the *sarnobat* of Shivaji was vigorously chased and wounded by the Mughal forces, and lost 300 horse to them,[135]

---

126 J C Grant Duff, *History of the Mahrattas*, I, p. 149.

127 J C Grant Duff, *History of the Mahrattas*, I, pp. 150-151.

128 J C Grant Duff, *History of the Mahrattas*, I, p. 151.

129 Paramananda Kavindra, *Shiva-bharata*, 29; also *Shiva-charitra-pradipa*, p. 51. See G S Sardesai, *New History of the Marathas*, I, pp. 143-144; J N Sarkar, *History of Aurangzib*, IV, p. 59.

130 G S Sardesai, *New History of the Marathas*, I, p. 144.

131 J N Sarkar, *History of Aurangzib*, IV, p. 60; G S Sardesai, *New History of the Marathas*, I, p. 149.

132 J N Sarkar, *History of Aurangzib*, IV, p. 60; G S Sardesai, *New History of the Marathas*, I, p. 145.

133 G S Sardesai, *New History of the Marathas*, I, p. 149.

134 J N Sarkar, *History of Aurangzib*, IV, p. 60; G S Sardesai, *New History of the Marathas*, I, p. 149.

135 J N Sarkar, *History of Aurangzib*, IV, p. 60.

although he was saved by the timely intervention of Rustam-i-Zaman.[136]

Shayista Khan was holding on to the occupied Maratha territories. Shivaji, with the help of his spies, collected intelligence regarding the movements in the Mughal camp, and the arrangements for his security. He devised a scheme on the basis of the intelligence thus gathered. On 15 April 1663,[137] he led fifty[138] of his devoted followers, including Babaji Bapuji and Chimnaji Bapuji of Khed as his bodyguards,[139] in a surprise attack on the *harem* of Shayista Khan around midnight. A thousand strong cavalry under Netaji Palkar, and a thousand strong Mavali infantry under Moropant Trimbak Pingle, were stationed on the two flanks of the Mughal encampment to provide assistance, as and when required.[140] A number of the family members (including his son, Abul Fath), soldiers, and attendants of the Mughal governor were killed, but Shayista Khan himself managed to escape with only minor injuries.[141]

---

136 J N Sarkar, *Shivaji and His Times*, pp. 87, 223.

137 G S Sardesai, Shivaji, Chapter IX, in R C Majumdar, J N Chaudhuri, and S Chaudhuri (ed), *The Mughul Empire* (The History and Culture of the Indian People, VII), p. 159. But 05 April 1663, according to J N Sarkar, *History of Aurangzib*, IV, pp. 62, 65. However, in his *New History of the Marathas*, I, p. 149, G S Sardesai has accepted the date given by J N Sarkar.

138 G S Sardesai, Shivaji, Chapter IX, in R C Majumdar, J N Chaudhuri, and S Chaudhuri (ed), *The Mughul Empire* (The History and Culture of the Indian People, VII), p. 259. But four hundred, according to J N Sarkar, *History of Aurangzib*, IV, p. 62; *Shivaji and His Times*, p. 88. However, in his *New History of the Marathas*, I, p. 149, G S Sardesai has accepted the figure given by J N Sarkar.

139 J N Sarkar, *Shivaji and His Times*, p. 88.

140 J N Sarkar, *History of Aurangzib*, IV, pp. 61-62; *Shivaji and His Times*, p. 88.

141 *Ma'asir-i-Alamgiri*, p. 28. See also J N Sarkar, *Shivaji and His Times*, pp. 88-92; J C Grant Duff, *History of the Mahrattas*, I, pp. 156-157; C A Kinkaid and D B Parasnis, *A History of the Maratha People*, I, pp. 62-64; N S Takakhav and Keluskar, *Life of Shivaji Maharaj*, pp. 229-234; Rawlinson, *Shivaji, the Maratha*, pp. 68-70; C V Vaidya, *Shivaji, the Founder of the Maratha Swarajya*, pp.

This success of Shivaji made the Mughals realize the hopelessness of their situation in Maharashtra. Shayista Khan was transferred to Bengal by the emperor, on 01 December 1663.[142] Muazzam was sent to replace him as the viceroy in the Deccan.[143] He was a man given to the pleasures of the senses.[144] Mughal activities in the Deccan came virtually to a standstill, and Shivaji was free to send Netaji Palkar to plunder the Mughal territories up to the very vicinity of Aurangabad and Ahmadnagar.[145] Shivaji was now the acknowledged master of all the regions up to Kolhapur in the Deccan, and up to Goa in the Konkan.[146]

Shivaji was informed by his chief spy, Bahirji Nayak, of the insecurity of Surat, the richest port on the western coast,[147] and 'the gateway to the holy places of Arabia' for the Indian Muslim pilgrims.[148] Along with five thousand of his followers, he struck camp at Nasik, and secretly proceeded towards Surat, on the banks of the river Tapti. Early in January 1664, he arrived near Surat, and, on 5 January 1664, demanded rich payments from its local governor, Inayat Khan, and three prosperous merchants,

---

134-142; David Kincaied, *Shivaji, the Founder of the Maratha Empire*, pp. 145ff; G S Sardesai, *New History of the Marathas*, I, pp. 149-151; also G S Sardesai, Shivaji, Chapter IX, in R C Majumdar, J N Chaudhuri, and S Chaudhuri (ed), *The Mughul Empire* (The History and Culture of the Indian People, VII), pp. 259-260.

142 J N Sarkar, *History of Aurangzib*, IV, p. 66; *Shivaji and His Times*, p. 92; G S Sardesai, *New History of the Marathas*, I, pp. 150-151.

143 J N Sarkar, *Shivaji and His Times*, p. 92.

144 See David Kincaied, *Shivaji, the Founder of the Maratha Empire*, p. 157.

145 G S Sardesai, *New History of the Marathas*, I, p. 156; R V Nadkarni, *The Rise and Fall of the Maratha Empire*, pp. 59-60.

146 G S Sardesai, Shivaji, Chapter IX, in R C Majumdar, J N Chaudhuri, and S Chaudhuri (ed), *The Mughul Empire* (The History and Culture of the Indian People, VII), pp. 259-260; R V Nadkarni, *The Rise and Fall of the Maratha Empire*, p. 60.

147 G S Sardesai, *New History of the Marathas*, I, p. 151.

148 J N Sarkar, *History of Aurangzib*, IV, pp. 66-67; *Shivaji and His Times*, p. 92.

Haji Sayyid Beg, Baharji Borah, and Haji Qasim.[149] When his demands were not met with, and even an attempt was made on his life,[150] he attacked the city the next day, wrecked havoc, and plundered the rich, while the governor and his forces were kept confined to the fort, and thus rendered ineffective, by the Maratha musketeers.[151] It was only in the morning of 10 January 1664, when he heard of the imminent arrival of Mughal forces from Burhanpur, that Shivaji repaired to Raigadh with the large amount of booty.[152] Although this expedition proved very successful for Shivaji in terms of booty, it also earned him the wrath of the Mughal emperor, who decided to put an end to the Maratha menace, once and for all.[153] Shortly after these successes against the Mughals, Shivaji suffered the loss of his father, Shahji, on 23 January 1664.[154] Some time later, after having observed the prescribed period of mourning, Shivaji assumed the title of *raja*, and started issuing coins in his own name.[155]

Early in 1663, Ali Adilshah II of Bijapur embarked on a military expedition to recover the territories lost to Shivaji, but could not gain much success. He sent a large force under Ikhlas Khan to capture Kudal, and instructed his minister, Khavas Khan, and Baji Ghorpade to assist him. Vyankoji of Thanjavur, the half brother of Shivaji, also came out to fight on the side of the Adilshahi *sultan*. Shivaji, in November 1664, attacked Mudhol, where he made short work of the Ghorpades, ostensibly for Baji Ghorpade's rôle in the arrest of Shahji at Jinji in 1648.[156]

---

149 J N Sarkar, *Shivaji and His Times*, pp. 95-96; G S Sardesai, *New History of the Marathas*, I, pp. 152-153.

150 J N Sarkar, *Shivaji and His Times*, pp. 97-98,

151 J N Sarkar, *History of Aurangzib*, IV, p. 69-60.

152 J N Sarkar, *History of Aurangzib*, IV, pp. 66-73; David Kincaied, *Shivaji, the Founder of the Maratha Empire*, pp. 160ff; G S Sardesai, *New History of the Marathas*, I, pp. 151-155.

153 G S Sardesai, Shivaji, Chapter IX, in R C Majumdar, J N Chaudhuri, and S Chaudhuri (ed), *The Mughul Empire* (The History and Culture of the Indian People, VII), pp. 260-261.

154 For the death of Shahji, see above, Chapter I.

155 J C Grant Duff, *History of the Mahrattas*, I, p. 160.

156 G S Sardesai, *New History of the Marathas*, I, pp. 157-158; J N Sarkar, *Shivaji and His Times*, pp. 228ff.

Shivaji then proceeded against Khavas Khan, overtook and defeated him in December 1664, and went on to plunder Khanapur, Hubli, and other places.[157] He himself narrates his actions in the following words : 'Thereupon Khavas Khan marched upon me, and I on my part answered his charge vigorously. A stiff battled ensued in which the enemy was completely routed and ran back to Bijapur after losing some brave commanders under him. I then turned to punish the Sawant for his wanton desertion of my cause, plundered his territory and captured his forts and towns. As the Portuguese sheltered him I blew their fort of Ponda with gunpowder and captured it by sheer force. They negotiated for peace and gave me some guns. Pitambar Shenvai came to me as an envoy of peace to treat both for the Savant and the Portuguese. I annexed half the territories of the Savant and restored the other half to him. I reminded him that he was a son of the Bhosles and ought to join me in saving our country and religion.'[158] He, however, took no action against Vyankoji for the time being.[159] Early in 1665, Shivaji also led a naval expedition to plunder ports like Bassur on the Malabar coast.[160]

Towards the close of 1664, Aurangzeb despatched an expedition against Shivaji under Jay Singh,[161] and instructed Diler Khan and the Italian traveller, Nicholo Manucci,[162] to assist him. While Shivaji was busy in a war against Bijapur, Jay Singh occupied the Maratha dominions. Shivaji came to learn of the activities of the Mughal general while he was worshipping the deity of Gokarna at Karwar in February 1665. He immediately repaired to Raigadh, which was by then becoming the seat of his power. But Jay Singh arrived at Poona in March 1665, besieged

---

157 Balkrishna, *Shivaji the Great*, I, p. 533.

158 G S Sardesai (ed), *Shivaji Souvenir*, p. 144.

159 G S Sardesai, *New History of the Marathas*, I, p. 159.

160 G S Sardesai, Shivaji, Chapter IX, in R C Majumdar, J N Chaudhuri, and S Chaudhuri (ed), *The Mughul Empire* (The History and Culture of the Indian People, VII), p. 261.

161 *Ma'asir-i-Alamgiri*, p. 31.

162 *Storia do Mogor*, II, pp. 120-125, 132-137. See J N Sarkar, *Shivaji and His Times*, p. 105n.

Purandar,[163] and, within months, was able to secure the allegiance and support of all those, who felt overawed or wronged by Shivaji.[164] Manucci was sent to bribe the chiefs of the coastal forest areas to conduct raids on the Maratha outposts.[165] It appears that even the Portuguese of Goa, who had been helping Shivaji against the Mughals, found it wise to withdraw their support to the Maratha.[166] On 13 and 14 April 1665, the Mughals captured Vajragadh, the 'very strong sister enclosure' of the fort of Purandar.[167] In order to harass the Mughals besieging Purandar, Netaji Palkar led a cavalry attack on Parenda, but was repulsed and chased away by a Mughal detachment from Supa.[168] Shivaji found himself bereft of allies; he had also heard that Aurangzeb had despatched heavy artillery to help Jay Singh at Purandar.[169] Under the circumstances, he thought it wise to make peace with Jay Singh, who, however, played hard to get.[170] Thereupon, after Murar Baji and a number of Maratha soldiers had sacrificed their lives in a valiant defence of the fort of Purandar,[171] Shivaji went unarmed to meet Jay Singh in his quarters below the fort, on 11 June 1665. He

---

163 For the siege of Purandar, see J N Sarkar, *Shivaji and His Times*, pp. 113ff; David Kincaied, *Shivaji, the Founder of the Maratha Empire*, pp. 191ff. See also J N Sarkar, *House of Shivaji*, pp. 117ff.

164 J N Sarkar, *History of Aurangzib*, IV, pp. 78ff; *Shivaji and His Times*, pp. 106ff.

165 David Kincaied, *Shivaji, the Founder of the Maratha Empire*, p. 187.

166 *Proceedings of the Indian History Congress*, XXI, pp. 187-188.

167 J N Sarkar, *History of Aurangzib*, IV, p. 85; *Shivaji and His Times*, p. 114; G S Sardesai, *New History of the Marathas*, I, p. 162.

168 J N Sarkar, *History of Aurangzib*, IV, p. 87; *Shivaji and His Times*, p. 117; G S Sardesai, *New History of the Marathas*, I, p. 162.

169 J N Sarkar, *History of Aurangzib*, IV, p. 91.

170 J N Sarkar, *Shivaji and His Times*, p. 121 and n.

171 J C Grant Duff, *History of the Mahrattas*, I, pp. 175-176; G S Sardesai, *New History of the Marathas*, I, pp. 162-163. According to J N Sarkar (*History of Aurangzib*, IV, pp. 91-92) and R V Nadkarni (*The Rise and Fall of the Maratha Empire*, p. 63), 300 Mavalis lost their lives with Murar Baji. The date for this event is given as 02 June 1665. See J N Sarkar, *History of Aurangzib*, IV, p. 92.

succeeded in meeting Jay Singh through the good offices of Diler Khan.[172] Terms of peace were agreed upon,[173] and the treaty of Purandar was signed on 12 June 1665.[174] Under this treaty, Shivaji was to surrender 23 of his forts to the Mughals,[175] retaining control over only 12 minor ones.[176] He agreed to enter the service of the Mughal emperor, and provide assistance to Jay Singh in his future military actions against Bijapur; his son, Shambhuji was to enter the Mughal service as a *panchhazari mansabdar*.[177] Shivaji also accepted Jay Singh's advice[178] to seek the pardon of Aurangzeb by making a personal visit to him at Agra.[179]

---

172 G S Sardesai, *New History of the Marathas*, I, pp. 163ff.

173 For the terms of the treaty, see J N Sarkar, *House of Shivaji*, pp. 126ff.

174 *Ma'asir-i-Alamgiri*, p. 33; J N Sarkar, *Shivaji and His Times*, pp. 123-124.

175 *Ma'asir-i-Alamgiri*, p. 33. See also J N Sarkar, *House of Shivaji*, p. 121.

176 V K Rajwade (*Marathyanchya Itihasanchi Sadhane*, VIII, p. 14) and M G Ranade (*Rise of the Maratha Power*, p. 106), however, say that Shivaji had to surrender only 20 of his forts to the Mughals. For a list of the 23 forts surrendered to the Mughals by Shivaji, see J N Sarkar, *History of Aurangzib*, IV, p. 95; *Shivaji and His Times*, p. 126.

177 J N Sarkar, *History of Aurangzib*, IV, pp. 94ff.

178 J N Sarkar, *History of Aurangzib*, IV, pp. 98-99.

179 G S Sardesai, Shivaji, Chapter IX, in R C Majumdar, J N Chaudhuri, and S Chaudhuri (ed), *The Mughul Empire* (The History and Culture of the Indian People, VII), pp. 261-262. Regarding Shivaji's purpose behind the treaty of Purandar, M G Ranade observes : '[T]here must have been some deep-laid scheme of policy which justified him and his councillors the course he pursued. Shivaji might well have thought that his temporary submission and visit to Delhi would introduce him to a larger sphere of action or at least would enable him to make the acquaintance of the great Rajput nobles of the Empire. Jay Singh's friendship cemented by such an act of self-sacrifice might prove helpful in the furtherance of his larger designs. Shivaji had been always urging his claims to Chowth and Sardeshmukhi and though these claims had not been recognized either by Aurangzeb or Shah Jehan, hopes had been held out which encouraged him to think that

Shivaji did cooperate with Jay Singh in his war against Bijapur in November 1665.[180] Accompanied by Netaji Palkar, Shivaji led a 9,000 strong Maratha force, which 'formed the left centre of the Mughal army'.[181] Diler Khan and Netaji Palkar even succeeded in defeating the combined forces of Bijapur (led by Sharza Khan and Khavas Khan), Maloji Ghorpade of Mudhol, and Vynakoji of Thanjavur, at Mangalvedhe, in December 1665.[182] Jay Singh did not desire to engage his services in the siege of Bijapur. He was also aware of the danger to the freedom and life of Shivaji, posed by some Mughal officers like Diler Khan. Therefore, he permitted Shivaji to storm the fort of Panhala, in an effort to divert the armies of Bijapur.[183] The Maratha forces assaulted the fort, some three hours before sunrise, on 16 January 1666.[184] Although Shivaji was unable to capture it, his scheme of creating a diversion was successful, in that a Bijapuri force of 6,000 men was sent under Siddi Masud and Ranadaula Khan to defend Panhala. Shivaji gave up the assault, and repaired to the Maratha fort of Vishalgadh.[185]

According to J N Sarkar, the failure of the Maratha attempt to capture Panhala should be ascribed to Netaji Palkar, who was absent from his assigned position, when Shivaji assaulted that fort. As a consequence of the absence of Netaji Palkar, the garrison of the fort could afford to spare men from the sector he was supposed to storm, and send these men to the defence of the sector assaulted by Shivaji.[186]

---

by temporary submission he might secure a legitimate basis for the assertion of these claims.' See R V Nadkarni, *The Rise and Fall of the Maratha Empire*, p. 64; also J N Sarkar, *History of Aurangzib*, IV, p. 99.

180 *Ma'asir-i-Alamgiri*, p. 38. See J N Sarkar, *History of Aurangzib*, IV, pp. 97-98; *Shivaji and His Times*, pp. 126-130.

181 J N Sarkar, *Shivaji and His Times*, pp. 127-128; G S Sardesai, *New History of the Marathas*, I, p. 168.

182 G S Sardesai, *New History of the Marathas*, I, p. 168.

183 J N Sarkar, *Shivaji and His Times*, pp. 130-131.

184 G S Sardesai, *New History of the Marathas*, I, p. 168.

185 J N Sarkar, *History of Aurangzib*, IV, p. 137.

186 J N Sarkar, *Shivaji and His Times*, pp. 131-132.

Sabhasad, however, says that Netaji Palkar showed this negligence, when Shivaji stormed the siege trenches of Siddi Jauhar near Panhala, and angered by this, Shivaji removed him from the post of *sarnobat*, and appointed Prataprao Gujar to that post.[187] The *91 Qalmi Bakhar* also gives a similar account, but states that negligence occurred on the part of the brother-in-law of Netaji Palkar. When Shivaji suspended the payment of his salary for a month as punishment, Netaji Palkar behaved in an unseemly manner, for which he was immediately dismissed from his position. These two Marathi sources would indicate that the dismissal of Netaji Palkar occurred in 1660, when Shivaji assaulted the siege trenches of Siddi Jauhar near Panhala. But that Netaji Palkar was in the service of Shivaji till January 1666, is indicated, not only by Jay Singh referring to Netaji Palkar as 'the second Shiva' several times in 1665, but also by the *English Factory Records*. Therefore, J N Sarkar rightly suggests that the negligence on the part of Netaji Palkar occurred during the Maratha assault on Panhala on 16 January 1666, and not in 1660 when Shivaji stormed the siege trenches of Siddi Jauhar.[188]

Angered by his summary dismissal, Netaji Palkar went over to Bijapur, where he was offered four lac of *huns* by the Adilshahi *sultan*, and became active against the Mughals.[189] Troubled by this development, Jay Singh won him over to his side by granting him the position of a *panchhazari*, fifty thousand of rupees in cash,[190] and a *jaghir*.[191]

On receipt of favourable reports of the conduct of Shivaji from Jay Singh, and on the latter's passionate entreaties,[192]

---

187 *Sabhasad-bakhar*, p. 59.

188 J N Sarkar, *Shivaji and His Times*, pp. 131-132.

189 G S Sardesai, *New History of the Marathas*, I, p. 169.

190 In his *History of Aurangzib*, IV, p. 138, J N Sarkar gives the amount of cash payment to Netaji Palkar as thirty eight thousand of rupees.

191 J N Sarkar, *Shivaji and His Times*, p. 131; G S Sardesai, *New History of the Marathas*, I, p. 169.

192 *Ma'asir-i-Alamgiri*, p. 36. There is a suggestion that Jay Singh was greatly alarmed by the defection of Netaji Palkar to Bijapur, and feared that Shivaji, too, might go over to the Adilshah. He, therefore, advised Aurangzeb to show imperial favour to the

Aurangzeb agreed to grant an audience to Shivaji.[193] After hectic consultations with his advisors, and on Jay Singh and his sons, Ram Singh and Kirat Singh,[194] guaranteeing the safety of Shivaji at Agra,[195] the Maratha chief and his entourage left Raigadh for Agra on 05 March 1666,[196] leaving behind Jijabai as regent.[197] Sabhasad says that Netaji Palkar was left behind by Shivaji in charge of his army. But this is not possible, for, as seen above, Netaji Palkar had been dismissed from his position by Shivaji immediately after the failure at Panhala, and he had defected over, first to Bijapur, and then to the Mughals, early in 1666.[198] It would have been Prataprao Gujar, the new *sarnobat*, who would have been left behind in charge of the Maratha army in Maharashtra.[199] On 12 May 1666, Aurangzeb received Shivaji and his son in the *Divan-i-Khas*,[200] and accepted the *nazar* offered by the Maratha. However, trouble broke out when Shivaji was not treated like a *shahzada*, as promised, but asked

---

Maratha by granting him an audience. J N Sarkar, *Shivaji and His Times*, pp. 132-133. G S Sardesai, *New History of the Marathas*, I, pp. 173-174.

193 G S Sardesai, Shivaji, Chapter IX, in R C Majumdar, J N Chaudhuri, and S Chaudhuri (ed), *The Mughul Empire* (The History and Culture of the Indian People, VII), p. 262.

194 G S Sardesai, *New History of the Marathas*, I, p. 174.

195 J N Sarkar, *History of Aurangzib*, IV, p. 100.

196 G S Sardesai, Shivaji, Chapter IX, in R C Majumdar, J N Chaudhuri, and S Chaudhuri (ed), *The Mughul Empire* (The History and Culture of the Indian People, VII), pp. 262-263. For the journey of Shivaji to Agra, see J N Sarkar, *Shivaji and His Times*, pp. 137ff.

197 J N Sarkar, *History of Aurangzib*, IV, p. 100.

198 J N Sarkar, *Shivaji and His Times*, p. 132n.

199 See G S Sardesai, *New History of the Marathas*, I, p. 175.

200 G S Sardesai, *New History of the Marathas*, I, p. 178; also G S Sardesai, Shivaji, Chapter IX, in R C Majumdar, J N Chaudhuri, and S Chaudhuri (ed), *The Mughul Empire* (The History and Culture of the Indian People, VII), p. 263. J N Sarkar (*History of Aurangzib*, IV, p. 101), however, says that Shivaji met Aurangzeb in the *Divan-i-Am*. But in his *Shivaji and His Times*, p. 142, the meeting is described as having taken place in the *Divan-i-Khas*.

to stand in the third row of the nobles.[201] Aurangzeb took strong exception to the vehement protestations of Shivaji,[202] and he was confined in the garden of Ram Singh.[203]

Aurangzeb planned to move Shivaji to a secluded place, the house of Radandaz Khan,[204] and quietly put him to death. But Shivaji was planning his escape. He pretended illness, and, to get rid of the anxiety regarding the safety of his attendants, sent most of them away.[205] Then, on 19 August 1666,[206] a day before he was to be shifted to the house of Fidai Husain,[207] he and his son escaped from prison, hiding in baskets of sweetmeats,[208] which he sent out everyday to be distributed among the poor as charity.[209] His escape could be detected only about the noon of

---

201 For the lukewarm reception offered Shivaji by Aurangzeb, see V K Rajwade, *Marathyanchya Itihasanchi Sadhane*, VIII, p. 23.

202 For the furor created by Shivaji in the Mughal court, see *Ma'asir-i-Alamgiri*, p. 36. Also J N Sarkar, *History of Aurangzib*, IV, pp. 101-102; *Shivaji and His Times*, pp. 142-144; David Kincaied, *Shivaji, the Founder of the Maratha Empire*, p. 220; G S Sardesai, *New History of the Marathas*, I, pp. 178-179.

203 G S Sardesai, Shivaji, Chapter IX, in R C Majumdar, J N Chaudhuri, and S Chaudhuri (ed), *The Mughul Empire* (The History and Culture of the Indian People, VII), p. 263. For some details of Shivaji's visit to Aurangzeb, see J N Sarkar, *House of Shivaji*, pp. 136ff.

204 J N Sarkar, *Shivaji and His Times*, p. 145; G S Sardesai, *New History of the Marathas*, I, p. 180.

205 J N Sarkar, *History of Aurangzib*, IV, pp. 107-108; David Kincaied, *Shivaji, the Founder of the Maratha Empire*, p. 226; G S Sardesai, *New History of the Marathas*, I, p. 182.

206 On 17 August 1660, according to G S Sardesai, *New History of the Marathas*, I, p. 183.

207 G S Sardesai, *New History of the Marathas*, I, pp. 185-186.

208 See G S Sardesai, *New History of the Marathas*, I, p. 184, for this device used by Shivaji, as described by the French traveller, Thevenot, who was present at Agra at that time.

209 J N Sarkar, *History of Aurangzib*, IV, p. 108; *Shivaji and His Times*, pp. 149-150. However, *contra* David Kincaied, *Shivaji, the Founder of the Maratha Empire*, p. 228, who says that the baskets were apparently being sent to a Mughal court official. *Cf* J C Grant Duff (*History of the Mahrattas*, I, p. 183, numbering of pages is

20 August 1666.[210] There was earlier some uncertainty about the route he took while escaping. However, now it is generally believed that, '[i]nstead of moving due south-west from Agra, through Malwa and Khandesh or Gujrat, he travelled *northwards* to Mathura, then *eastwards* to Allahabad, and finally south-westwards through Bundelkhand, Gondwana, and Golkonda, describing a curve east of the public highway to the Deccan, in returning to Rajgadh'.[211] At Mathura, Shivaji was met by Tanaji Malasure,[212] and, entrusting an exhausted Shambhuji in the care of Krishnaji, Kashi, and Visaji, the brothers-in-law of Moropant Trimbak Pingle,[213] the Maratha chief, travelling in the garb of a *samnyasin*, reached Jijabai at Raigadh on 12 September 1666.[214] The incident had an adverse effect on the reputation of Aurangzeb. But the prestige of Shivaji was greatly enhanced,[215] so much so that the sultanates of both Bijapur and Golkunda agreed to pay him an annual *chauth*.[216]

---

faulty in 1912 edition of the work), who says that the baskets of sweetmeats were sent both to the Mughal nobles and to the poor.

210 J N Sarkar, *Shivaji and His Times*, p. 150. *Ma'asir-i-Alamgiri* (p. 37) makes only a passing reference to the escape, and reveals that Aurangzeb held Ram Singh responsible for it.

211 J N Sarkar, *Shivaji and His Times*, p. 152; *cf* J N Sarkar, *History of Aurangzib*, IV, p. 111.

212 R V Nadkarni, *The Rise and Fall of the Maratha Empire*, p. 66.

213 J N Sarkar, *History of Aurangzib*, IV, p. 111. The three brothers were, later on, amply rewarded. J N Sarkar, *Shivaji and His Times*, p. 153.

214 For details of Shivaji in the presence of Aurangzeb and his escape from Agra, see C A Kinkaid and D B Parasnis, *A History of the Maratha People*, I, pp. 72-78; J N Sarkar, *Shivaji and His Times*, pp. 134-154; N S Takakhav and Keluskar, *Life of Shivaji Maharaj*, pp. 274-294; Rawlinson, *Shivaji, the Maratha*, pp. 73-74; G S Sardesai, *New History of the Marathas*, I, pp. 183ff; G S Sardesai, Shivaji, Chapter IX, in R C Majumdar, J N Chaudhuri, and S Chaudhuri (ed), *The Mughul Empire* (The History and Culture of the Indian People, VII), pp. 263-264.

215 G S Sardesai, *New History of the Marathas*, I, p. 188.

216 G S Sardesai, Shivaji, Chapter IX, in R C Majumdar, J N Chaudhuri, and S Chaudhuri (ed), *The Mughul Empire* (The History and Culture of the Indian People, VII), pp. 264-265.

Immediately after the escape of Shivaji from Agra, Aurangzeb instructed Jay Singh to arrest Netaji Palkar,[217] who had by then entered the service of the Mughals. The former Maratha *sarnobat* was imprisoned at Dharur in October 1666, and sent to Delhi as a captive. In February 1667, he was forced to convert to Islam, as the only means of saving his life.[218] Even his family was brought from Maharashtra, and forcibly converted.[219] Netaji Palkar was given the name of Muhammad Quli Khan,[220] and was sent to serve in Afghanistan,[221] from where he could return only about ten years later.[222]

Suspecting Jay Singh himself of disloyalty, Aurangzeb recalled him, and the Rajput *raja* died at Burhanpur, on 28 August 1667,[223] on his way to Agra.[224] Shivaji, however, came to an understanding with Muazzam,[225] and Shambhuji was sent to Aurangabad, as agreed in the treaty of Purandar.[226] According to the *Jedhe Sakavali*, in August 1665, a Maratha contingent, under Prataprao Gujar and Niraji Raoji, was also sent to Aurangabad,[227] the two officers acting as guardians of Shambhuji.[228]

---

217 *Ma'asir-i-Alamgiri*, p. 37. See also J N Sarkar, *House of Shivaji*, p. 154.

218 J N Sarkar, *History of Aurangzib*, IV, p. 138; *House of Shivaji*, pp. 154-155.

219 J N Sarkar, *House of Shivaji*, p. 155.

220 *Ma'asir-i-Alamgiri*, pp. 38, 40.

221 G S Sardesai, *New History of the Marathas*, I, p. 190.

222 J N Sarkar, *Shivaji and His Times*, p. 157.

223 J N Sarkar, *Shivaji and His Times*, p. 160.

224 *Ma'asir-i-Alamgiri*, p. 41. J N Sarkar, *History of Aurangzib*, IV, pp. 112-113.

225 G S Sardesai, *New History of the Marathas*, I, pp. 191-192.

226 J N Sarkar, *History of Aurangzib*, IV, pp. 115-117; J N Sarkar, *Shivaji and His Times*, pp. 161-163; G S Sardesai, *New History of the Marathas*, I, pp. 190ff; also G S Sardesai, Shivaji, Chapter IX, in R C Majumdar, J N Chaudhuri, and S Chaudhuri (ed), *The Mughul Empire* (The History and Culture of the Indian People, VII), pp. 264-265.

227 J N Sarkar, *History of Aurangzib*, IV, p. 198; G S Sardesai, *New History of the Marathas*, I, p. 192.

228 G S Sardesai, *New History of the Marathas*, I, p. 195.

For two years following his escape from Agra, Shivaji was relatively inactive, a fact noted even in the English factory records.[229] However, the peace was broken when Aurangzeb instructed Muazzam to arrest Prataprao Gujar and Niraji Raoji, and take them as hostages along with Shambhuji. According to Sabhasad, Muazzam conveyed this information to Niraji Raoji.[230] On learning of this development, Shivaji instructed Prataprao Gujar to escape from Aurangabad, with his contingent. The Maratha soldiers stationed in Shambhuji's *jaghir* in Berar also slipped away.[231] On 09 April 1669, Aurangzeb had issued general orders, which signalled an unprecedented persecution of the Hindus. A number of Hindu temples, including the famous Visvanatha temple at Varanasi, and the Keshav Rai temple at Mathura, were pulled down, and mosques were built in their place.[232] Retaliating against this,[233] in February 1670, Shivaji attacked and captured the fort of Singhgadh, which he had earlier handed over to the Mughals, although, in the process, he lost one of his most trusted officers, Tanaji Malasure, who had scaled the walls of the fort, with the help of an iguana, along with 300 soldiers.[234] Shivaji is reported to have remarked that he had come in possession of [Singh]gadh, but had lost the lion (*simha*).[235] Subsequently, he reoccupied Purandar on 08 March 1670,[236]

---

229 J N Sarkar, *History of Aurangzib*, IV, pp. 198-199.

230 G S Sardesai, *New History of the Marathas*, I, p. 195.

231 J N Sarkar, *History of Aurangzib*, IV, pp. 199-200; *Shivaji and His Times*, p. 164.

232 G S Sardesai, *New History of the Marathas*, I, p. 196.

233 But *contra* J N Sarkar, *Shivaji and His Times*, p. 164n.

234 The account of the capture of Singhgadh forms the subject matter of the famous Ballad of Singhgadh, composed by Tulasidas, a bard from Poona. See Rawlinson, *Shivaji, the Maratha*, Appendix I. See also *Sabhasad-bakhar*, pp. 56-57; S N Sen, *Shiva Chhatrapati*, pp. 72-74; J N Sarkar, *Shivaji and His Times*, pp. 165-166; G S Sardesai, *New History of the Marathas*, I, pp. 198-200.

235 *Gadh ala, simha gela*. See J C Grant Duff, *History of the Mahrattas*, I, p. 197; David Kincaied, *Shivaji, the Founder of the Maratha Empire*, p. 256n. Also R V Nadkarni, *The Rise and Fall of the Maratha Empire*, p. 67.

236 *Ma'asir-i-Alamgiri*, p. 62. See J N Sarkar, *History of Aurangzib*, IV, p. 203; *Shivaji and His Times*, p. 166.

Kalyan on 30 March 1670,[237] and Mahuli on 16 June 1670.[238] After recovering a number of other places in northern Konkan, Shivaji attacked Surat,[239] with an army of 15,000 men, looted the recently fortified city for three days, early in October 1670, carrying away booty worth almost 66 lac of rupees.[240] The plunder of several towns in the possession of the Mughals continued for well nigh three years (1670-1673).[241]

In the course of these three years, Shivaji won some successes against the Mughals and the Adilshahi *sultan* of Bijapur. On 17 October 1670, Ikhlas Khan, the commander of the vanguard of the Mughal forces under Daud Khan, attacked the Maratha rearguard commanded by Prataprao Gujar and some other officers, near Vani Dindori. However, he was no match to the Maratha general, and was soon wounded and had to be rescued by Daud Khan himself.[242] Shortly afterwards, the fort of Trimbak was captured by Moropant Trimbak Pingle.[243] In the month of December 1670, a Maratha contingent, under Prataprao Gujar, captured some forts in Baglan, including Ahivant, and attacked Khandesh. The Maratha force looted the village of Bahadurpura in the vicinity of Burhanpur, the capital of Khandesh, and Karinja in Berar; the residents of those regions agreed to pay *chauth* to the Marathas in future.[244] Meanwhile, Moropant Trimbak Pingle was involved in similar activities in western Khandesh and Baglan. The Maratha forces, led by these

---

237 J N Sarkar, *History of Aurangzib*, IV, p. 203.

238 J N Sarkar, *Shivaji and His Times*, pp. 166-167. For these three forts, see G S Sardesai, *New History of the Marathas*, I, p. 200.

239 *Ma'asir-i-Alamgiri*, p. 66.

240 J N Sarkar, *History of Aurangzib*, IV, pp. 211-216; *Shivaji and His Times*, pp. 170-175; G S Sardesai, *New History of the Marathas*, I, p. 201.

241 G S Sardesai, Shivaji, Chapter IX, in R C Majumdar, J N Chaudhuri, and S Chaudhuri (ed), *The Mughul Empire* (The History and Culture of the Indian People, VII), pp. 265-266.

242 J N Sarkar, *History of Aurangzib*, IV, pp. 216-218; *Shivaji and His Times*, pp. 176-178.

243 J N Sarkar, *History of Aurangzib*, IV, p. 218.

244 J C Grant Duff, *History of the Mahrattas*, I, pp. 200-201; J N Sarkar, *History of Aurangzib*, IV, pp. 219-220; G S Sardesai, *New History of the Marathas*, I, pp. 202-203.

two Maratha officers, converged on Salher, a strategically important fort on the borders of Khandesh and Gujarat. Early in January 1671, the Marathas won a notable victory at Salher.[245] The Mughals tried to reoccupy it in 1672, and the resultant conflict took a heavy toll on both the sides. Prataprao Gujar and Moropant Trimbak Pingle exhibited rare valour in a cavalry action against Ikhlas Khan, who was captured.[246]

Following the death of Ali Adilshah II in 1672, Shivaji also reopened a front against Bijapur, and captured the fort of Panhala in 06 March 1673.[247] It was during this capture of Panhala, that a young officer, Santaji Ghorpade, who later rose to the position of *senapati* under Rajaram, exhibited rare valour.[248] In April 1673, Khavas Khan, the regent of the boy *sultan*, Sikandar Adilshah, of Bijapur, sent Bahlol Khan and three other generals to recover the fort of Panhala. Shivaji sent Prataprao Gujar and some other Maratha officers against Bahlol Khan. The Maratha *sarnobat* attacked the Bijapuri forces at Umbrani, about 36 miles to the west of the city of Bijapur. The battle raged till nightfall. Bahlol Khan secretly conveyed to Prataprao Gujar that he did not want to fight against the Marathas, but was only making a show for the benefit of the Bijapuri authorities. He succeeded in convincing Prataprao Gujar to allow the Bijapuri forces to retreat to their base at Tikota, for which the Maratha general was reprimanded by Shivaji.[249]

---

245 J N Sarkar, *History of Aurangzib*, IV, pp. 221-222; *Shivaji and His Times*, pp. 179-180; G S Sardesai, *New History of the Marathas*, I, p. 203.

246 J N Sarkar, *History of Aurangzib*, IV, pp. 224-226; J N Sarkar, *Shivaji and His Times*, p. 185; Rawlinson, *Shivaji, the Maratha*, p. 81; G S Sardesai, *New History of the Marathas*, I, pp. 203ff; R V Nadkarni, *The Rise and Fall of the Maratha Empire*, pp. 67-68.

247 J N Sarkar, *Shivaji and His Times*, p. 193; G S Sardesai, *New History of the Marathas*, I, pp. 209-210; also G S Sardesai, Shivaji, Chapter IX, in R C Majumdar, J N Chaudhuri, and S Chaudhuri (ed), *The Mughul Empire* (The History and Culture of the Indian People, VII), p. 266.

248 Below, Chapter III.

249 J N Sarkar, *Shivaji and His Times*, pp. 194-195; G S Sardesai, *New History of the Marathas*, I, pp. 210-211. According to Sarkar, Prataprao Gujar was bribed by Bahlol Khan.

The Marathas were much emboldened by these successes. In May 1673, Prataprao Gujar led a Maratha force into Bijapuri Kanara, and looted Hubli and a number of other places.[250] However, in June 1673, the Marathas also suffered some reverses at the hands of the Bijapuri general, Bahlol Khan, near Kolhapur.[251] Shivaji's raids on the Kanara region during October to December 1673, were also unsuccessful due to the strong defence provided by the Bijapuri generals, like Bahlol Khan, Sharza Khan, and others.[252]

In January 1674, Shivaji despatched an angry letter to Prataprao Gujar, censuring him for not destroying Bahlol Khan at Umbrani, when he had him in his power, and ordering him to inflict a crushing defeat on the Bijapuri general.[253] On 24 February 1674, Prataprao Gujar encountered Bahlol Khan at Nesari. In his anger, he rushed upon the Bijapuri general with only six or seven horsemen, and all of them were slain by the enemy.[254] The Bijapuri forces then attacked the Maratha army, and there was much bloodshed. The survivors returned to Shivaji under the command of Anandrao Makaji.[255] Shivaji sent him with a Maratha force to give battle to Bahlol Khan, but he could not achieve any success, and was forced to retreat towards Kanara, where the Marathas indulged in large scale plunder and loot in the *jaghir* of Bahlol Khan. Anandrao even succeeded in robbing the entire army of Bahlol Khan, but had to abandon the

---

250 J N Sarkar, *Shivaji and His Times*, p. 238.

251 J N Sarkar, *History of Aurangzib*, IV, pp. 235-236; *Shivaji and His Times*, p. 195.

252 J N Sarkar, *Shivaji and His Times*, p. 195.

253 J C Grant Duff, *History of the Mahrattas*, I, p. 210; G S Sardesai, *New History of the Marathas*, I, p. 211.

254 G S Sardesai, *New History of the Marathas*, I, p. 211.

255 In the *Sabhasad-bakhar* and the *Chitnis-bakhar*, we find Hansaji Mohite (later on, famous as Hambirrao Mohite) in place of Anandrao. See J N Sarkar, *Shivaji and His Times*, p. 196n. *Cf* J C Grant Duff, *History of the Mahrattas*, I, p. 211. But J N Sarkar (*Shivaji and His Times*, p. 196n) gives greater credence to the information supplied by Narayan Shenvi, in whose account of the event, written only a month after its occurrence, the credit has been given to Anandrao.

booty when he was counterattacked by the Bijapuri general.[256] Shivaji was deeply saddened by the loss of the gallant Prataprao Gujar, and made suitable provisions for his family, even marrying his daughter to Rajaram.[257] On 08 April 1674, Hansaji Mohite, with the title of *Hambirrao*, was appointed to succeed Prataprao Gujar as *sarnobat*.[258] Nevertheless, the Marathas did not lose heart at these reverses, continued their efforts, and, shortly afterwards, occupied the Bijapuri territories as far as Miraj.[259]

After almost thirty years of incessant struggles against the Bijapuri *sultans*, the Mughals, and his own Maratha compatriots, Shivaji ultimately decided to give a legal form to his status as the independent sovereign ruler of the kingdom,[260] over which he had been exercising authority for the last over twenty years. After he had secured evidence of the descent of his family from the Sisodia Ranas of Udaipur, which gave him kshatriya status,[261] he was formally coronated, with the titles of *chhatrapati*, *maharaja*, *kshatriyakulavatamsa*, *simhasanadhisvara*, etc, on 06 June 1674,[262] by Gagabhatt of Varanasi, at a grand ceremony, which is reputed to have cost around five crores.[263] Shivaji also founded

---

256 J N Sarkar, *Shivaji and His Times*, pp. 195-198; G S Sardesai, *New History of the Marathas*, I, pp. 211-212.

257 J N Sarkar, *Shivaji and His Times*, p. 196.

258 See *Sabhasad-bakhar*, p. 79. See also J C Grant Duff, *History of the Mahrattas*, I, p. 211; J N Sarkar, *Shivaji and His Times*, p. 198.

259 R V Nadkarni, *The Rise and Fall of the Maratha Empire*, p. 68. See also J N Sarkar, *Shivaji and His Times*, pp. 240ff.

260 For the disadvantages of not being the formally crowned king, see J N Sarkar, *Shivaji and His Times*, pp. 201-202.

261 J N Sarkar, *Shivaji and His Times*, pp. 202-203.

262 This is the date given by J N Sarkar, *Shivaji and His Times*, p. 207. G S Sardesai (*New History of the Marathas*, I, p. 219) gives the date as 05 June 1674.

263 This is the information provided by Sabhasad. It is believed that about 50 lac was spent on the actual ceremony, and the balance of the figure given by Sabhasad was spent on the fortifications of the capital, Raigadh, and on other construction activities. A reliable, eyewitness account of the coronation ceremony has been given by Henry Oxinden, the English ambassador from the East India Company, who is believed to have gone to Raigadh to negotiate for

an era, commencing from the date of his coronation, and came to be known as *sakakarta*, 'founder of an era'.[264] On the occasion, Shivaji formally announced the following as the *ashta-pradhana* or the council of eight ministers:

1. *Peshva* (prime minister)—Moropant Trimbak/Trimal Pingle;
2. *Amatya* (revenue minister)—Ramchandra Nilkanth;
3. *Sachiv* (finance minister)—Annaji Datto;
4. *Mantri* (minister for interior)—Dattaji Trimbak;
5. *Senapati* (commander-in-chief)—Hambirrao Mohite;
6. *Sumant* (minister for external affairs)—Ramchandra Trimbak;
7. *Nyayadhish* (the chief judge)—Niraji Raoji; and
8. *Panditrao* (minister for religious affairs)—Raghunath Pandit.[265]

---

peace between the Marathas and the English. See R V Nadkarni, *The Rise and Fall of the Maratha Empire*, p. 70. For the details of the preparations and the ceremony itself, see J N Sarkar, *Shivaji and His Times*, pp. 203ff; also G S Sardesai, *New History of the Marathas*, I, p. 216ff.

264 G S Sardesai, Shivaji, Chapter IX, in R C Majumdar, J N Chaudhuri, and S Chaudhuri (ed), *The Mughul Empire* (The History and Culture of the Indian People, VII), pp. 266-268. See also Rawlinson, *Shivaji, the Maratha*, pp. 84-85. For a reported second coronation of Shivaji, this one on 24 September 1674, see J N Sarkar, *Shivaji and His Times*, pp. 211-214; G S Sardesai, *New History of the Marathas*, I, pp. 224-225.

265 G S Sardesai, Shivaji, Chapter IX, in R C Majumdar, J N Chaudhuri, and S Chaudhuri (ed), *The Mughul Empire* (The History and Culture of the Indian People, VII), p. 268. On the basis of the use of Sanskrit designations and terminology, it has been surmised by some scholars that the *svarajya* of Shivaji was based on the provisions laid down in the ancient Indian *sastras*. *Cf* G S Sardesai, *New History of the Marathas*, I, pp. 111-112. However, this is challenged by others, who believe that Shivaji followed the model of the Muslim sultanates of the Deccan. See V G Dighe and S N Qanungo, Administrative and Military System of the Marathas, Chapter XVII, in R C Majumdar and V G Dighe (ed), *The Maratha Supremacy* (The History and Culture of the Indian People, VIII), p. 542.

The *peshva* was to receive an annual salary of 15,000 of *huns* in cash, and the *amatya*, 12,000 of *huns*; each of the other six ministers were to receive 10,000 of *huns*.[266] All the payments were to be made in cash, Shivaji being against the allotment of *jaghirs* in *lieu* of salary.[267] None of these offices was to be hereditary.[268]

Aurangzeb took the formal coronation as a personal affront. Bahadur Khan posed a threat to the newly founded sovereign Maratha state from the east. Shivaji had launched a campaign against the Koli country of northern Konkan, Baglan, and Khandesh.[269]

According to G S Sardesai, after the coronation of Shivaji, some forts held by Bijapur, like those of Satara and Parli, were occupied by the Marathas, in 1674.[270] However, J N Sarkar writes that these places had been captured by July 1673, months before the coronation.[271] Shivaji also had a conflict with the Portuguese of Goa.[272] He is reported to have wrested Ponda, probably from the Portuguese themselves,[273] in May 1675.[274] Shortly after the capture of Ponda, a number of places, like

---

266 G S Sardesai, *New History of the Marathas*, I, pp. 223-224, 280.

267 G S Sardesai, *New History of the Marathas*, I, p. 282.

268 G S Sardesai, *New History of the Marathas*, I, p. 282. See also V G Dighe and S N Qanungo, Administrative and Military System of the Marathas, Chapter XVII, in R C Majumdar and V G Dighe (ed), *The Maratha Supremacy* (The History and Culture of the Indian People, VIII), p. 542.

269 J N Sarkar, *History of Aurangzib*, IV, pp. 227ff; *Shivaji and His Times*, pp. 215ff.

270 G S Sardesai, Shivaji, Chapter IX, in R C Majumdar, J N Chaudhuri, and S Chaudhuri (ed), *The Mughul Empire* (The History and Culture of the Indian People, VII), p. 269.

271 J N Sarkar, *Shivaji and His Times*, p. 193.

272 J N Sarkar, *Shivaji and His Times*, p. 218.

273 J N Sarkar (*Shivaji and His Times*, p. 241), however, calls Ponda 'the most important *Bijapuri* fort near Goa' [*italics* mine].

274 G S Sardesai, Shivaji, Chapter IX, in R C Majumdar, J N Chaudhuri, and S Chaudhuri (ed), *The Mughul Empire* (The History and Culture of the Indian People, VII), p. 269. *Cf* J N Sarkar, *Shivaji and His Times*, pp. 241-243.

Ankola, Siveshvar, Karwar, and Kadra, also fell into the hands of the Marathas.[275]

It has been observed that, despite his grand coronation and lofty titles, in 1674, Shivaji's 'actual dominion was hardly more than two hundred miles in length and far less in breadth'.[276] Therefore, he wanted to extend the boundaries of his kingdom. The Mughals in the north, and the Siddis of Janjira and the Portuguese of Goa in the west, were great hurdles in his plans for the expansion of his authority. The south, however, provided an opportunity to the Maratha chief. Conquests towards the south would not only extend his dominions, but also provide him with a safe base against both the Mughals and Bijapur.[277] In that direction, the two main players were Bijapur and Golkunda. Shivaji's half brother, Vyankoji, who had been appointed to succeed Shahji in Karnataka,[278] had probably declared himself an independent sovereign in Thanjavur, but was still favourably inclined towards Bijapur.[279]

In 1672, the rulers of both Bijapur and Golkunda died, and their death was followed by a struggle for succession and anarchy in both the sultanates. So strong was the anti-Maratha feeling in Bijapur, that its new ruler 'would rather sell the State

---

275 J N Sarkar, *Shivaji and His Times*, p. 243.

276 G S Sardesai, Shivaji, Chapter IX, in R C Majumdar, J N Chaudhuri, and S Chaudhuri (ed), *The Mughul Empire* (The History and Culture of the Indian People, VII), p. 269.

277 According to J N Sarkar (*Shivaji and His Times*, p. 277; *History of Aurangzib*, IV, p. 247), the main aim of Shivaji behind his Karnataka expedition, so far removed from his kingdom in Maharashtra, was plunder, in order to replenish his treasury exhausted by his grand coronation. See J N Sarkar, *History of Aurangzib*, IV, p. 238. However, scholars like S N Sen and C V Vaidya (see *Shivaji, the Founder of the Maratha Swarajya*, p. 279) are of the view that Shivaji undertook the expedition to make fresh conquests. See also J N Sarkar, *Shivaji and His Times*, p. 276, where he states that Shivaji was 'looking about for some fresh field of gain'. G S Sardesai (*New History of the Marathas*, I, p. 233) strikes a balance between the two views.

278 David Kincaied, *Shivaji, the Founder of the Maratha Empire*, p. 291.

279 G S Sardesai, *New History of the Marathas*, I, p. 236.

to Aurangzib and his nominee Diler Khan than let it fall into the hands of Shivaji'.[280] In Golkunda, Abul Hasan Qutbshah was not capable of providing leadership to his kingdom, and defending it against the Mughals, although his sultanate was being ably managed by two of his Hindu ministers, the brothers Madanna and Akkanna.[281]

In Thanjavur, Raghunathpant Hanumante, the loyal minister of Vyankoji,[282] tried his best to veer his master around to supporting Shivaji. Failing miserably in his endeavour due to the influence of some unscrupulous Muslim advisors of Vyankoji, Raghunathpant Hanumante left the side of his king. He first went to Bijapur to muster support for Shivaji, and, thereafter, to Golkunda, where he was welcomed by Madanna and Akkanna, and the three of them convinced Abul Hasan Qutbshah to meet Shivaji and join forces with him for the mutual benefit of both the powers. Raghunathpant Hanumante went to Raigadh in 1676, and revealed his plan to an enthusiastic Shivaji,[283] who travelled to Haidarabad, in the company of Hambirrao Mohite, Yesaji Kank, Suryaji Malasure, Anandrao Makaji, and other military officers,[284] to meet Abul Hasan Qutbshah, leaving behind Moropant Trimbak Pingle to take care of the main kingdom, and Annaji Datto, of the conquered territories in the Konkan.[285] An understanding was reached between Shivaji and Abul Hasan Qutbshah,[286] according to which, they were to form a joint front,

---

280 G S Sardesai, Shivaji, Chapter IX, in R C Majumdar, J N Chaudhuri, and S Chaudhuri (ed), *The Mughul Empire* (The History and Culture of the Indian People, VII), p. 270.

281 *Cf* J C Grant Duff, *History of the Mahrattas*, I, p. 221; G S Sardesai, *New History of the Marathas*, I, p. 235.

282 J N Sarkar (*Shivaji and His Times*, p. 282) doubts the loyalty of Raghunathpant Hanumante, and says that the minister, during his long tenure as regent of Vyankoji, had prospered by unscrupulous means.

283 G S Sardesai, *New History of the Marathas*, I, p. 237.

284 J N Sarkar, *Shivaji and His Times*, p. 287; G S Sardesai, *New History of the Marathas*, I, p. 239.

285 J N Sarkar, *Shivaji and His Times*, p. 285.

286 According to some scholars, Prahlad Niraji, Shivaji's envoy in the Qutbshahi court at Haidarabad, also had an important rôle to play in this understanding reached between Shivaji and Golkunda. See J

both to resist the Mughal advance and to make new conquests. It was agreed that the two would divide, equally among themselves, all the new acquisitions, to which Shivaji had no claims as inheritance from Shahji.[287] The Maratha also promised to pay an annual tribute of six lac of *huns* to the Qutbshahi *sultan*.[288] The *sultan* was to pay 3,000 of *huns* per day towards military expenses on the expedition,[289] and also provide support in the form of 5,000 soldiers, and artillerymen together with the necessary equipments.[290] Bahadur Khan, the Mughal viceroy in the Deccan, was paid a handsome amount to maintain neutrality.[291]

Shivaji spent about a month at Haidarabad. One day, following a dinner thrown by some Qutbshahi noble in honour of Shivaji, Yesaji Kank fought with an inebriated elephant of the Qutbshah, and, after facing it for some time, hacked off its trunk with his sword. The nobles were suitably impressed by this demonstration of the prowess of Yesaji Kank.[292] After some

---

N Sarkar, *History of Aurangzib*, IV, pp. 245ff; R V Nadkarni, *The Rise and Fall of the Maratha Empire*, p. 75.

287 J C Grant Duff, *History of the Mahrattas*, I, p. 223; J N Sarkar, *History of Aurangzib*, IV, p. 246; *Shivaji and His Times*, p. 290.

288 J N Sarkar, *History of Aurangzib*, IV, p. 247; G S Sardesai, *New History of the Marathas*, I, p. 240; also G S Sardesai, Shivaji, Chapter IX, in R C Majumdar, J N Chaudhuri, and S Chaudhuri (ed), *The Mughul Empire* (The History and Culture of the Indian People, VII), pp. 270-271.

289 J N Sarkar, *History of Aurangzib*, IV, p. 246; *Shivaji and His Times*, p. 290; G S Sardesai, *New History of the Marathas*, I, p. 240; R V Nadkarni, *The Rise and Fall of the Maratha Empire*, p. 75.

290 J C Grant Duff, *History of the Mahrattas*, I, p. 224; J N Sarkar, *History of Aurangzib*, IV, p. 246; G S Sardesai, *New History of the Marathas*, I, p. 240.

291 J C Grant Duff, *History of the Mahrattas*, I, p. 222; J N Sarkar, *History of Aurangzib*, IV, p. 245; *Shivaji and His Times*, pp. 284-185; R V Nadkarni, *The Rise and Fall of the Maratha Empire*, p. 74.

292 J N Sarkar, *Shivaji and His Times*, p. 291 and n; also David Kincaied, *Shivaji, the Founder of the Maratha Empire*, pp. 305-306.

time, in March 1677, the Maratha and Qutbshahi forces embarked upon a joint military campaign under the command of Shivaji. He first reached Jinji, and induced its Bijapuri captain, Nasir Muhammad Khan, to surrender the fort, in May 1677.[293] Shivaji then besieged Vellore, the capture of which, however, could be affected by the Maratha army only after a fourteen month long sustained effort, on 22 July 1678.[294]

In the meantime, in June 1676, Netaji Palkar returned to Maharashtra. It is believed that he was sent against the Marathas by Aurangzeb himself. But he came over to Shivaji, was accepted within the Maratha fold, and 'remade a Hindu' by certain purificatory rites, on 19 June 1676.[295] There is a view that he might have been given some high military position, although there is no evidence to support such a suggestion.[296] He is, however, believed to have accompanied Shivaji during his southern expedition.[297]

Receiving delegations from the French of Pondicherry and the Nayaks of Madura, Shivaji finally reached Thirumalvadi, about 10 miles north of Thanjavur.[298] There, he was welcomed by Vyankoji, who came out to meet him, and stayed in his camp for about a week.[299] However, due to the influence of his Muslim advisors, who pressed him not to desert Bijapur and side with Shivaji, Vyankoji secretly left for Thanjavur one night,[300] and all the efforts of Shivaji, to bring his half brother around to support

---

293 J N Sarkar, *Shivaji and His Times*, p. 293. Shivaji had offered him a *jaghir* with an annual income of fifty thousand of rupees. See G S Sardesai, *New History of the Marathas*, I, p. 244.

294 G S Sardesai, *New History of the Marathas*, I, p. 245; J N Sarkar, *Shivaji and His Times*, pp. 293ff, 302. J N Sarkar (*Shivaji and His Times*, p. 302) gives the date of the capture of this fort as 21 August 1678.

295 G S Sardesai, *New History of the Marathas*, I, p. 227.

296 J N Sarkar, *Shivaji and His Times*, p. 285.

297 G S Sardesai, *New History of the Marathas*, I, p. 239.

298 G S Sardesai, Shivaji, Chapter IX, in R C Majumdar, J N Chaudhuri, and S Chaudhuri (ed), *The Mughul Empire* (The History and Culture of the Indian People, VII), p. 272.

299 G S Sardesai, *New History of the Marathas*, I, pp. 246-247.

300 J N Sarkar, *Shivaji and His Times*, pp. 298-299; David Kincaied, *Shivaji, the Founder of the Maratha Empire*, p. 309.

his scheme, came to nothing.[301] He even refused to share with Shivaji, the territories their father, Shahji, had acquired in Karnataka.[302]

Towards the end of July 1677, Shivaji had, perforce, to return to Maharashtra to deal with some urgent business,[303] leaving behind his *senapati*, Hambirrao Mohite, his viceroy at Jinji, Santaji Bhonsle,[304] and his representative, Raghunathpant Hanumante,[305] to look into the matter of Vyankoji. On his way to Maharashtra, Shivaji occupied most of the territories held by Vyankoji in the Mysore plateau. He met with a slight resistance at Belvadi, near Belgam, which was subjugated by a month long effort on the part of Dadji Raghunath Prabhu Mahadkar, in December 1677.[306] Savitribai Thanedar of Belvadi was taken under his wing by Shivaji. Dadji Raghunath Prabhu Mahadkar played a prominent rôle against the Siddis of Janjira, in the first half of 1782, during the reign of Shambhuji.[307] In an attempt to take advantage of the absence of Shivaji from Thanjavur, Vyankoji attacked Hambirrao Mohite at Valigandpuram on 16 November 1677. After some initial success against Santaji Bhonsle, Vyankoji's forces were completely routed with heavy losses.[308] After a hectic exchange of correspondence between the two brothers, Dipabai, the wife of Vyankoji, brought about reconciliation between the two brothers, and, on her advice, her husband handed over the administration of his kingdom to Raghunathpant Hanumante.[309] The *senapati*, Hambirrao Mohite

---

301 G S Sardesai, Shivaji, Chapter IX, in R C Majumdar, J N Chaudhuri, and S Chaudhuri (ed), *The Mughul Empire* (The History and Culture of the Indian People, VII), p. 272.

302 G S Sardesai, *New History of the Marathas*, I, p. 247.

303 J N Sarkar, *Shivaji and His Times*, p. 302; G S Sardesai, *New History of the Marathas*, I, p. 248.

304 An illegitimate son of Shahji. See J C Grant Duff, *History of the Mahrattas*, I, p. 96.

305 J N Sarkar, *Shivaji and His Times*, p. 303.

306 G S Sardesai, *New History of the Marathas*, I, p. 258.

307 Below, Chapter III.

308 J N Sarkar, *Shivaji and His Times*, p. 304; G S Sardesai, *New History of the Marathas*, I, p. 248.

309 G S Sardesai, *New History of the Marathas*, I, pp. 249-250; also G S Sardesai, Shivaji, Chapter IX, in R C Majumdar, J N Chaudhuri,

was recalled by his sovereignto Maharashtra, where his services were urgently required.[310]

Although death prevented Shivaji from executing his grand plans for the Karnataka region, this successful southern expedition, which, according to some scholars, placed Shivaji 'in the front rank of the world's greatest generals',[311] proved beneficial to the Marathas in that, later on, it provided a safe haven to Rajaram at Jinji, when Maharashtra was overrun by Aurangzeb.[312]

After his return to Maharashtra from the Karnataka expedition, Shivaji, in order to connect his old dominion in Maharashtra and the Konkan with the newly acquired territories in Karnataka, made a more concerted effort to conquer the southern corner of the sultanate of Bijapur, comprising Kopbal to the north of the river Tungabhadra, and parts of Dharwar and Belgaum between Kopbal and Panhala. The Kopbal region was under the charge of the powerful Afghan brothers, Husain Khan Miana and Qasim Khan Miana, who were related to Bahlol Khan. Already in January 1677, Shivaji had despatched two Maratha contingents, under Hambirrao Mohite and Dhanaji Jadhav, against the Miana brothers.[313] Hambirrao Mohite[314] had invaded the Gadag region, and was challenged by Husain Khan Miana near Yelbarga. The Marathas were, however, victorious in this engagement. Husain Khan Miana tried to escape on his elephant, but Nagoji Jedhe wounded his mount. Although Nagoji

---

and S Chaudhuri (ed), *The Mughul Empire* (The History and Culture of the Indian People, VII), p. 272; David Kincaied, *Shivaji, the Founder of the Maratha Empire*, pp. 309-310. However, *contra* J N Sarkar, *Shivaji and His Times*, p. 308.

310 J N Sarkar, *Shivaji and His Times*, p. 305.

311 See C A Kinkaid and D B Parasnis, *A History of the Maratha People*, I, pp. 96, 103; R V Nadkarni, *The Rise and Fall of the Maratha Empire*, p. 76; etc.

312 Below, Chapter IV. For other benefits of the expedition in Karnataka, see G S Sardesai, *New History of the Marathas*, I, pp. 258ff.

313 G S Sardesai, *New History of the Marathas*, I, p. 238.

314 In the *Jedhe Shakavali* and the *91 Qalmi-bakhar*, the name is given as Bahirrao, which has been taken as an error for Hambirrao, the name given by Sabhasad.

Jedhe was killed in the encounter, Husain Khan Miana was captured. Shivaji tried to convince him to make arrangements for handing over the fort of Kopbal to the Marathas, in exchange for his freedom, but he refused to agree to these terms. Finally, on 03 March 1679, as a result of bribery and some negotiations between Moropant Trimbak Pingle and Qasim Khan Miana, with the son of Husain Khan Miana acting as an intermediary, the Marathas were able to gain control the fort. Husain Khan Miana was set free, and he entered the service of the Marathas.[315]

With the Marathas controlling Kopbal, 'the gate of the south' according to Sabhasad, it was relatively easy for Shivaji to extend his dominion right up to the river Tungabhadra, and even further, into the Bellary and Chittaldurg regions, and reduce the *poligars* of Kanakgiri, Harpanhalli, Raidurg, Chittaldurg, and other places, to submission.[316]

Shambhuji, the elder son of Shivaji and a 'profligate, capricious and violent youth',[317] was a source of trouble to his father,[318] and was living at Shringarpur near Sangameshvar in Konkan, under strict supervision, and studying at the feet of Keshav Bhatt Upadhyaya, the deputy *panditrao*.[319] Even his stay with Ramdas at Sajjangadh failed to have any beneficial influence on him.[320] Enticed by Diler Khan to desert his father, and join the Mughals, Shambhuji, in the company of his wife, Yesubai, left Panhala on 13 December 1678,[321] and is reported to have joined Diler Khan near Pandharpur.[322] Together, in April

---

315 J N Sarkar, *Shivaji and His Times*, pp. 312-313. G S Sardesai (*New History of the Marathas*, I, p. 238), however, says that the fort of Kopbal was seized in 1677 itself. *Cf* J C Grant Duff, *History of the Mahrattas*, I, p. 229), who would date the event to 1678.

316 J N Sarkar, *Shivaji and His Times*, p. 313.

317 R V Nadkarni, *The Rise and Fall of the Maratha Empire*, p. 77.

318 J C Grant Duff, *History of the Mahrattas*, I, p. 235; G S Sardesai, *New History of the Marathas*, I, p. 261.

319 J N Sarkar, *Shivaji and His Times*, p. 316. The *Prabhat Shakavali* (article 58, p. 59 of *Prabhat-bakhar*) says that Shambhuji was tutored by Umaji Pandit. See G S Sardesai, *New History of the Marathas*, I, p. 230.

320 J N Sarkar, *Shivaji and His Times*, p. 317.

321 G S Sardesai, *New History of the Marathas*, I, p. 261.

322 J N Sarkar, *History of Aurangzib*, IV, p. 252.

1679, Diler Khan and Shambhuji captured, plundered, and devastated Bhupalgadh, to the east of Satara.[323] In the second half of 1679, they also led their armies against Bijapur, where they were, however, repulsed by Shivaji.[324]

After saving Bijapur from falling into the hands of Diler Khan, Shivaji, accompanied by Anandrao, led 18,000 Maratha horsemen into the Mughal Deccan, indulging in plunder, and captured Jalna, about 40 miles east of Aurangabad. But the Marathas had to repair, ultimately to Raigadh, leaving behind much of the booty, and with Hambirrao Mohite wounded,[325] due to the pressure of Mughal officers like Ranmast Khan, Kesari Singh, and Sardar Khan.[326]

The atrocities Diler Khan visited upon the innocent people at Tikota near Bijapur, and in the market town of Athni,[327] disgusted Shambhuji. The Maratha prince was also informed by his friends about Diler Khan's intention to hand him over to Aurangzeb as a prisoner.[328] Shambhuji and Yesubai escaped from the Mughal camp one night, and, on 04 December 1679, were brought to Panhala by some agents of Shivaji.[329]

Shivaji knew that Shambhuji was incapable of carrying on the work begun by his father.[330] He visited his son at Panhala, where Shambhuji was being kept under strict vigil, and tried to impress upon him the great responsibility that he was to inherit

---

323 J N Sarkar, *History of Aurangzib*, IV, pp. 253-255; *Shivaji and His Times*, pp. 319-320; G S Sardesai, *New History of the Marathas*, I, p. 261.

324 J N Sarkar, *History of Aurangzib*, IV, pp. 255-256; *Shivaji and His Times*, pp. 323-325; David Kincaied, *Shivaji, the Founder of the Maratha Empire*, pp. 317ff.

325 J N Sarkar, *History of Aurangzib*, IV, p. 258.

326 See J N Sarkar, *Shivaji and His Times*, pp. 327-329.

327 J N Sarkar, *Shivaji and His Times*, p. 326; G S Sardesai, *New History of the Marathas*, I, pp. 262-263.

328 G S Sardesai, *New History of the Marathas*, I, p. 263.

329 J N Sarkar, *History of Aurangzib*, IV, p. 256; *Shivaji and His Times*, pp. 326-327; G S Sardesai, Shivaji, Chapter IX, in R C Majumdar, J N Chaudhuri, and S Chaudhuri (ed), *The Mughul Empire* (The History and Culture of the Indian People, VII), p. 273.

330 J N Sarkar, *History of Aurangzib*, IV, pp. 259-260.

as the successor of Shivaji,[331] but to no avail.[332] Much perturbed by the hopelessness of the situation, Shivaji tried unsuccessfully to find solace in the company of Ramdas at Sajjangadh.[333] A dejected Shivaji returned to Raigadh in February 1680. On 23 March 1680, he suffered an acute attack of fever and blood dysentery,[334] and succumbed to it on 04 April 1680.[335]

Such was the personality of this 'last great constructive genius and nation-builder that the Hindu race has produced',[336] that, on hearing of his death, even his bitterest enemy, Aurangzeb, is reported to have observed :

> 'He was a great captain and the only one who has had the magnanimity to raise a new kingdom, while I have been endeavouring to destroy the ancient sovereignties of India. My armies have been employed against him for nineteen years (1660-1679) and nevertheless his state has been increasing.'[337]

---

331 J N Sarkar, *History of Aurangzib*, IV, p. 260; *Shivaji and His Times*, pp. 330-331.

332 G S Sardesai, *New History of the Marathas*, I, pp. 264-265.

333 G S Sardesai, *New History of the Marathas*, I, p. 266.

334 Rawlinson, *Shivaji, the Maratha*, p. 88; J N Sarkar, *History of Aurangzib*, IV, p. 261; *Shivaji and His Times*, p. 331.

335 J N Sarkar, *History of Aurangzib*, IV, p. 261; *Shivaji and His Times*, p. 331; G S Sardesai, Shivaji, Chapter IX, in R C Majumdar, J N Chaudhuri, and S Chaudhuri (ed), *The Mughul Empire* (The History and Culture of the Indian People, VII), pp. 273-274. J C Grant Duff, *History of the Mahrattas*, I, p. 238) gives the date of the death of Shivaji as 05 April 1680, and the *Ma'asir-i-Alamgiri* (p. 120), as 14 May 1680.

336 J N Sarkar, *Shivaji and His Times*, p. 388.

337 *Vide* G S Sardesai, *New History of the Marathas*, I, pp. 296-297.

Chapter III

Senapatis under Shambhuji and Rajaram

I. The Reign of Shambhuji

Shivaji wanted to divide his kingdom on his death, with his elder son, Shambhuji, succeeding him in the newly acquired territories in Karnataka, and his younger son, Rajaram, succeeding him in Maharashtra and Konkan. But Shambhuji was not amenable to this arrangement, as the acceptance of this division would entail a life away from his homeland, working ceaselessly to secure the Maratha position in the newly acquired, and, as yet largely unsubdued, territories in Karnataka.[1] Shivaji died without nominating an heir, which resulted in intrigue within the royal family. His eldest son, Shambhuji, had earned the wrath of his father, and was kept confined in the fort of Panhala.[2] In April 1680, Soyarabai, the widow of Shivaji, contrived to place her own son, Rajaram, then only ten years of age, on the throne at Raigadh. Balaji Avji, the confidential secretary of Shivaji, supported her cause, and arranged with the *qiledar* of Panhala to keep vigil on the activities of Shambhuji. But when Shambhuji came to learn of his father's death, and the accession of Rajaram, he killed the *qiledar* of Panhala, and made preparation to

---

1 J N Sarkar, *Shivaji and His Times*, pp. 316-317. *Cf* G S Sardesai, *New History of the Marathas*, I, p. 266.

2 G S Sardesai, *Marathi Riyasat*, I, p. 539; G S Sardesai, *New History of the Marathas*, I, p. 303.

proceed towards the capital.[3] At that time, *Senapati* Hambirrao Mohite was at Karhad, in the neighbourhood of Panhala. Being ignorant of Soyarabai's plans, he joined Shambhuji.[4]

Soyarabai ordered the *peshva*, Moropant Trimbak Pingle, and another minister, Annaji Datto, to proceed to Panhala, to keep a check on the activities of Shambhuji.[5] They were, however, captured by the prince, and detained at Panhala. Shambhuji then marched upon Raigadh with 20,000 soldiers, and occupied the capital on 18 June 1680. Rajaram and his mother were taken prisoners. Shambhuji ascended the throne on 20 July 1680,[6] and the formal coronation took place on 10 January 1681.[7]

In the meantime, in August 1680, the Marathas snatched 25 cannons from the Mughals.[8] In October-November 1680, it is learnt that Shambhuji's *senapati*, Hambirrao Mohite, led some Maratha soldiers against the Mughals, and succeeded in divesting them of their arms, ammunitions, and provisions.[9] Moropant Trimbak Pingle had, meanwhile, died in October 1680, and Shambhuji appointed his son, Nilopant as his *peshva*.[10] In January 1681, Hambirrao Mohite is again seen

---

3 G S Sardesai, *Marathi Riyasat*, I, p. 542. According to R V Nadkarni, (*The Rise and Fall of the Maratha Empire*, p. 119), the soldiers in the fort of Panhala supported the cause of Shambhuji.

4 G S Sardesai, *New History of the Marathas*, I, p. 303.

5 Both Annaji Datto and Moropant Trimbak Pingle were well aware of the temperament of Shambhuji, and they set aside their rivalry to support the cause of Soyarabai. G S Sardesai, *Marathi Riyasat*, I, pp. 539-542.

6 But some scholars regard 28 July 1680 as the date of his accession to the throne (R V Nadkarni, The *Rise and Fall of the Maratha Empire*, p. 119). *Bombay Factory Records* inform that Shambhuji had been publicly declared king on 12 July 1680. See J N Sarkar, *House of Shivaji*, p.p. 215-216.

7 G S Sardesai, *New History of the Marathas*, I, pp. 303-304. J N Sarkar, however, places the coronation in February 1681. See *History of Aurangzib*, IV, p. 243.

8 *Akhbarat*, year 23, Shaban 17.

9 *Shiva-charitra-pradipa*, p. 31.

10 G S Sardesai, *New History of the Marathas*, I, p. 304.

leading Maratha bands in northern Khandesh, and attacking and plundering the suburbs of Burhanpur, like Bahadurpur.[11]

Shambhuji lacked the abilities that had made his father a great warrior and a statesman. He had a suspicious nature, and suspected all his officials and advisors of treason and disloyalty.[12] In the August of 1681, there occurred an incident, which confirmed the worst fears of the new king. European merchants report that someone tried to assassinate him by poisoning a dish of fish meant for Shambhuji. The king somehow learnt of the attempt on his life, and was saved. He suspected Anaji Pandit, Kesho Pandit, Prahlad Pandit, Hiroji Farzand, Balaji Prabhu, Somaji Datto, and others, of conspiring against him, imprisoned them, and, in the first half of October 1681, had several of them trampled under elephant's feet. It is suspected that, towards the end of the same month, he was instrumental in the death of Soyarabai.[13] A number of influential persons, including Manaji More, Gangadharpant, Vasudevpant, Raoji Somnath, and Prahlad Niraji, suffered atrocities at the hand of Shambhuji, who suspected them of involvement in the plot to assassinate him.[14]

In this atmosphere of distrust, Shambhuji selected as his advisor, Kavi Kalash, a north Indian brahmana who had come to the Deccan and been employed to teach Shambhuji, Sanskrit and the puranic lore.[15] This Sanskrit scholar and poet was appointed as *chhandogyamatya*, or the minister of vedic learning, by

---

11 *Khafi Khan*, II, pp. 272-275; *Dilkasha*, II, pp. 167-168. See J N Sarkar, *History of Aurangzib*, IV, pp. 278ff.

12 G S Sardesai, *New History of the Marathas*, I, p. 308.

13 J N Sarkar, *House of Shivaji*, p. 220; G S Sardesai, *New History of the Marathas*, I, pp. 308-310.

14 G S Sardesai, *New History of the Marathas*, I, p. 310. See *Shiva-charitra-pradipa*, pp. 31, 33; *Sambhaji Kalina Patra Sarasamgraha*, p. 119.

15 According to some scholars, he had accompanied Shambhuji to the Deccan, when the Maratha escaped from Aurangzeb (Elliot and Dowson, *History of India, as told by its Own Historians*, VII, p. 305). But J N Sarkar (*History of Aurangzib*, IV, p. 253) holds that Kavi Kalash was present at Raigadh before the coronation of Shambhuji.

Shambhuji. He exercised a profound influence on the king,[16] and, according to some reports, introduced him to vices, like drugs.[17] G S Sardesai reports that, according to an old chronicle, a person named Keshavbhat Kabji, who was a north Indian brahmana and well versed in 'magic and incantation', possessed the mind of Shambhuji. From this, he concludes that Kavi Kalash and Keshavbhat Kabji must have been one and the same person, and that Keshavbhat must have been the real name of this person, and Kavi Kalash, his title.[18]

In 1679, Aurangzeb had started a war against the Rajputs, and made his favourite son, Akbar, in charge of the operations. The Mughal prince, after suffering heavy losses, conferred with the Rajputs, especially the Rathor chief, Durgadas, and they agreed to enter into a subordinate alliance with the Mughals, if they were left in peace. But Aurangzeb did not accept this, and made his displeasure known to Akbar.[19] The prince realized that the sole cause of the Mughal operations against the Rajputs was the emperor's 'deliberate resolution of putting down the Hindus', as he wrote to Shambhuji after crossing the river Narmada in May 1681.[20] He revolted against his father, but, on suffering reverses, fled towards the Deccan in the hope of seeking shelter with the new Maratha king.

In the beginning of June 1681, Akbar arrived at Pali, about 25 miles north of Raigadh, where he was met by Shambhuji's men, who made some arrangements for the stay of the Mughal prince there.[21] Shambhuji was himself busy solving the domestic

---

16 It is a general belief that Shambhuji abolished the posts of the *ashta-pradhana*, and handed over all their functions and powers to Kavi Kalash. But this is not correct. These ministers existed, but had almost no powers. V K Rajwade, *Marathyanchya Itihasachi Sadhane*, VIII, p. 40; XV, p. 342; G S Sardesai, *Marathi Riyasat*, I, pp. 559, 560-563; R V Nadkarni, *The Rise and Fall of the Maratha Empire*, p. 121, n. 14.

17 J N Sarkar (*History of Aurangzib*, IV, p. 254n) does not fully agree with this.

18 G S Sardesai, *New History of the Marathas*, I, pp. 310-311.

19 J N Sarkar, *House of Shivaji*, p. 179; G S Sardesai, *New History of the Marathas*, I, pp. 304-305.

20 G S Sardesai, *New History of the Marathas*, I, p. 305.

21 *Ma'asir-i-Alamgiri*, p. 130.

crisis arising out of the attempt at his assassination.[22] Netaji Palkar, the disgraced *senapati* of Shivaji, who had deserted his king, spent nearly ten years in the service of the Mughals, but finally returned to the Maratha fold,[23] had continued to serve under Shambhuji after the death of Shivaji; he was the only high ranking Maratha officer to have 'knowledge of the imperial life and manners of the Court'. He was sent by Shambhuji to look after the comforts of Akbar.[24]

The revolt of Akbar provided Shambhuji with an opportunity of ridding his kingdom of the Mughal menace, once and for all. Aurangzeb's faith in his family was 'totally shaken', and he was no longer sure as to which of his family member he could trust. As has been observed, the result of all this was that, for some time following his arrival in the Deccan in 1681-1682, his policy was 'hesitating, suspicious, watchful and seemingly capricious or self-contradictory'.[25] But Shambhuji remained embroiled in his domestic troubles, some of which were mere figments of his imagination and the result of his suspicious temperament, and failed to take advantage of this opportunity, with serious consequences to himself and the Marathas. Some significant letters have come to light in the archives of Jaipur. These were written by both Shambhuji and Kavi Kalash to Ram Singh of Amber, in 1682. The letters reveal that the Maratha king was trying to make grand alliances with Akbar and some Rajput chiefs, against Aurangzeb.[26] The initial attempt of Aurangzeb against Shambhuji and Akbar, through his eldest son, Shah Alam, proved to be an utter failure, and the Mughal emperor turned his attention towards the sultanates of Bijapur and Golkunda.[27] Shambhuji is known to have sent some force to the

---

22 See above.

23 See above, Chapter II.

24 G S Sardesai, *New History of the Marathas*, I, p. 306.

25 J N Sarkar, *History of Aurangzib*, IV, p. 304.

26 J N Sarkar, *House of Shivaji*, p. 184. Some other sources also reveal similar grand designs. See *Shiv-charitra-sahitya*, II, no. 271, p. 267; no. 222, p. 221; *Sambhaji Kalina Patra Sarasamgraha*, no. 126, p. 39; V K Rajwade, *Marathyanchya Itihasachi Sadhane*, XV, no. 281, p. 288; no. 342, pp. 371-372; etc.

27 G S Sardesai, *New History of the Marathas*, I, pp. 308-315.

help of Sikandar Adilshah.[28] But Aurangzeb succeeded in capturing Bijapur on 12 September 1686, and Golkunda on 01 October 1687.[29]

The Siddi of Janjira acted as the admiral of Aurangzeb, and had joined the emperor's war against the Marathas. He invested the Maratha territories as far as the foot of Raigadh, towards the close of 1681. Shambhuji threw his whole naval might—150 ships and around 5,000 sailors, against the Siddi. In this war, Dadji Raghunath Prabhu Mahadkar, a prominent military officer of Shambhuji, played a prominent rôle. As we have seen earlier,[30] Dadji Raghunath Prabhu Mahadkar had distinguished himself during the reign of Shivaji, when, in the December of 1677, he had succeeded in subjugating Savitribai Thanedar of Belvadi. He caused great consternation in the territories of the Siddi in the beginning on 1682, and placed the Siddi on the defensive. However, around this time, Aurangzeb arrived in the Deccan, and the Marathas were forced to raise their siege of Janjira to tackle the new situation.[31]

There was a Mughal-Maratha conflict at Titvala near Kalyan on 27 February 1683. In this conflict, *Senapati* Hambirrao Mohite, his brother-in-law, Rupaji Bhonsle, Manaji More, and others, participated on behalf of the Marathas, while Ruh-ullah Khan, Sayyad Izzat Khan, Ranmast Khan, Ram Singh Ratnawat, Padam Singh Hada, and others participated on behalf of the Mughals. Although the Marathas did not succeed in capturing the fort, the Mughals suffered heavy losses, and Padam Singh Hada, Bhagvant Singh (the son of Mankoji Dakkhani), Ram Singh, (the son of Ratan Rathor), and Hari Singh, (the son of

---

28 J N Chaudhuri, Muslim Resistance to Mughul Imperialism (II), Chapter XIV in R C Majumdar, J N Chaudhuri, and S Chaudhuri (ed), *The Mughul Empire*, The History and Culture of the Indian People, VII, pp. 412-485, on pp. 462-463.

29 J N Chaudhuri, Muslim Resistance to Mughul Imperialism (II), Chapter XIV in R C Majumdar, J N Chaudhuri, and S Chaudhuri (ed), *The Mughul Empire*, The History and Culture of the Indian People, VII, pp. 412-485, on pp. 478-479; above, Chapter I.

30 Above, Chapter II.

31 J N Sarkar, *History of Aurangzib*, IV, pp. 311-314.G S Sardesai, *New History of the Marathas*, I, p. 316.

Puranmal Bundela), died in action. Among the Marathas, Hambirrao Mohite was sustained an arrow wound; the dead included his brother-in-law, and three other chiefs, besides a Ghorpade chief.[32]

Aurangzeb had called upon the various European trading establishments—the British at Surat and Bombay, the Dutch at Vengurla, the Portuguese on the western coast, to help him against the Marathas. In 1683, Shambhuji himself led an expedition against the Portuguese at Chaul and Goa. The position of the Portuguese viceroy, Francisco de Tavora, became very precarious, and he prayed for divine intervention. Manucci informs us that, towards the end of 1683, the governor was about to surrender Goa to Shambhuji, when the Maratha received intelligence of the arrival of Shah Alam and the Mughal army to threaten his rear, and had to beat a hasty retreat.[33]

The rebel Mughal prince, Akbar, had been constantly urging Shambhuji to make a sudden attack upon Aurangzeb's central camp, and rout the Mughal army. But the Maratha king, though 'brave as a lion personally, lacked the patient calculating forethought and vigilance essential for the success of such an extensive and large scale undertaking',[34] and tarried, leading to gradual estrangement with Akbar.[35] The Rajputs were inviting him to Rajasthan, to lead an uprising against Aurangzeb. However, he realized that his position was becoming untenable, and, in the beginning of 1687,[36] the Mughal prince sailed aboard a British cargo ship from Rajapur, reaching Ispahan in Iran the next year. There, he led a miserable life, had correspondence with his father,[37] was entreated by his family members to return

---

32 *Shiva-charitra-pradipa*, p. 32; *Akhbarat*, 17 March, 02 April, 04 April, and 09 April 1683.

33 Manucci, *Storia do Mogor*, II, pp. 260-282. See J N Sarkar, *History of Aurangzib*, IV, p. 315-335; G S Sardesai, *New History of the Marathas*, I, pp. 316-317.

34 G S Sardesai, *New History of the Marathas*, I, p. 318.

35 For the developments in the relations between Shambhuji and Akbar, see J N Sarkar, *House of Shivaji*, pp. 186, 189; G S Sardesai, *New History of the Marathas*, I, pp. 319-320.

36 *Cf Ma'asir-i-Alamgiri*, p. 139.

37 Manucci, *Storia do Mogor*, IV, pp. 171-177.

to India, but chose to stay in Iran, where he died in November 1704.[38]

While the Mughal emperor was himself engaged in subjugating Bijapur and Golkunda, he had succeeded in winning over several high officials of Shambhuji through the offices of Shihab-ud-din Firoz Jang and his son, Chinqilich Khan.[39] The capture of the two Muslim kingdoms led to an increase, not only in the prestige of Aurangzeb, but also his resources, for he had amassed great wealth, trained warriors, and arms and equipments, as a result of these victories. He pitched his camps at Akluj on the river Bhima near Pandharpur, about 50 miles from Brahmapuri, and turned all his military might against Shambhuji. The Maratha affairs, especially financial ones, were in dire straits, due to mismanagement and internal strife during the seven years of Shambhuji's reign. Towards the end of 1687, Aurangzeb sent Sharza Khan, a former Bijapuri general, to invade Satara. Hambirrao Mohite, the *senapati* of Shambhuji, was sent to confront him. In December 1687, an engagement took place near Wai, in which Hambirrao Mohite lost his life,[40] leaving Shambhuji without a single staunch supporter.[41]

The Shirkes, who occupied the hilly terrain between Kolhapur and Satara, harboured inimical feelings against Shambhuji, because his stepmother, Soyarabai, whom Shambhuji had allegedly murdered, belonged to that family.[42] Shambhuji had defeated them near Sangameshvar towards the end of 1688, and retreated to the fort of Vishalgadh. The Shirkes reported the whereabouts of Shambhuji to Shaikh Nizam, a

---

38 *Khafi Khan*, II, pp. 286-290, 450, 546; *Ma'asir-i-Alamgiri*, pp. 320-321; Manucci, *Storia do Mogor*, II, pp. 279, 322. Se J N Sarkar, *History of Aurangzib*, IV, p. 467n; G S Sardesai, *New History of the Marathas*, I, pp. 317-321.

39 His actual name was Mir Qamar-ud-din. Later on, pleased with his services, Farrukhsiyar appointed him as viceroy of the six *subas* of the Deccan, and conferred on him the title of Nizam-ul-mulk Bahadur Fath Jang. See Yusuf Hussain, *The First Nizam* (1963), pp. 34-53.

40 G T Kulkarni, *The Mughal-Maratha Relations*, p. 68.

41 G S Sardesai, *New History of the Marathas*, I, p. 323.

42 Above.

former official of Golkunda, who had been posted at Kolhapur by Aurangzeb to attack Shambhuji at the first opportunity. The Maratha king was now bereft of all able generals, and had to depend solely on the advice on Kavi Kalash. Shaikh Nizam led a surprise attack on the Marathas, when they were halting at Sangameshvar, and captured Kavi Kalash and Shambhuji, perhaps at Khatola near Sangameshvar,[43] on 01 February 1689.[44] Aurangzeb met Shambhuji at Bahadurgadh, and had the captive Maratha king humiliated in public. He then offered Shambhuji to spare his life on the conditions that he would surrender all his forts and treasures to the Mughal, and reveal the names of the Mughal officers who were conspiring with him against the emperor. Shambhuji, who was infuriated at the public humiliation inflicted upon him by Aurangzeb, gave vent to his fury by using abusive language against the emperor, his faith, and his prophet, for which, he was blinded, tortured for about a fortnight, and then cruelly put to death at Koregaon, on 11 March 1689.[45]

Thus, it is seen that during the reign of Shambhuji, with Kavi Kalash managing to make himself almost the sole intermediary between the king and the ministers and other high officials, there was hardly any scope left for these ministers and high officials, including the *senapati*, to play any important rôle in the affairs of the time.

II. The Reign of Rajaram

At the time of the death of Shambhuji, his son, Shahu, was only six years old. Prominent Maratha officials, like Janardanrao Hanumante, Ramchandrapant Bavdekar, Khando Ballal Chitnis,

---

43 *Waqil Report*, 24 Rabi II, Hijri 1100. See G T Kulkarni, *The Mughal-Maratha Relations*, p. 74, n. 222.

44 For details of the capture of Shambhuji, see *Khafi Khan*, II, pp. 384-386; *Shiva-charitra-pradipa*, p. 34. Also see G S Sardesai, *New History of the Marathas*, I, p. 324.

45 *Ma'asir-i-Alamgiri*, pp. 193-196; *Khafi Khan*, II, p. 389. For the capture and execution of Shambhuji, see J N Sarkar, *House of Shivaji*, pp. 202ff. Also G S Sardesai, *New History of the Marathas*, I, pp. 324-326.

Mahadaji Nayak Pansambal, Dhanaji Jadhav, and Santaji Ghorpade, met with Prahlad Niraji, and decided, in consultation with Yesubai, the widow of Shambhuji, that Rajaram, the younger son of Shivaji, be appointed regent.[46] Rajaram, who had been imprisoned by Shambhuji at Raigadh, was released on 09 February 1689,[47] and he ascended the throne on 12 February 1689.[48]

Within a month and a half, on 25 March 1689, Aurangzeb despatched Etiqad Khan to capture Raigadh.[49] He immediately besieged the fort of Raigadh, where Rajaram and his family, as also Yesubai and Shahu, were residing. Keeping in mind the seriousness of the situation, Yesubai decided that, before the Mughal siege of the fort became impregnable, Rajaram and his family should leave Raigadh, but that she herself would remain behind with her son.[50]

The Maratha ministers felt that if Rajaram remained in Maharashtra, it would become increasing difficult to save him from falling into Mughal hands. Besides, they also wanted to divert Aurangzeb's attention away from Maharashtra, to give some respite to their homeland.[51] Therefore, they decided that the second line of Maratha defence against the Mughals at Karnataka, prepared during the last years of the reign of Shivaji, be revived, and that Rajaram should go to the fort of Jinji, which was regarded as impregnable. J N Sarkar believes that Rajaram also wanted to raise a large army with the help of the Karnataka chiefs, so that Bijapur and Golkunda may be occupied.[52] Shahji

---

46 J C Grant Duff, *History of the Mahrattas*, I, pp. 296-298; R V Nadkarni, *The Rise and Fall of the Maratha Empire*, p. 124.

47 *Shiva-charitra-pradipa*, pp. 34-35.

48 *Shiva-charitra-pradipa*, p. 35.

49 *Shiva-charitra-pradipa*, p. 35.

50 G S Sardesai, *New History of the Marathas*, I, pp. 329-330. When Raigadh was captured by Zulfiqar Khan on 03 November 1689, Yesubai, her seven year old son, Shahu, two illegitimate sons of Shambhuji, and Shivaji's widow, Sakvarbai, were carried away by Zulfiqar Khan, and had to spend 17 years in captivity. *Ibid.*, p. 359.

51 See *Madras Diary*, 06 December 1689; J N Sarkar, *History of Aurangzib*, V, p. 50.

52 *Madras Diary*, 14 November and 26 December 1689.

II, the ruler of Thanjavur, was a cousin of Rajaram. Several other chiefs in the region were afraid of the Mughals, and they feared for their political existence. These chiefs could easily be prevailed upon to assist Rajaram against the Mughals.[53] Rajaram left Raigadh, on 05 April 1689,[54] for Jinji, located about 40 miles from the coast of Pondicherry, and about 60 miles to the southwest of Chennai.[55]

In the early days of April 1689, Santaji Ghorpade, along with his brothers, Bahirji and Maloji, and also a Maratha chief, Vithoji Chavan, had a conflict with the Mughals. On 02 April 1689, the Mughal emperor was planning an inspection tour of the fort of Islamabad (Chakan).[56] But before he could leave from Koregaon, the Marathas, under Santaji Ghorpade, attacked the Mughal camp at night. According to some reports, they lifted the golden finials from the emperor's tent, and presented them to Rajaram, who was then at Vishalgadh.[57] This Maratha act caused consternation in the Mughal camp, and raised hope among the Marathas, barely two and a half months following the death of Shambhuji. Pleased with the daring of Santaji Ghorpade and other Marathas warriors, Rajaram conferred the title of *mamulkat-madar* on Santaji Ghorpade, *Hindurao* on Bahirji Ghorpade, *amir-ul-umrao* on Maloji Ghorpade, and *himmat bahadur* on Vithoji Chavan.[58] Santaji Ghorpade also attacked the Mughal general, Zulfiqar Khan, defeated him, and seized five elephants and some valuables from him. For this achievement also, he was honoured by Rajaram.[59]

On his way to Jinji, while Rajaram was staying on an island in the river Tungabhadra, the Mughals suddenly attacked him. Although Rajaram somehow succeeded in making good his escape, Hindurao, Vyankoji, the two brothers of Santaji Ghorpade, and some other Marathas, were captured.[60] Rajaram

---

53 *Rajaram-charitam*, p. 35.

54 *Shiva-charitra-pradipa*, p. 35.

55 G S Sardesai, *New History of the Marathas*, I, p. 333.

56 *Ma'asir-i-Alamgiri*, p. 197.

57 *Kavya Itihasa Samgraha Patre Yadya*, no. 3, p. 5.

58 G T Kulkarni, *The Mughal-Maratha Relations*, pp. 138-139.

59 G S Sardesai, *New History of the Marathas*, I, p. 331.

60 *Ma'asir-i-Alamgiri*, p. 198.

took refuge with the queen of Bednur. Aurangzeb sent Jan Nisar Khan, Sharza Khan, and Matlab Khan to capture him. But Santaji Ghorpade reached Bednur, and successfully repulsed the Mughal generals. Admitting the success of Santaji Ghorpade, the *Ma'asir-i-Alamgiri* states that the queen of Bednur had merely to pay some fine for providing refuge to Rajaram.[61] The Mughals placed the Maratha captives in the fort of Bijapur. The brothers of Santaji Ghorpade managed to escape, but the rest were put to death at the emperor's orders.[62]

From Bednur, Rajaram went to Vellore,[63] and from there, he reached Jinji, located about 50 miles to the southeast, on 01/02 November 1689.[64] Jinji was being administered by Harji Mahadik, the son-in-law of Shivaji.[65] But he had died,[66] on 19 September 1689,[67] about a month before the arrival of Rajaram at Jinji, and Jinji was in the charge of Ambikabai, the widow of Harji Mahadik. Rajaram took over government from her,[68] and made the following appointments as his *ashta-pradhana* :

1. Nilopant Moreshvar as *peshva*,
2. Janardanpant Hanumante as *amatya*,
3. Shankaraji Malhar as *sachiv*
4. Ramchandra Trimbak Pandey as *mantri*,
5. Mahadaji Gadadhar as *sumant*,

---

61 *Ma'asir-i-Alamgiri*, p. 198.

62 *Ma'asir-i-Alamgiri*, p. 198.

63 G S Sardesai, *Rajaram*, p. 26.

64 Detailed accounts of the flight of Rajaram, from Raigadh to Jinji, are available in *Rajaram-charitam* by Keshav Pandit, the chaplain of Rajaram; G S Sardesai, *New History of the Marathas*, I, pp. 333ff; J N Sarkar, *House of Shivaji*, p. 225; R V Nadkarni, *The Rise and Fall of the Maratha Empire*, pp. 124-126; G T Kulkarni, *The Mughal-Maratha Relations*, pp. 95-97.

65 Harji Mahadik had been appointed to administer Jinji by Shambhuji early in 1681. J N Sarkar, *History of Aurangzib*, V, p. 42.

66 *Shiva-charitra-pradipa*, p. 35.

67 See J N Sarkar, *History of Aurangzib*, V, pp. 49-50.

68 Ambikabai handed over the government reluctantly. See J N Sarkar, *History of Aurangzib*, V, pp. 49-50; R V Nadkarni, *The Rise and Fall of the Maratha Empire*, p. 126.

6. Balaji Sundar as *nyayadhish*,
7. Khandoji (or Mahadaji, according to J C Grant Duff[69] and J N Sarkar[70]) Nayak Pansambal as *senapati*, and
8. Khandoji Ballal as *chitnis*.[71]

But the list of the *ashta-pradhana* given by J C Grant Duff differs from the above list in some aspects. In Duff's list, besides mentioning Niraji Raoji as *nyayadhish*, and Santaji Ghorpade as *senapati*, in the eighth place, mention is made of Srikaracharya holding the office of *panditrao*.[72] The same is the information provided by C S Srinivasachari.[73] It has been argued that *panditrao* was not a cabinet position,[74] and it is surprising to find these two scholars including it among the *ashta-pradhana*. But in the list of the *ashta-pradhana* of Shivaji, *panditrao* does occupy the eighth place.[75] However, it is relatively easy to understand the reason behind the confusion regarding the person appointed to the office of *senapati*. It appears that Rajaram initially appointed Mahadaji Nayak Pansambal as his *senapati*. But, one of the earliest news to reach him from Maharashtra after his arrival at Jinji, was that of the death of Mahadaji Nayak Pansambal.[76] Consequently, he appointed Santaji Ghorpade to the office of *senapati* with immediate effect.[77] Here, I would also like to point out an account given by Malhar Ramrao Chitnis, which has some bearing on this issue. He says that when Rajaram left for Jinji, he instructed Santaji Ghorpade and his two brothers to stay in Maharashtra and obey Ramchandrapant Amatya, whom he had left behind as *Hukumat-panah*, with the

---

69 J C Grant Duff, *History of the Mahrattas*, I, p. 300.

70 J N Sarkar, *House of Shivaji*, pp. 228-229.

71 See G T Kulkarni, *The Mughal-Maratha Relations*, pp. 98-99; for Khandoji Nayak Pansambal as *senapati*, see *ibid.*, p. 93.

72 J C Grant Duff, *History of the Mahrattas*, I, p. 301.

73 C S Srinivasachari, *A History of Gingee and its Rulers*, p. 265.

74 G T Kulkarni, *The Mughal-Maratha Relations*, p. 178, n. 21.

75 G S Sardesai, Shivaji, Chapter IX, in R C Majumdar, J N Chaudhuri, and S Chaudhuri (ed), *The Mughul Empire* (The History and Culture of the Indian People, VII), p. 268.

76 J C Grant Duff, *History of the Mahrattas*, I, p. 301.

77 V K Rajwade, *Marathyanchya Itihasachi Sadhane*, XV, p. 45.

charge of the governance of Maharashtra.[78] But when Ramchandrapant Amatya tried to raise the Mughal siege of Panhala, Santaji Ghorpade rendered him no assistance; he spent his time in military activities in the Sandur region up to the river Tungabhadra. He captured the fort of Gunti, and occupied the neighbouring *thanas*. Ramchandrapant Amatya informed Rajaram of Santaji Ghorpade's indiscpline, and the king removed Santaji Ghorpade from the position of *senapati*, and, in 1690, appointed Mahadaji Nayak Pansambal in his stead. Rajaram apprised Ramchandrapant Amatya of his decision, and deprived Santaji Ghorpade of the *sikke-katar*. For about a fortnight or a month, Santaji Ghorpade tried to meet Ramchandrapant Amatya, but in vain. He then reached Jinji to meet the king, assured him of his loyalty and satisfactory service, and started helping Rajaram against the Mughals at Jinji.[79] Later on, when Mahadaji Nayak Pansambal fell in battle, Santaji Ghorpade was again designated *senapati*.[80] If the account of Chitnis is correct,[81] it would imply that Rajaram had initially appointed Santaji Ghorpade as his *senapati*, but, due to his indiscipline, replaced him with Mahadaji Nayak Pansambal. But when Mahadaji Nayak Pansambal was killed in battle, Santaji Ghorpade was reinstated as *senapati*.

The Ghorpade family, to which Santaji Ghorpade belonged, was related to the Bhonsle family in which Shivaji was born. We have seen above, that according to a tradition, supported by copies of some Persian *firmans* in the possession of the Mudhol royal family, when Alauddin Khilji captured Chittor in 1303, Sajjan Singh or Sujan Singh, a scion of the ruling family of Udaipur, went to the south in search of employment. His fifth descendant was one Ugrasena, who had two sons, Karna Singh and Shubha Krishna. Shubha Krishna's descendants became

---

78 *Chitnis-bakhar*, II, p. 40.

79 *Chitnis-bakhar*, II, p. 34.

80 *Chitnis-bakhar*, II, p. 40.

81 J N Sarkar (*House of Shivaji*, p. 228) believes that the dates and names supplied by Chitnis are usually not reliable. But he does not specifically doubt the correctness of this account of Chitnis (*House of Shivaji*, pp. 228-229).

known as Bhonsles.[82] Karna Singh's son, Bhima Singh, entered the service of the Bahmani *sultan*. He showed great bravery while participating in a war in Konkan, by scaling the walls of an inaccessible fort using a hill iguana (Marathi, *ghorapad*),[83] for which he received the title of *Raja Ghorpade Bahadur* and a *jaghir* of 84 villages at Mudhol.[84] Thus, the descendants of Bhima Singh came to be styled Ghorpades.

Although the Bhonsles and the Ghorpades were offshoots of the same family, initially, the Ghorpades of Mudhol were not on friendly terms with the Bhonsles. We find Baji Ghorpade of Mudhol playing a rôle in the capture of Shahji in 1648,[85] and in an attempt by the Adilshah to suppress Shivaji in 1660.[86] In 1664, Shivaji attacked Mudhol, defeated and killed Baji Ghorpade, and captured and plundered Mudhol, before setting it on fire. Such a large number of members of the Ghorpade family were killed that the incident is labelled as the 'massacre of the Ghorpades'.[87] Later, in March 1677, Shivaji successfully tried to

---

82 G S Sardesai, *New History of the Marathas*, I, p. 52; however, writers, like Orme and David Kincaied, have expressed doubts regarding the authenticity of this tradition. See David Kincaied, *Shivaji, the Founder of the Maratha Empire*, p.25.

83 A similar device was used by Tanaji Malusare to enter the fort of Singhgadh. See David Kincaied, *Shivaji, the Founder of the Maratha Empire*, pp. 254-255.

84 J C Grant Duff, *History of the Mahrattas*, I, pp. 67-68.

85 Muhammad Juhur, *Muhammad-namah* (*Shivaji Nibandhavali*, II), p. 124; Muhammad Ibrahim Zubairi, *Basatin-us-Salatin*, pp. 325-326; R V Nadkarni, *The Rise and Fall of the Maratha Empire*, p. 35; Paramananda Kavindra, *Shiva-bharata*, canto 12; see J N Sarkar, *House of Shivaji*, p. 61; D C Varma, *History of Bijapur*, p. 154; etc. For details, see Nidhi Srivastava, *Santaji Ghorpade : Vyaktitva evam Krititva* (unpublished Ph D thesis, University of Lucknow, 2002), pp. 35-38.

86 R V Nadkarni, *The Rise and Fall of the Maratha Empire*, pp. 58-59. For details, see Nidhi Srivastava, *Santaji Ghorpade : Vyaktitva evam Krititva* (unpublished Ph D thesis, University of Lucknow, 2002), pp. 38-39.

87 *Sabhasad-bakhar*, pp. 68-69. J C Grant Duff, *History of the Mahrattas*, I, p. 148. See also J N Sarkar, *Shivaji and His Times*, p. 229. For details, see Nidhi Srivastava, *Santaji Ghorpade :*

bring about reconciliation between the Bhonsles and the Ghorpades of Mudhol, by writing to Maloji Ghorpade, the son and successor of Baji Ghorpade, and denying his rôle in the 'massacre of the Ghorpades'.[88]

Besides the Ghorpades of Mudhol, there was another branch of the family at Kapshi, which seems to have been earlier eclipsed by the Ghorpades of Mudhol, but which rose to prominence after the Ghorpades of Mudhol had been suppressed by Shivaji. But while the Ghorpades of Mudhol mostly harboured inimical feelings against the Bhonsles, these Ghorpades of Kapshi were favourably included towards the Bhonsles, and we see Santaji Ghorpade of this family, and his younger brothers, fighting alongside Rajaram against the Mughals.[89]

In this context, it would not be out of context to recall the Mughal-Maratha conflict at Titvala near Kalyan on 27 February 1683.[90] Although the Marathas did not succeed in capturing the fort, the Mughals suffered heavy losses. Among the Marathas, the *senapati*, Hambirrao Mohite sustained an arrow wound; the dead included his brother-in-law, and three other chiefs, besides a Ghorpade chief.[91] This slain Ghorpade chief does not appear to belong to the Mudhol branch of that family. Although there existed a number of branches of the Ghorpade family,[92] it is quite possible that the Ghorpade chief, who gave up his life, belonged to the Kapshi branch of the Ghorpades, on the grounds that the Ghorpades of Kapshi had always been loyal to the Bhonsles, and that, even though unnamed, this Ghorpade chief has been accorded so much importance in the account of the

---

Vyaktitva evam Krititva (unpublished Ph D thesis, University of Lucknow, 2002), pp. 39-41.

88 G S Sardesai (ed), *Shivaji Souvenir*, p. 146.

89 Of course, at times, Santaji Ghorpade is seen giving vent to his ire against the Maratha king, but he never sided with the enemies of Rajaram. See below.

90 Above.

91 *Shiva-charitra-pradipa*, p. 32; *Akhbarat*, 17 March, 02 April, 04 April, and 09 April 1683.

92 David Kincaied, *Shivaji, the Founder of the Maratha Empire*, p. 254, n. 1.

conflict that there seems to be little likelihood of his hailing from some minor branch of the family. Could this slain Ghorpade chief have been the father of Santaji Ghorpade ? It is difficult to reach any definite conclusion in the present state of our knowledge.

During the period between April 1685 and December 1688, when Aurangzeb was engaged in his campaigns against the sultanates of Bijapur and Golkunda, and could ill afford to pay attention towards Maharashtra, two chiefs, named Rahuloji Ghorpade and Tukoji Yashvantrao Ghorpade, were active in Karnataka, and their valour has been praised in a letter issued by Shambhuji.[93] There is no information about their antecedents, but, in view of their affiliations with the family of Shivaji, it may be surmised that they, too, belonged to the Ghorpade family of Kapshi. Besides, these two chiefs exhibited their valour in Karnataka, and, later on, Santaji Ghorpade, too, made an attempt to establish his chiefdom in the Bellary region of Karnataka.[94]

In 1676-1677, during his campaigns in Karnataka, Shivaji had encouraged a number of promising young warriors—Hambirrao Mohite, Janardanpant Hanumante, Keshav Trimal Pingle, Harji Mahadik, Santaji Bhonsle. Two such dashing young men were Santaji Ghorpade of the Ghorpade family of Kapshi, and Dhanaji Jadhav, the great grandson of the brother of Jijabai. These young men were provided practical training in military and civil administration, in order to groom them as future warrior-administrators.[95]

The death of the *senapati*, Mahadaji Nayak Pansambal, provided young and able Maratha warriors, like Santaji Ghorpade and Dhanaji Jadhav, to play significant rôle in Maratha history and polity. Realizing their importance, Rajaram honored them. Dhanaji Jadhav, who was related to Rajaram, as he was the great grandson of the brother of Jijabai, the mother of Shivaji, had started his career under Prataprao Gujar, the commander-in-chief of Shivaji. He first achieved military distinction, when, in 1689, he defeated a Mughal detachment in the plains of Phaltan, and was conferred the title

---

93 *Sambhaji Kalina Patra Sarsamgraha*, no. 298, p. 66.
94 J N Sarkar, *House of Shivaji*, p. 229.
95 G S Sardesai, *New History of the Marathas*, I, p. 258.

of *Jaysinghrao.*[96] As the eldest member of the Ghorpade family of Kapshi, Santaji Ghorpade was appointed to the post of *senapati*, and conferred *zari-patka*, that is 'golden banner', besides other honours.[97] Dhanaji Jadhav and Santaji Ghorpade were sent to Maharashtra, with instructions to raise a large army, and harass the Mughals there.[98]

In 1689, the Bijapuri general, Sharza Khan, the son of Sayyad Ilyas Khan, entered the services of Aurangzeb, and received from the emperor, the title of *Rustam Khan.* In May 1690, he made an attempt to capture the fort of Satara for his new master. Santaji Ghorpade, together with Dhanaji Jadhav, Ramchandrapant, and Shankaraji, led a combined attack on him.[99] Rustam Khan sent his son, Ghalib, to resist the Marathas, but he had very few and ill equipped soldiers with him.[100] The Maratha generals targeted the Mughal war elephants, causing the rout of the Mughal army. However, when the Mughal soldiers saw Rustam Khan bravely fighting with the Maratha, they took courage, and made a counter-attack on the Marathas. The Marathas pretended to give ground, and an overconfident Rustam Khan, mounted on his elephant, moved ahead with only a few soldiers.[101] But about that time, his clothes suddenly caught fire. The Berads started attacking and looting the confused Mughal soldiers, who took to flight. Rustam Khan fell down from his elephant, and was taken prisoner by Babaji More, perhaps the same as Manaji More. Rustam Khan's son, Ghalib, was also captured.[102] The Maratha captain of the fort of Satara

---

96 J N Sarkar, *House of Shivaji*, p. 224.

97 J C Grant Duff, *History of the Mahrattas*, I, p. 302; G S Sardesai, *New History of the Marathas*, I, p. 331.

98 J C Grant Duff, *History of the Mahrattas*, I, p. 302; R V Nadkarni, *The Rise and Fall of the Maratha Empire*, p. 126.

99 J N Sarkar (*History of Aurangzib*, V, pp. 21-23) has given a detailed account of this military engagement, on the basis of the information provided by the *Ma'asir-i-Alamgiri* (p. 202), *Jedhe Shakavali*, and *Ishvardas* (pp. 141a-143a).

100 J N Sarkar, *History of Aurangzib*, V, p. 22. *Cf* Bhimasena, *Dilkasha*, p. 146b, who discusses the weaponry of the Deccan soldiers.

101 J N Sarkar, *History of Aurangzib*, V, p. 22.

102 G T Kulkarni, *The Mughal-Maratha Relations*, p. 144.

also rallied out with his 5,000 soldiers, and captured the mother, wife, and children of Rustam Khan. Around 1,500 Mughal soldiers lost their life in this battle, and the Marathas carried away 4,000 Mughal horses, eight war elephants, and the tents of Rustam Khan.[103] After a few days, Rustam Khan managed to gain his freedom on promising to pay a ransom on one lac of rupees.[104] Some members of his family succeeded to escape capture at the hands of the Marathas by taking advantage of the confusion resulting due to the plunder of the Mughal camp by the victors.[105] The Marathas achieved this victory on 11 May 1690.[106] Aurangzeb sent Feroz Jang to help Rustam Khan. But the Mughal forces were attacked by Rupaji Bhonsle. The Mughals lost around 50 soldiers, and the Marathas carried away their provisions.[107]

Again, with the help of Ramchandrapant and Shankaraji, Santaji Ghorpade and Dhanaji Jadhav also succeeded in capturing the forts of Wai, Pratapgadh, Torna, and Rohida in April-May 1690,[108] and Rajgadh[109] and Vichitragadh[110] in July 1690, from the Mughals.

Worried by these developments in Maharashtra, the Mughal emperor appointed Lutf-ullah Khan as the *thanedar* of Khatav, and, on 30 May 1690, ordered him to take charge of his new posting.[111] On reaching Khatav on 06 July 1690, Lutf-ullah Khan ordered his tired soldiers to rest on a while. Due to heavy rains, it was not possible to establish a regular military camp, or to dig a ditch for protection. *Insha-i-Madhuram* informs us that, at night, Santaji Ghorpade, with 10,000 horsemen and a large number of

---

103 J N Sarkar, *History of Aurangzib*, V, pp. 22-23.

104 J N Sarkar, *House of Shivaji*, p. 226; G T Kulkarni, *The Mughal-Maratha Relations*, p. 144.

105 J N Sarkar, *History of Aurangzib*, V, p. 23.

106 J N Sarkar, *House of Shivaji*, p. 226.

107 J N Sarkar, *History of Aurangzib*, V, p. 23.

108 *Shiva- charitra-pradipa*, p. 36.

109 *Khafi Khan*, II, p. 392.

110 V K Rajwade, *Marathyanchya Itihasachi Sadhane*, XV, no. 283, p. 290.

111 *Ma'asir-i-Alamgiri*, p. 203.

footsoldiers, suddenly attacked the sleeping Mughal soldiers.[112] The attack lasted for about three hours, after which, Santaji Ghorpade wisely retreated to Vardhangadh, about 8 miles to the northwest of Khatav, while his soldiers went homeward. This battle did not result in any advantage to the Marathas; rather, they lost around 500 soldiers, while another 100 were captured and killed. They also lost 300 horses, 40 spears, 200 muskets, and some war drums and standards to the Mughals. On the Mughal side, 67 soldiers lost their lives, and 170 were wounded. After repulsing this Maratha attack, Lutf-ullah Khan began the task of establishing Mughal military posts in the area.[113]

Although this adventure of Santaji Ghorpade proved to be a failure, he consolidated his power, and became active in eastern Satara region. Aurangzeb ordered Lutf-ullah Khan to drive away the Marathas from there. The Mughal *thanedar* encamped in the village of Piliv, 12 miles to the east of Mhasvad and 15 miles to the south of Akluj. At dawn the next day, a Maratha force of 20,000 horsemen and a large body of infantry, reached the Mughal camp. It was being led by Santaji Ghorpade, Dhanaji Jadhav, Dafle, More, and some other Maratha chiefs. Lutf-ullah Khan ordered his soldiers to strike camp before the Marathas could attack. But the Marathas surrounded the Mughal soldiers, and started attacking them. Around sunset, Santaji Ghorpade and Dhanaji Jadhav led 5,000 select Maratha horsemen against Lutf-ullah Khan, but were repulsed. In this engagement, the Marathas lost 1,000 soldiers. On the Mughal side, around 200 soldiers lost their lives, and over 300 were wounded.[114] The dispatch, through which the Mughal emperor was informed of this incident, is undated. J N Sarkar suggests that, as Santaji Ghorpade and Dhanaji Jadhav were in the Kanara region during the second posting of Lutf-ullah Khan (16 October to 15 December 1692) as the *thanedar* of Akluj, they could not possibly have participated in any conflict in 1692. Therefore, the conflict would have taken place during the first posting of Lutf-ullah Khan as the *thanedar* of Akluj in 1690.[115] He is also of the view that, due to these

---

112 See J N Sarkar, *History of Aurangzib*, V, pp. 28-30.
113 See J N Sarkar, *History of Aurangzib*, V, pp. 28-30.
114 J N Sarkar, *History of Aurangzib*, V, pp. 29-30.
115 J N Sarkar, *History of Aurangzib*, V, p. 30n.

reverses, Santaji Ghorpade and Dhanaji Jadhav had to remain inactive for about six months, from October 1690 to April 1691.[116]

On 24 September 1691, 3,000 horsemen and 2,000 footsoldiers, led by Santaji Ghorpade, attacked a village in the neighbourhood of Nandaj in Ahmadnagar. The Mughal *kotwal* of the area tried to repulse the Maratha attack, but was unsuccessful. Gopal, the *gumashta* of that village, acted as Santaji Ghorpade's informer. The villagers had to pay 5,500 of rupees to Santaji Ghorpade as *chauth*. The Maratha also carried away all the camels from the fortress.[117]

In September-October 1691, Rajaram ordered Sarjarao Jedhe Deshmukh of Rohirakhore to reassert Maratha authority over Maval, Purandar, and Junnar regions, and instructed Santaji Ghorpade to render all possible help to the Jedhe Deshmukh in this endeavour.[118] On 05 October 1691, Muhammad Azam marched towards Bahadurgadh to suppress the Marathas. When he received the intelligence that Santaji Ghorpade was in the neighbourhood of Satara, he proceeded *post haste* to meet him in battle.[119] But the Marathas succeeded in defeating the Mughal officers at Chakhandi,[120] Parasgadh,[121] Parenda,[122] and other places.[123] Thus, the Maratha generals had again become active in Maharashtra, causing much worry to the Mughal emperor.[124]

Some time after February 1692, the Marathas succeeded in capturing the fort of Panhala.[125] Encouraged by this success, they started attacking Akluj. On 08 May 1692, Aurangzeb sent Prince

---

116 J N Sarkar, *History of Aurangzib*, V, p. 30n.

117 V K Rajwade, *Marathyanchya Itihasachi Sadhane*, XV. See G T Kulkarni, *The Mughal-Maratha Relations*, pp. 146-147.

118 V K Rajwade, *Marathyanchya Itihasachi Sadhane*, XV, no. 352, p. 382.

119 *Akhbarat*, year 35, Muharam 23.

120 *Akhbarat*, year 35, Muharam 29.

121 *Akhbarat*, year 35, Safar 2.

122 *Akhbarat*, year 35, Safar 2.

123 *Akhbarat*, year 35, Rabi II, 5.

124 *Waqil Report*, year 36, Ziqad 27. See G T Kulkarni, *The Mughal-Maratha Relations*, pp. 145-149.

125 *Shiva-charitra-pradipa*, p. 36.

Muiz-ud-din to Akluj to end the Maratha menace. Santaji Ghorpade had made the Mahadev hill region, to the northeast of Akluj, the centre of his activities, and raided the Bijapuri plains from there. Muiz-ud-din did not prove very effective against Santaji Ghorpade, and Aurangzeb was forced to appoint Lutf-ullah Khan as the *thanedar* of Akluj for the second time, on 16 October 1692.[126]

On 08 October 1692, Santaji Ghorpade, in concert with Dhanaji Jadhav, led 7,000 soldiers, and captured some fortresses in and around Belgam. They also attacked the cities of Belgam and Dharwad. It is learnt from the contemporary *Akhbarat*, that Aurangzeb sent Hamid-ud-din Khan to Belgam, and Matlab Khan to Dharwad to deal with the Marathas. Qasim Khan, the *fauzdar* of Bijapuri Karnataka, was instructed to make adequate arrangements for the defence of Bankapur and its neighbouring areas.[127] Of these three Mughal officers, Matlab Khan was able to achieve some success against the Marathas.[128] Shortly afterwards, Santaji Ghorpade and Dhanaji Jadhav had to be recalled from Maharashtra due to certain developments in Karnataka.[129]

In 1690, the Mughals besieged Jinji. But it proved to be a long drawn out affair.[130] In October 1692, the Mughals suddenly became quite active, and reached the wall of the fort. When Shankaraji received this information, he sent Dhanaji Jadhav to Jinji on 13 December 1692, and Santaji Ghorpade, on 14 December 1692.[131] From the Marathi sources, it is learnt that

---

126 J N Sarkar, *History of Aurangzib*, V, p. 31.

127 *Akhbarat*, 16 October 1692.

128 J N Sarkar, *History of Aurangzib*, V, p. 32n.

129 G T Kulkarni, *The Mughal-Maratha Relations*, pp. 102-107. See Nidhi Srivastava, *Santaji Ghorpade : Vyaktitva evam Krititva* (unpublished Ph D thesis, University of Lucknow, 2002), pp. 68ff.

130 For details of the siege, see Nidhi Srivastava, *Santaji Ghorpade : Vyaktitva evam Krititva* (unpublished Ph D thesis, University of Lucknow, 2002), pp. 69-72.

131 *Shiva-charitra-pradipa*, p. 36.

Santaji Ghorpade had with him a 15,000 strong cavalry.[132] Khafi Khan describes the cruel attacks of Santaji Ghorpade and Dhanaji Jadhav on the Mughal forces, and says that each of these two Maratha chiefs led a body of horsemen, numbering between 15,000 and 20,000; according to him, Santaji Ghorpade was the overall leader of these Maratha forces.[133] The Mughal soldiers were aware of the reputation of these two Maratha warriors, and the news of their arrival in Karnataka caused them much fear.[134]

Santaji Ghorpade and Dhanaji Jadhav first reached Kanchi, and struck so much terror in the inhabitants of that city that they fled, a large number of them taking shelter at Chennai. Ali Mardan Khan, the Mughal *fauzdar* of Kanchi, unaware of the military strength of the Marathas, left the shelter of his city, and came out to give fight to the Marathas. Martin has given a graphic account of the strategy of Santaji Ghorpade against Ali Mardan Khan.[135] Some information is also available in the *Madras Diary*,[136] *Jedhe Shakavali*, and a few other sources.[137] When the Mughal *fauzdar* realized that he was ill-matched to face the Marathas, he tried to retreat to the city, but Santaji Ghorpade surrounded the Mughal forces, and captured Ali Mardan Khan.[138] According to Martin, Santaji Ghorpade carried away five war elephants and 300 horses of superior breed, from the Mughals.[139] The Mughal *fauzdar* was taken to Jinji, and set free only after the payment of a ransom of one lac of *huns* by his brother-in-law, Ali Qadir.[140]

---

132 *Shiva-charitra-pradipa*, p. 36. According to J N Sarkar, (*House of Shivaji*, p. 226), both Santaji Ghorpade and Dhanaji Jadhav led 15,000 horsemen each to Jinji.

133 *Khafi Khan*, II, p. 415.

134 G T Kulkarni, *The Mughal-Maratha Relations*, p. 107.

135 François Martin, *Memoires*, III, pp. 268-269.

136 *Madras Diary*, 13, 17, 23 December 1692, and 04 August 1693. See J N Sarkar, *History of Aurangzib*, V, p. 62.

137 Bhimasena, *Dilkasha*, p. 108b.

138 *Khafi Khan*, II, p. 416.

139 J N Sarkar, *History of Aurangzib*, V, p. 62. But in some other sources, the number of captured elephants is given as six, and that of the horses, 1,500. See J N Sarkar, *House of Shivaji*, p. 226.

140 *Ibid*. But in some sources, the ransom amount is said to be as much as two lac of *huns*. *Shiva-charitra-pradipa*, p. 36; *Waqil Report*,

When the Marathas reached Jinji, Zulfiqar Khan decided to order a retreat. Sayyid Lashkar Khan and Kakkad Khan retreated with him. But Ismail Khan Mak, posted at the western gate of the fort, received the instructions for retreat rather late. On 09 Janurary 1693, Dhanaji Jadhav attacked him with a Maratha force, numbering between 7,000 and 8,000 soldiers, and wounded and captured Ismail Khan Mak.[141] The Marathas carried away two Mughal war elephants, and 500 horses.[142] In the *Ma'asir-i-Alamgiri*, the credit for capturing Ismail Khan Mak has been given to Santaji Ghorpade.[143] But, according to the account of François Martin,[144] as also the *Shiva-charitra-sahitya*,[145] and the *Jedhe Shakavali*,[146] the feat was performed by Dhanaji Jadhav. The information of the *Ma'asir-i-Alamgiri* appears to be erroneous.[147]

The Mughal forces besieging Jinji were beset with both internal and external troubles. Prince Kam Bakhsh was suspected of intrigue with the Marathas, and imprisoned by Zulfiqar Khan and Asad Khan. Santaji Ghorpade, along with 20,000 Maratha soldiers, led almost daily raids on the Mughals, keeping them occupied.[148] When provisions became scarce in the Mughal camp, Zulfiqar Khan went to Wandiwash, 24 miles to the northeast of Jinji, looted the grain merchants there, and marched back towards Jinji on 05 January 1693.[149] But he found Santaji Ghorpade blocking his way at Desur, about 10 miles to the south of Wandiwash, and was forced to take refuge in the fort there. When the Mughals resumed their marched towards Jinji, the Marathas attacked them with all their might, their musketeers

---

year 36, Jamadi II, 24. See G T Kulkarni, *The Mughal-Maratha Relations*, p. 107.

141 François Martin, *Memoires*, III, pp. 266-269. See J N Sarkar, *House of Shivaji*, p. 226.

142 *Akhbarat*, year 36, Shaban 1.

143 *Ma'asir-i-Alamgiri*, p. 216.

144 François Martin, *Memoires*, III, pp. 266-269.

145 *Shiva-charitra-sahitya*, V, no. 778, p. 23.

146 *Jedhe Shakavali*, p. 36.

147 See G T Kulkarni, *The Mughal-Maratha Relations*, p. 179, n. 55.

148 *Ma'asir-i-Alamgiri*, pp. 216ff.

149 J N Sarkar, *History of Aurangzib*, V, p. 69.

targeting the elephants on which the Mughal commanders were riding. On the contrary, the Mughals faced a shortage of ammunitions.[150] Before the Mughals could suffer further losses, Sarfaraz Khan reached the spot, and engaged the Marathas in a grim battle. Taking advantage of this diversion, Rao Dalpat sent the Mughal soldiers towards Jinji, and the Marathas decided to give up the offensive.[151]

Due to the shortage of provisions, the Mughal *wazir*, Asad Khan, who was the highest general of the Mughal forces besieging Jinji, sent a message to Rajaram, offering to pay a heavy amount to the Maratha king, if he allowed the Mughal forces to retreat to Wandiwash. He also bribed some brahmana Maratha ministers to plead before Rajaram on behalf of the Mughals.[152] Rajaram agreed to the Mughal request, despite of the advice of his commanders to continue the struggle against the demoralized Mughals, and drive them away.[153] Bhimasena has given a graphic account of the lifting of the Mughal siege of Jinji,[154] which was effected on 22 or 23 January 1693.[155] Thus, Santaji Ghorpade and Dhanaji Jadhav played a prominent rôle in the lifting of the Mughal siege of Jinji.

Thereafter, Santaji Ghorpade, at his own initiative, laid siege to Trichinapoly, in March 1693. The chief of that place was on inimical terms with Shahji II, the ruler of Thanjavur and a cousin and ally of Rajaram.[156] Rajaram himself reached Trichinapoly from Jinji to take part in this battle. Realizing the hopelessness of his situation, the Nayak of Trichinapoly entered into a treaty with Rajaram.[157]

---

150 Bhimasena, *Dilkasha*, p. 109b.

151 See J N Sarkar, *History of Aurangzib*, V, pp. 68-70.

152 François Martin, *Memoires*, III, pp. 285-287.

153 G T Kulkarni, *The Mughal-Maratha Relations*, p. 110.

154 Bhimasena, *Dilkasha*, p. 110b.

155 Bhimasena, *Dilkasha*, p. 110b. Aurangzeb was so enraged on receiving this news, that he ordered the recovery of three lac of rupees from Asad Khan, and one lac fifty thousand of rupees from Zulfiqar Khan, as fine. *Akhbarat*, year 37, Ramzan 4.

156 J N Sarkar, *House of Shivaji*, p. 228.

157 J N Sarkar, *History of Aurangzib*, V, p. 75.

Rajaram had allowed the Mughals to retreat from Jinji to Wandiwash at the advice of his brahmana ministers, ignoring the protests of *Senapati* Santaji Ghorpade and other military commanders. This proved to be one of the major issues leading to an estrangement between Rajaram and Santaji Ghorpade.[158] From the *Jedhe Shakavali*, it appears that by March 1693, the situation at the Maratha court had become untenable for Santaji Ghorpade, and some time in April or May 1693, he decided to leave Rajaram to his own devices at Jinji.[159] An angry Rajaram conferred the office of *senapati* on Dhanaji Jadhav.[160] According to Chitnis, Santaji Ghorpade was always quarreling with the courtiers of Rajaram. The king found this attitude of the general unbearable, and sent Mane to teach him a lesson. But the other officers prevailed upon him, not to take such a harsh step. Hence, Santaji Ghorpade was only censored, and replaced by Dhanaji Jadhav as *senapati*.[161] The same source reveals that this state of affairs continued for about two to three years.[162]

Santaji Ghorpade carved out a principality for himself in the Bellary region, and started acting like practically an independent ruler. In this period, he did not deign to obey the orders of Rajaram.[163] He did not even help his king in relieving the siege of Panhala.[164]

In October 1693, Santaji Ghorpade started raiding the regions around Bhupalgadh, around 65 miles to the northwest of Bijapur, and 76 miles to the southeast of Satara. Aurangzeb despatched Himmat Khan to stop him. Santaji Ghorpade had

---

158 G S Sardesai, *New History of the Marathas*, I, p. 342-343.

159 *Shiva-charitra-pradipa*, p. 37.

160 J N Sarkar, *History of Aurangzib*, V, p. 75; J N Sarkar, *House of Shivaji*, p. 228 and n. However, G S Sardesai (*New History of the Marathas*, I, pp. 346-347) places the dismissal of Santaji Ghorpade from the position of *senapati*, and the appointment of Dhanaji Jadhav on that position, some time in 1696, citing *Peshwa Daftar*, 31. 68, dated 27 October 1696; and Mawjee and Parasnis, *Sanads and Letters*, p. 177.

161 *Chitnis-bakhar*, II, p. 42.

162 *Chitnis-bakhar*, II, p. 42. J N Sarkar (*House of Shivaji*, p. 229) does not regard this account of Chitnis, as completely reliable.

163 J N Sarkar, *House of Shivaji*, p. 229.

164 J N Sarkar, *House of Shivaji*, p. 229.

forced Himmat Khan to take shelter near Mangaon, when Hamid-ud-din Khan and Khwaja Khan arrived with reinforcements, and the Marathas decided to retreat. The Mughals pursued them, and defeated them near Vikramahalli. Aurangzeb was informed of this victory in the *Akhbarat* of 19 November 1693.[165] But after this, differences cropped up among the Mughal commanders, and Hamid-ud-din Khan and Khwaja Khan went to Gulbarga, leaving Himmat Khan alone. However, he succeeded in forcing Santaji Ghorpade to seek refuge in the fort of Alur on 21 November 1693.[166] The Maratha commander had to face some further reverses at the hands of the Mughals in 1694, and had to retreat to the Mahadev hills.[167] In August 1694, we find Santaji Ghorpade active in Satara.[168]

The most notable military achievement of Santaji Ghorpade against the Mughals was his victory over the Mughal commanders, Qasim Khan and Khanazad Khan.[169] He spent the months of October and November 1695, raiding the Mughal occupied regions of the Deccan. After plundering the regions to the south of the river Krishna, he went towards his *jaghir* in northwestern Karnataka to deposit it there safely. Aurangzeb ordered Qasim Khan, his governor of Sera in western Karnataka, to seize the booty from Santaji Ghorpade. Khanazad Khan, who was, later, conferred the title of *Ruh-ullah Khan II*, and some other young commanders, were sent to assist him. They tried to intercept Santaji Ghorpade, but the Maratha received intelligence of their plans, and decided to inflict a crushing defeat on these Mughal commanders. The Mughals were unable to withstand the

---

165 J N Sarkar, *History of Aurangzib*, V, pp. 32-33.

166 J N Sarkar, *History of Aurangzib*, V, p. 33.

167 J N Sarkar, *History of Aurangzib*, V, pp. 32-33.

168 J N Sarkar, *History of Aurangzib*, V, p. 34. The events mentioned in this paragraph are not desribed in detail, as, at the time of their occurrence, Santaji Ghorpade was not serving Rajaram as his *senapati*, but acting in his individual capacity; Dhanaji Jadhav had been appointed as *senapati* by Rajaram (above).

169 For details of this event, see Nidhi Srivastava, *Santaji Ghorpade : Vyaktitva evam Krititva* (unpublished Ph D thesis, University of Lucknow, 2002), pp. 124ff.

Maratha onslaught the next day.[170] Santaji Ghorpade then sent some soldiers to attack and plunder the advance Mughal camp, where Qasim Khan had made elaborate arrangements for entertaining the Mughal officials sent to his help.[171] He kept some soldiers in reserve, and himself led a large Maratha force against the main Mughal army, meeting Qasim Khan while the Mughal officer was on his way to provide help to the advance camp. Barmappa Nayak of Chittaldurg came to the support of Santaji Ghorpade, and the Mughals were surrounded on all sides.[172] On the basis of the account given in the *Ma'asir-i-Alamgiri*,[173] J N Sarkar has described the battle that followed, as below :

'A great battle was fought and many were slain on both sides. In spite of the steadiness of the imperialists and the destruction done by them, the enemy did not yield one foot of ground or sow the least wavering. Then the reserve division of Santā fell upon the camp and baggage left behind and looted everything. This news reached Qasim and Khānazād in the heat of the battle and shook their firmness. They took counsel together and decided to go to the small fort of Dodderi close to which their advanced-tents had been sent and where there was a tank. Fighting for two miles they reached the tank in the evening and halted; the enemy retired from the attack but encamped nearby.'[174]

But the imperial forces stationed in the fort of Dodderi did not permit the fugitive Mughals to enter the fort, and the latter had to face shortage of provisions. On the fourth day, the *kala piada* musketeers wrecked great havoc on the Mughal forces.[175]

---

170 J N Sarkar, *History of Aurangzib*, V, p. 87.

171 *Ma'asir-i-Alamgiri*, pp. 227-228. See also, G T Kulkarni, *The Mughal-Maratha Relations*, p. 124.

172 *Ma'asir-i-Alamgiri*, p. 228; Bhimasena, *Dilkasha*, p. 117b.

173 *Ma'asir-i-Alamgiri*, pp. 227-230. See also, Bhimasena, *Dilkasha*, p. 118a.

174 J N Sarkar, *History of Aurangzib*, V, pp. 88-89.

175 *Ma'asir-i-Alamgiri*, pp. 227-229. See J N Sarkar, *History of Aurangzib*, V, p. 89. Khafi Khan (II, p. 429) gives a slightly different account of the battle. But J N Sarkar (*History of Aurangzib*, V, p. 89n) gives greater credence to the information

According to Khafi Khan, finding their position untenable, Qasim Khan, Khanazad Khan, and Saf Shikan Khan decided to enter the fort using shameful means.[176] There was severe scarcity of provisions in the fort.[177] The *Ma'asir-i-Alamgiri* informs us that Qasim Khan was addicted to opium, and he died of deprivation.[178] But there is also a view that he committed suicide to escape the wrath of Aurangzeb.[179] When there was no water left in the fort, Khanazad Khan sued for peace. Santaji Ghorpade demanded twenty lac of rupees, and all the elephants, horses, and jewels in the fort.[180] The Mughal officers were allowed to leave, only after signing notes of ransom.[181] They tried to meet the emperor, but he, in his anger, refused to give them audience.[182] This defeat of Qasim Khan at the hands of the Marathas is mentioned in the *Madras Diary* for 15 December 1695, from which we can get some idea of the date of this event.[183]

The Mughal emperor ordered Himmat Khan to avenge the defeat of Qasim Khan.[184] But this Mughal commander had very few soldiers at his disposal, and when he realized that it would not be possible for him to obey the orders of Aurangzeb, he took shelter in the fort of Basavpatan. It is known from the *Akhbarat* of 03 February 1696, that Santaji Ghorpade reached Basavpatan with 10,000 cavalry and an equal number of footsoldiers. His *kala piada* musketeers took position on a hillock, but were forced to retire by Himmat Khan, who then ordered his elephant

---

supplied by the *Ma'asir-i-Alamgiri* and the *Akhbarat*, mainly because the account of Khafi Khan was written about 30 years after the event.

176 *Khafi Khan*, II, p. 331. See J N Sarkar, *History of Aurangzib*, V, pp. 90-91.

177 J N Sarkar, *History of Aurangzib*, V, p. 91.

178 *Ma'asir-i-Alamgiri*, p. 228.

179 J N Sarkar, *History of Aurangzib*, V, p. 91.

180 J N Sarkar, *History of Aurangzib*, V, pp. 91-92. Khafi Khan (II, p. 433) mentions seven lac of rupees, and the *Jedhe Shakavali*, only one lac, in this context. See *Shiva-charitra-pradipa*, p. 38. G T Kulkarni, *The Mughal-Maratha Relations*, p. 182, n. 112.

181 J N Sarkar, *History of Aurangzib*, V, pp. 91-92.

182 G T Kulkarni, *The Mughal-Maratha Relations*, p. 128.

183 J N Sarkar, *History of Aurangzib*, V, p. 93 and n.

184 *Ma'asir-i-Alamgiri*, p. 230.

be taken near Santaji Ghorpade. But he was wounded, and fell down, and died around midnight. Another Mughal officer, Ali Baqi, was also wounded and captured. The Mughals stopped fighting, and the Marathas retired after plundering the camp of Himmat Khan.[185] On 22 January 1696, Aurangzeb sent Hamid-ud-din Khan to Basavpatan, where Sayyad Azmat-ullah and Muhammad Euz were bravely holding the fort. According to the *Akhbarat*, Santaji Ghorpade attacked the Mughals about 20 miles from Basavpatan, perhaps as Chakargola on the Tungabhadra,[186] but was repulsed with heavy losses. He again attacked Hamid-ud-din Khan at Basavpatan, but was again defeated.[187] But these reverses did not douse the spirit of Santaji Ghorpade, and we learn from the *Akhbarat* that, on 06 March 1696, Santaji Ghorpade yet again attacked Hamid-ud-din Khan, with similar results.[188]

We have seen above, that Zulfiqar Khan had once made a bid to capture the fort of Jinji, but had not succeeded in his endeavour, mainly because the Mughals could not suppress the supporters of Rajaram in the neighbouring areas. In the middle of 1694, Zulfiqar Khan again reached the neighbourhood of Jinji. By September 1694, he had consolidated his position there, made ample preparations for the second siege of Jinji, and occupied the Vetvalam forest, thus blocking the supply line to the fort of Jinji.[189] In October 1694, Zulfiqar Khan actually besieged the fort. The Marathas carried away some Mughal horses from the main camp of Zulfiqar Khan, which had been pitched to the north of the Changamon fort, about 42 miles to the west of Jinji. This led to speculations that Zulfiqar Khan had

---

185 J N Sarkar, *History of Aurangzib*, V, pp. 93-94; J N Sarkar, *House of Shivaji*, p. 237. J N Sarkar has based his description of the event on the *Akhbarat*, rejecting the account of Khafi Khan (II, pp. 433-434) as 'gossipy fabrication' (J N Sarkar, *House of Shivaji*, p. 237n).

186 J N Sarkar, *History of Aurangzib*, V, p. 95n.

187 J N Sarkar, *History of Aurangzib*, V, pp. 94-95.

188 *Akhbarat*, year 39, Shaban 2. See G T Kulkarni, *The Mughal-Maratha Relations*, p. 129.

189 Bhimasena, *Dilkasha*, p. 115b; *Akhbarat*, year 38, Safar 12.

entered into an intrigue with Rajaram.[190] But a number of scholars do not accept this as true.[191] The Mughals had a strong presence in Karnataka, and Rajaram feared for the defense of Jinji. But the Maratha position was improved by the arrival of Hindurao Ghorpade. Appeals were also made to Santaji Ghorpade and Dhanaji Jadhav to come to the rescue of the Maratha king, in all haste.[192] Shankarajipant ordered Santaji Ghorpade, with a strong Maratha force, to leave for Jinji. Some other Maratha commanders, like Yemaji Malhar and Hanumantrao Nimbalkar, were also sent to reinforce the defense of Jinji.[193]

Zulfiqar Khan himself was facing internal dissensions, and, consequently, there were no military engagements between the Mughals and the Marathas at Jinji in 1695. In October-November 1695, Zulfiqar Khan besieged Vellore. But shortly afterwards, the news of the arrival of Santaji Ghorpade and Dhanaji Jadhav, at the head of a large Maratha army, in eastern Karnataka, reached the Mughal camp, causing consternation among the Mughal soldiers.[194] Towards the end of December 1695, Dhanaji Jadhav reached Vellore, and Zulfiqar Khan was forced to lift the siege.[195] Thereafter, Dhanaji Jadhav besieged the Mughal *fauzdar* at Teruvadi, but Zulfiqar Khan reached there, and defended him against the Marathas.[196] Zulfiqar Khan then went to Arcot.[197] In March 1696, Santaji Ghorpade reached Jinji, and expressed his loyalty to Rajaram.[198] The arrival of Santaji Ghorpade and Dhanaji Jadhav raised the hopes of the Marathas. Meanwhile, Zulfiqar Khan was not receiving any help,

---

190 J N Sarkar, *History of Aurangzib*, V, pp. 78-79.

191 Eg, G T Kulkarni, *The Mughal-Maratha Relations*, pp. 114ff.

192 *Shiva-charitra-sahitya*, V, no. 729, pp. 81-82.

193 *Shiva-charitra-pradipa*, p. 31.

194 *Madras Diary*, 05 December 1695.See J N Sarkar, *History of Aurangzib*, V, p. 80.

195 *Shiva-charitra-pradipa*, p. 38.

196 *Akhbarat*, 18 January 1696.

197 J N Sarkar, *History of Aurangzib*, V, p. 80; G T Kulkarni, *The Mughal-Maratha Relations*, pp. 115-116.

198 *Shiva-charitra-pradipa*, p. 38; J N Sarkar, *History of Aurangzib*, V, p. 80.

financial and military, from Aurangzeb. He unsuccessfully tried to raise one lac of *huns* from the English at Chennai.[199] In April 1696, Zulfiqar Khan and Santaji Ghorpade faced each other at Arni, in which the former achieved some success against the Maratha commander. Despite of this, Zulfiqar Khan confined himself in the fort of Arcot, and took a defensive stance.[200]

In August 1696, the Maratha position weakened once again. There was rivalry between Santaji Ghorpade and Dhanaji Jadhav, in which Rajaram supported the latter. Santaji Ghorpade demanded that he be reinstated as *senapati*. The *pratinidhi*, Prahlad Niraji, was an able diplomat, and during his lifetime, he tried his best to maintain peace between Santaji Ghorpade and Dhanaji Jadhav, with some success. It was his endeavour that no action of the government could be construed by either of the rivals as a fovour conferred upon the other. But after his death, no minister of Rajaram possessed such a quality.[201] Consequently, there was an open conflict between Santaji Ghorpade and Dhanaji Jadhav at Evargudi to the northwest of Vriddhachalam near Kanchi,[202] in May 1696, in which Rajaram openly supported Dhanaji Jadhav.[203] According to the *Ma'asir-i-Alamgiri*, Santaji Ghorpade emerged victorious in this conflict, and he ordered that Amritrao Nimbalkar, the brother-in-law of Dhanaji Jadhav's ally, Nagoji Mane, be trampled to death by an elephant.[204] Santaji Ghorpade also took Rajaram captive, but Dhanaji Jadhav escaped. The next day, Santaji Ghorpade approached Rajaram with his own hands bound together, said

---

199 *Madras Diary*, 03 March 1696; J N Sarkar, *History of Aurangzib*, V, p. 81.

200 J N Sarkar, *History of Aurangzib*, V, p. 81; G T Kulkarni, *The Mughal-Maratha Relations*, p. 116.

201 J C Grant Duff, *History of the Mahrattas*, I, p. 315; G S Sardesai, *Rajaram*, p. 72.

202 G S Sardesai, *Rajaram*, pp. 80-82.

203 J N Sarkar, *History of Aurangzib*, V, p. 97; J N Sarkar, *House of Shivaji*, p. 238.

204 *Ma'asir-i-Alamgiri*, p. 243. From Khafi Khan (II, p. 445), it appears as if Santaji Ghorpade got the brother-in-law of Nagoji Mane killed only in 1697, a year before his own death. But J N Sarkar (*History of Aurangzib*, V, p. 97; *House of Shivaji*, p. 238), believes this to have occurred in May 1696.

that he remained, as before, a loyal servant of the Maratha king, and agreed to obey his orders in future. He then freed Rajaram, and sent him to Jinji with all honours.[205] According to certain writers, Santaji Ghorpade left Jinji for Maharashtra in May 1696.[206] But J N Sarkar gives an account of the activities of Santaji Ghorpade in Karnataka up to the end of 1696.[207] After his success against Rajaram and Dhanaji Jadhav, Santaji Ghorpade remained in the Arcot region, up to nearly the end of 1696. It appears that there is some confusion somewhere, and actually, it was Dhanaji Jadhav, who had been forced by Santaji Ghorpade and his supporters to go to Maharashtra in May 1696.[208] According to J N Sarkar, Santaji Ghorpade reached Maharashtra, in March 1697.[209] Thereafter, Santaji Ghorpade had no rôle to play in the Mughal-Maratha engagement at Jinji, and, hence, it would be sufficient to complete the account of the fall of Jinji in brief.[210]

It appears from some *Factory Records* that Zulfiqar Khan sent Ram Singh and a few other chiefs, with his proposal to lift the siege of Jinji. He promised to pay to Rajaram one lac of rupees, and to set his wife free, if he agreed to hand over the fort of Jinji to the Mughals.[211] But J N Sarkar is of the opinion that, as it was Rajaram who was in need of money, the proposal would have originated with him.[212] However, Aurangzeb was not ready to enter into an alliance with the Marathas. As a result, the attempts of Zulfiqar Khan and Rajaram at a *rapprochement* bore

---

205 In the *Ma'asir-i-Alamgiri* (p. 243), the battle is said to have taken place in October 1689, which J N Sarkar (*History of Aurangzib*, V, p. 97n; *House of Shivaji*, p. 238) treats as erroneous.

206 G T Kulkarni, *The Mughal-Maratha Relations*, p. 116.

207 J N Sarkar, *History of Aurangzib*, V, p. 81.

208 J N Sarkar, *History of Aurangzib*, V, p. 82.

209 *History of Aurangzib*, V, p. 98.

210 For details, see Nidhi Srivastava, *Santaji Ghorpade : Vyaktitva evam Krititva* (unpublished Ph D thesis, University of Lucknow, 2002), pp. 143-149.

211 The letter sent on 29 July 1697, from Fort Saint David to Fort Saint George. See *Proceedings of the Indian Historical Records Commission*, XIX, pp. 160-161; G T Kulkarni, *The Mughal-Maratha Relations*, p. 117.

212 J N Sarkar, *History of Aurangzib*, V, p. 82.

no fruit, and, early in November 1967, Zulfiqar Khan started making serious preparations to capture the fort of Jinji.[213] Rajaram was alerted of his attack, and he left Jinji for Vellore on 26 December 1697. But his family had to be left behind. The Mughals first captured the forts of Krishnagiri, Kalakot, and Chandrayana, at Jinji, forcing the Maratha royal family and the defenders to take refuge in the highest fort, Rajgadh.[214] When Ram Singh Hada succeeded in entering that fort, he was requested to grant safe passage for the royal family. After the fort was taken, four of Rajaram's wives, three sons, and two daughters were brought out of the fort, and 'kept in honourable captivity'. One of the wives of Rajaram refused to be captured by the Mughals, and gave up her life by jumping down from the summit of the fort.[215] J N Sarkar, on the basis of the *Ma'asir-i-Alamgiri*, proposes that the fort of Jinji fell to the Mughals on 07/08 February 1698,[216] while G T Kulkarni suggests 30 December 1697.[217] Bhimasena reports that Jinji fell on a *samkranti*, which, according to J N Sarkar, should be 02 January 1698 or 31 January 1698.[218] It is clear from the *Madras Diary*, that up to 02 January 1698, Zulfiqar Khan had captured all but one (Rajgadh ?) forts at Jinji. On 05 January 1698, it was written in the *Letters to Fort Saint George*, that Zulfiqar Khan had captured Jinji.[219] From this, it may safely be concluded that the Mughals succeeded in capturing Jinji some time between 02 January 1698 and 05 January 1698.[220]

---

213 Bhimasena, *Dilkasha*, p. 122b; *Madras Diary*, 26 October 1697; *Shiva-charitra-pradipa*, p. 39.

214 Bhimasena, *Dilkasha*, p. 124a. See J N Sarkar, *History of Aurangzib*, V, p. 83.

215 Bhimasena, *Dilkasha*, p. 124b. See J N Sarkar, *History of Aurangzib*, V, p. 84.

216 J N Sarkar, *History of Aurangzib*, V, p. 84n.

217 G T Kulkarni, *The Mughal-Maratha Relations*, p. 183, n. 125.

218 J N Sarkar, *History of Aurangzib*, V, p. 84n.

219 C S Srinivasachari, *A History of Gingee and its Rulers*, pp. 346-347.

220 See Nidhi Srivastava, *Jinji Durg ke Patan ki Tithi* (Hindi), in R C Tripathi, Agam Prasad, and Shalini Awasthi (ed), *Triratna—Heritage, Governance and Equity* (Hon'ble Shri T N Chaturvedi *Festschrift*), (Delhi, 2003), IV, pp. 1153-1160.

Although Santaji Ghorpade had defeated Dhanaji Jadhav (above), the power of the latter was not totally destroyed. He was able to win over several Maratha officials and chiefs, who had been insulted by the impetuous Santaji Ghorpade.[221] In March 1697, Dhanaji Jadhav and Hanumantrao Nimbalkar, whose brother, Amritrao Nimbalkar, had been killed by Santaji Ghorpade,[222] attacked a detachment of Santaji Ghorpade near Satara, following which, a number of the supporters of Santaji Ghorpade joined forces with Dhanaji Jadhav. Santaji Ghorpade lost several of his loyal supporters in the battle, and his soldiers took to flight. Santaji Ghorpade also fled towards Mhasvad,[223] where he sought refuge with Nagoji Mane, whose wife, Radhabai, was a sister of Amritrao Nimbalkar.[224] Radhabai sent Hanumantrao Nimbalkar after Santaji Ghorpade. The available sources are not in agreement regarding the circumstances of the death of Santaji Ghorpade.[225] But from their combined testimony, it may be concluded that, some time in June 1697,[226] when Santaji Ghorpade was bathing in a natural stream near the Shambhu Mahadev hill, Hanumantrao Nimbalkar beheaded

221 J N Sarkar, *History of Aurangzib*, V, p. 98; *House of Shivaji*, pp. 239-240.

222 J N Sarkar, *History of Aurangzib*, V, p. 97; *House of Shivaji*, p. 238.

223 J N Sarkar, *History of Aurangzib*, V, p. 97; *House of Shivaji*, p. 240. The description of J N Sarkar is based on the account of *Khafi Khan*, II, p. 445.

224 J N Sarkar, *History of Aurangzib*, V, p. 97; *House of Shivaji*, p. 240. The description of J N Sarkar is based on the account of *Khafi Khan*, II, p. 445.

225 *Ma'asir-i-Alamgiri*, p. 244; *Khafi Khan*, II, p. 448; records of the Mane family, in Parasnis, *Itihasa Samgraha, Junya Aitihasika Goshthi*, II, p. 45. See J N Sarkar, *History of Aurangzib*, V, pp. 98-99; *House of Shivaji*, p. 240.

226 For details of the death of Santaji Ghorpade, and its date, see Nidhi Srivastava, *Maratha Senapati Santaji Ghorpade : Katipaya Aityhasika Paksha* (Hindi), in S P Shukla, R S Bisht, M P Joshi, and Prashant Srivastava (ed), *History and Heritage* (in Honour of Professor Kiran Kumar Thaplyal), (Delhi, 2007), II, pp. 407-410.

him.[227] He lost the head of Santaji Ghorpade, which he was taking to Dhanaji Jadhav. It was found by Feroz Jang, who took it to Lutf-ullah Khan. When it was presented to Aurangzeb, he ordered it to be paraded before the Mughal army and the inhabitants of the various cities of southern India.[228]

Comparing Santaji Ghorpade and Dhanaji Jadhav, J N Sarkar[229] writes:

> 'The two life-long rivals, Santa and Dhana were both army leaders and organizers of the highest ability, courage and activity, but with contrasted characters. Dhana Jadhav made war like a gentleman; he knew that the fickle goddess of Fortune might desert him in the field any day; therefore, he never went to an extreme. He was moderate in victory, generous to the vanquished, polite in his address, practiced in self-control, and capable to taking long views and making statesmanly settlements. His inborn courtesy to the Mughal generals who had the misfortune to encounter him, is noticed with praise by the Muslim historians. Moreover, he served his country's Government unselfishly for many years.
>
> Santaji Ghorpare, on the other hand, was in comparison with Dhana, a barbarian devoid of culture or generosity, unable to restrain his passions or to take thought of the distant future. He loved to hustle all whom he met with, not even sparing his king. The hour of his victory was the Hour of the gratification of his vindictiveness. He showed no mercy and expected none. Therefore, he excited among the Mughal generals, as well as his Maratha adversaries, a feeling of mingled horror and repulsion....He lived and died merely as a

---

227 *Khafi Khan* (II, p. 448) erroneously calls him Mane. But J N Sarkar (*House of Shivaji*, p. 240) regards him as Hanumantrao Nimbalkar.

228 *Khafi Khan*, II, pp. 447-448; *Ma'asir-i-Alamgiri*, p. 244; Bhimasena, *Dilkasha*, II, p. 112a.

229 J N Sarkar, *House of Shivaji*, pp. 241-242; *Cf History of Aurangzib*, V, pp. 100-101.

> most successful raid-leader[230] and selfish adventurer, and exercised no influence on the political history of the Marathas....'

J N Sarkar seems to be a trifle too harsh in his above assessment of Santaji Ghorpade, and in denying him any influence on Maratha history.[231] G S Sardesai observes :

> 'Santāji is now remembered as the past master of guerilla warfare, the highest and best instrument which enabled the Marathas to attain a rapid rise before the development of artillery warfare in India. The death of this unmatched hero was a severe blow to the Maratha fortunes.'[232]

According to J N Sarkar, consequent to the death of Santaji Ghorpade, his brother, Bahirji Ghorpade, and son, Ranoji Ghorpade, began a war of attrition against Dhanaji Jadhav. In the last days of December 1700, there was a military conflict between Dhanaji Jadhav and Bahirji Ghorpade, at a place about 10 or 12 miles from Islampuri, in which both the sides lost a number of soldiers, but Dhanaji emerged victorious. Bahirji Ghorpade and Ranoji Ghorpade were put to flight towards Ahirvadi, about 13 miles to the south of Sholapur.[233] About three weeks later, on 16 January 1701, Ranoji Ghorpade is seen at Jagjivani near Bijapur, again making plans to avenge his defeat at the hands of Dhanaji Jadhav.[234] But shortly afterwards, Dhanaji Jadhav went to meet Ranoji Ghorpade at Ferozabad, about 20 miles to the south of Gulbarga, and made an attempt at

---

230 In his *History of Aurangzib*, V, p. 101, J N Sarkar uses, for Santaji Ghorpade, the term 'brigand', instead of 'raid-leader' used in *House of Shivaji*, p. 242.

231 *Cf* R V Nadkarni, *The Rise and Fall of the Maratha Empire*, p. 144, n. 94.

232 G S Sardesai, *New History of the Marathas*, I, p. 348.

233 J N Sarkar, *History of Aurangzib*, V, pp. 155-156. J C Grant Duff (*History of the Mahrattas*, I, p. 317), and G T Kulkarni (*The Mughal-Maratha Relations*, p. 162), merely allude to this event.

234 J N Sarkar, *History of Aurangzib*, V, p. 156.

a *rapprochement* in the wider interest of the Maratha kingdom.[235] The extent of his success in this endeavour is not known for certain. But in September 1701, Ranoji Ghorpade and Bahirji Ghorpade made inconclusive overtures to join the Mughal camp,[236] perhaps to escape the pressure of their Maratha rivals, especially Dhanaji Jadhav.[237]

It is, however, difficult to agree with J N Sarkar, when he says that main cause of the conflict of Bahirji Ghorpade and Ranoji Ghorpade with Dhanaji Jadhav was the rôle of Dhanaji Jadhav in the death of Santaji Ghorpade. For, after the death of Santaji Ghorpade in June 1697, and before the conflict between the Ghorpades and Dhanaji Jadhav in the last days of December 1700, we find Dhanaji Jadhav and Ranoji Ghorpade side by side, giving battle to Hamid-ud-din Khan, at Sangola, and putting him to flight on 20/21 December 1699.[238] Again, on 09/10 January 1700, Dhanaji Jadhav and Ranoji Ghorpade together gave battle to Zulfiqar Khan near Rehmatpur.[239] At Ferozabad, too, Dhanaji Jadhav and Ranoji Ghorpade helped each other against the Mughals.[240] G S Sardesai is of the view that the members of the Ghorpade family did not 'entertain any traces of hatred towards Dhanāji Jādhav, who had been already exalted to the position of the Senapati. They all joined him in continuing the war with full cordial co-operation, and when after the fall of Jinji, Rājārām and his Court returned to Mahārāshtra, it was the combined effort of all the Ghorpades that conquered and saved the distant Karnatak lands for the Maratha dominion….'[241] Santaji Ghorpade's brother, Bahirji Ghorpade, his son, Sidhoji Ghorpade, and grandson, Murarrao Ghorpade, exercized

---

235 Bhimasena, *Dilkasha*, II, p. 130b.

236 J N Sarkar, *History of Aurangzib*, V, p. 156.

237 J N Sarkar, *History of Aurangzib*, V, p. 156.

238 G T Kulkarni, *The Mughal-Maratha Relations*, pp. 164-165.

239 J N Sarkar, *History of Aurangzib*, V, p. 126; G T Kulkarni, *The Mughal-Maratha Relations*, p. 165.

240 S Pagdi, *Mughal ani Marathe* (Marathi translation of the *Dilkasha* of Bhimasena), p. 146, cited by G T Kulkarni, *The Mughal-Maratha Relations*, pp. 165-166.

241 G S Sardesai, *New History of the Marathas*, I, pp. 349-350.

authority over the greater part of Karnataka, till Balajirao's Karnataka expedition (below).[242]

When Rajaram reached Maharashtra from Jinji, in 1698, he made the fort of Satara the seat of his power, as Raigadh had been lost to the Mughals, and the inaccessible Vishalgadh would not have been a good choice as the new Maratha capital.[243] During the Dussehra season of 1696, Rajaram, accompanied by Dhanaji Jadhav, Khanderao Dabhade, Parsoji Bhonsle, and others, set out towards Surat, and had a number of encounters with the Mughal forces. On being resisted by Zulfiqar Khan, he moved towards Brahmapuri with the aim of raiding the Mughal camp, and rescuing Shahu. On 22 December 1699, he wrote to Vithoji Babar that Dhanaji Jadhav had succeeded in storming the imperial camp at Brahmapuri, and carried away captive, a daughter of the emperor, besides some members of the families of some prominent Mughal officials.[244] But camp life proved too arduous for Rajaram, who fell ill, and had to be taken to Singhgadh, where he died on 02 March 1700.[245]

While at Jinji, Rajaram took to a life given to the pleasures of the senses, just like his elder brother. Consequently, his authority was not undisputed, and it was very difficult for him to refuse any kind of favour to the various Maratha chiefs. He tried to keep them happy by awarding them high sounding titles, positions in his army, and extensive *jaghirs*.[246] We can get an idea of the feeling of insecurity, from which the king was suffering, from the fact that he often conferred the same title on more than one person, and appointed more then one person to the same post. He very frequently replaced his high officials.[247] In his brief reign of 11 years, he changed his *senapati* at least five

---

242 G S Sardesai, *New History of the Marathas*, II, p. 87.

243 G S Sardesai, *New History of the Marathas*, I, pp. 350-351. Soon, Satara, too, was occupied by the Mughals, but was repossessed by the Marathas in 1704, and again became the seat of Maratha power in 1708 on the return of Shahu from Mughal captivity.

244 *History of the Pratinidhis*, III, p. 451. See G S Sardesai, *New History of the Marathas*, I, pp. 351-352.

245 See G S Sardesai, *New History of the Marathas*, I, p. 352.

246 *Chitnis-bakhar*, II, p. 35.

247 *Chitnis-bakhar*, II, pp. 40-41.

times. There were several officials, like *sena-sahib-suba*, *sar-i-lashkar*, *sena-dhurandhar*, etc, whose designations were almost equivalent to that of the *senapati*,[248] and who enjoyed the same powers and privileges as the *senapati*.[249] This led to intense rivalries between the Maratha ministers, generals/commanders, and chiefs. This is clearly reflected in the account of Bhimasena, who laments the lack of unity among the Marathas about this time. He says that everyone calls oneself *sardar*, and raids and plunders for his personal profit.[250] Rajaram did not inherit the qualities of valour, bravery, and statesmanship from his father. He lacked the ability and spirit to provide leadership to the Marathas. Fortunately, he received the services of Prahlad Niraji as *pratinidhi*, Ramchandra Nilkanth as *amatya*, and Santaji Ghorpade and Dhanaji Jadhav as *senapati*, which alone prevented Aurangzeb from suppressing the Marathas, once and for all. These two Maratha generals played such a significance rôle in the Mughal-Maratha conflict during the period 1689 to 1697, that some scholars regards the history of the Deccan during this decade as 'the biography of these two men'.[251] But the rivalry between them adversely affected the Maratha cause, and even led to the death of Santaji Ghorpade.

---

[248] J N Sarkar, *History of Aurangzib*, V, p. 151n. Parsoji Bhonsle was *sena-sahib-suba*, Sidhoji Nimbalkar was *sar-i-lashkar*, and Khanderao Dhabhade was *sena-dhurandhar*. See G T Kulkarni, *The Mughal-Maratha Relations*, p. 9.

[249] J N Sarkar, *History of Aurangzib*, V, pp. 150-151.

[250] Bhimasena, *Dilkasha*, II, p. 122a.

[251] J N Sarkar, *House of Shivaji*, p. 224.

Chapter IV

Senapatis under the Successors of Rajaram

On the death of Rajaram on 02 March 1700, his four year old son, Shivaji II, was placed on the throne at Vishalgadh, as per the wishes of his wife, Tarabai, 'although the rightful succession of Shahu was not excluded'.[1] This son of Tarabai 'was deficient in mental power and not competent to manage the concerns of the State'. The queen-regent, a daughter of the valiant Hambirrao Mohite,[2] however, rose to the occasion, and inspired the Marathas by her conduct.

As seen above,[3] when Raigadh was captured by Zulfiqar Khan on 03 November 1689, Yesubai, her seven year old son, Shahu, two illegitimate sons of Shambhuji, and Shivaji's widow, Sakvarbai, were carried away by Zulfiqar Khan, and had to spend 17 years in captivity.[4] But Aurangzeb did not treat Shahu as he had treated his father. He made arrangements for the comfortable stay of the Maratha royal captives in his camp,[5]

---

1 G S Sardesai, *New History of the Marathas*, I, p. 358. See G T Kulkarni, *The Mughal-Maratha Relations*, p. 190.

2 R V Nadkarni, *The Rise and Fall of the Maratha Empire*, p. 146. See Brij Kishore, *Tara Bai and Her Times*, Bombay, 1963.

3 Above, Chapter III.

4 G S Sardesai, *New History of the Marathas*, I, p. 359.

5 *Ma'asir-i-Alamgiri*, p. 200. See J N Sarkar, *History of Aurangzib*, V, p. 156 and n.

under the supervision of his daughter, Zinat-un-nisa. Declaring Shahu as the legitimate king of the Marathas, he tried, though largely unsuccessfully, to take advantage of every opportunity to create dissension among the Marathas.[6] It is clear from the family papers of various Marathas families, that, not unoften, the Mughals made a claim on their services and loyalty by 'right of conquest', and the Marathas, by 'right of possession', thus revealing a political picture of 'double government'.[7]

The years following the death of Rajaram were quite disappointing for the Mughal emperor.[8] Of course, between 1700 and 1704, in spite of the brave resistance offered by Maratha officers and chiefs, like Dhanaji Jadhav,[9] he had succeeded in capturing the forts of Satara, Parli, Panhala, Vishalgadh, Singhgadh, Rajgadh, and Torna, from the Marathas, but was unable to retain his mastery over them for long.[10] Under the able guidance of Tarabai, the Marathas achieved successes against the Mughals.[11] In 1702, Dhanaji Jadhav is found harassing Zulfiqar Khan near Singhgadh and Miraj.[12] The son of Dhanaji Jadhav besieged Sultanpur and Nandurbar. Zulfiqar Khan marched to suppress them. However, he was informed that the Marathas had moved towards Baglan. Zulfiqar Khan decided to chase them,

---

6 J N Sarkar, *History of Aurangzib*, V, pp. 157-159. G S Sardesai, *New History of the Marathas*, I, pp. 360-361; G T Kulkarni, *The Mughal-Maratha Relations*, pp. 227ff.

7 G S Sardesai, *New History of the Marathas*, I, p. 363.

8 J N Sarkar, *History of Aurangzib*, V, pp. 12-14.

9 For Dhanaji Jadhav's resistance during the siege of Satara, see J N Sarkar, *History of Aurangzib*, V, p. 126. For Dhanaji Jadhav's resistance during the siege of Panhala, see J N Sarkar, *History of Aurangzib*, V, pp.136-138; G T Kulkarni, *The Mughal-Maratha Relations*, pp. 197-198. For Dhanaji Jadhav's resistance during the siege of Vishalgadh, see G T Kulkarni, *The Mughal-Maratha Relations*, pp. 202, 205. For Dhanaji Jadhav's resistance during the siege of Singhgadh, see G T Kulkarni, *The Mughal-Maratha Relations*, p. 223.

10 J N Sarkar, *History of Aurangzib*, V, pp. 123-148; G S Sardesai, *New History of the Marathas*, I, p. 357; G T Kulkarni, *The Mughal-Maratha Relations*, pp. 188-239.

11 R V Nadkarni, *The Rise and Fall of the Maratha Empire*, p. 146.

12 G T Kulkarni, *The Mughal-Maratha Relations*, p. 225.

and reached Abula (?).[13] There, he received the intelligence that the son of Dhanaji Jadhav was moving towards the imperial camp near Poona, and was able to drive them away.[14] In the first half of 1703, Aurangzeb ordered the conversion of Shahu to Islam,[15] but relented when Dhandoji and Jagjivan, the two sons of Shivaji's *senapati*, Prataprao Gujar, converted in his stead.[16] Some time after November 1703, he released Shahu, and authorized Kam Bakhsh, to whom he had entrusted the affairs of southern India, to negotiate with Dhanaji Jadhav for his release.[17] Dhanaji Jadhav, on behalf of the Marathas, agreed to swear allegiance to the Mughal emperor and protect the country,[18] if the Maratha king was given the right to collect *chauth* and *sardeshmukhi* from the six *subas* of the Deccan, and the prominent Maratha leaders were received and honoured by Aurangzeb in his court. The Mughal emperor acceded to these conditions, but when the Marathas assembled in large numbers in the vicinity of the imperial camp, he suspected them of some foul play, and reneged, to the evident joy of the Marathas, who were not happy to accept the suzerainty of the Mughals.[19]

During these last years of Aurangzeb, the Marathas led expeditions into Gujarat and Malwa; the Ghorpade family

---

13 Bhimasena mentions the name of the place as Abola. G T Kulkarni (*The Mughal-Maratha Relations*, p. 238, n. 68) proposed to identify it as Abhone near Baglan, or Ranola near Nandurbar.

14 G T Kulkarni, *The Mughal-Maratha Relations*, p. 226.

15 J N Sarkar, *History of Aurangzib*, V, p. 157.

16 G S Sardesai, *New History of the Marathas*, I, p. 364-365; G T Kulkarni, *The Mughal-Maratha Relations*, pp. 228-229. But, according to J N Sarkar (*History of Aurangzib*, V, p. 157 and n), the conversion of these two brothers was already reported in the *Akhbarat* of 27 May 1700 and 22 July 1700.

17 *Ma'asir-i-Alamgiri*, p. 281; Bhimasena, *Dilkasha*, II, pp. 145b, 147a. J N Sarkar, *History of Aurangzib*, V, p. 158.

18 Some scholars are of the view that in 1703, Dhanaji Jadhav made overtures to join the Mughal camp. See J N Sarkar, *History of Aurangzib*, V, p. 156.

19 See *Khafi Khan*, II, p. 520. J N Sarkar, *History of Aurangzib*, V, p. 158; G S Sardesai, *New History of the Marathas*, I, pp. 366-367. Also the account of Bhimasena, *Dilkasha*, II, p. 145b. G T Kulkarni, *The Mughal-Maratha Relations*, pp. 227-228.

extended its authority towards the south in Karnataka.[20] In June-July 1703, the Marathas raided and plundered the camp of Prince Azam, while he was marching from Rajewadi to Poona.[21] In November-December 1703, they captured Sharza Khan, and realized a ransom of three lac of rupees for his release.[22] In January 1704, they crossed the river Narmada, and caused much depredation in Malwa, till Firoz Jang defeated and repulsed them.[23] Towards the end of 1704, the Marathas attacked and plundered the imperial Mughal camp at Bahadurgadh, while Aurangzeb was proceeding towards Wagingera, the capital of the Bedars, to suppress the rebellion of Pidya Nayak in Karnataka.[24] On 08 March 1705, a Maratha force, led by Dhanaji Jadhav and Hindurao Ghorpade, arrived at Wagingera,[25] and attacked the imperial camp several times, till they were repulsed by Zulfiqar Khan and Daud Khan.[26] Prince Muhammad Azam, the *subedar* of Gujarat, was absent from his *suba* from November 1705 to March 1706, as he had gone to meet Aurangzeb. Dhanaji Jadhav led a strong Maratha force into Gujarat during the absence of Muhammad Azam. On 15 March 1706, a fierce battle was fought near Rajpipla on the eastern bank of the river Narmada, in which a large number of Mughal soldiers were either killed or wounded. Two Mughal officers, Safdar Khan Babi and Naar Ali Khan, were taken captive, and later set free on payment of a heavy ransom. The Mughal camp was mercilessly plundered.[27] The Marathas also captured Abdul Hamid Khan, the deputy governor of Gujarat, who had rushed to the rescue of the Mughal forces near Rajpipla, and plundered his camp. They then realized *chauth* from the villages in the region, and retired.[28] Taking

---

20 G S Sardesai, *New History of the Marathas*, I, p. 369-370.

21 *Miscellaneous Sources of Indian History*, III, no. 287, pp. 33-35.

22 G T Kulkarni, *The Mughal-Maratha Relations*, p. 244.

23 *Ma'asir-i-Alamgiri*, p. 286; Bhimasena, *Dilkasha*, II, p. 148b; *Shiva-charitra-pradipa*, p. 68.

24 Bhimasena, *Dilkasha*, II, p. 149b.

25 *Ma'asir-i-Alamgiri*, p. 297.

26 G T Kulkarni, *The Mughal-Maratha Relations*, p. 248.

27 *Shiva-charitra-pradipa*, p. 69; Bhimasena, *Dilkasha*, II, p. 156a; Manucci, *Storia do Mogor*, IV, p. 246.

28 *Khafi Khan*, II, p. 518.

advantage of the absence of Aurangzeb from Maharashtra, the Marathas recaptured most of the forts seized from them by the Mughals.[29] In fact, the Marathas had become so bold that, when Aurangzeb was returning from Bahadurgadh to Ahmadnagar, a strong Maratha contingent followed the imperial army, attacking and killing a large number of Mughal soldiers sent under Hamid-ud-din Khan to punish them.[30] In April-May 1706, Dhanaji Jadhav, and some other Maratha commanders, appeared in the vicinity of the imperial camp at Ahmadnagar. Khan-i-Alam was sent to repulse them, but was unsuccessful, and the Marathas withdrew of their own accord.[31] Some time before April 1706, Balaji Vishvanatha put the Mughals to flight in the Nashik region, and ravaged the village of Dindori near Vani, where the Mughals were encamped.[32] In July 1706, the Marathas, under Hindurao Ghorpade, captured the fort of Penukonda from the Mughals.[33]

In 1706 again, Aurangzeb tried to divide the Marathas and start a civil war, by removing Shahu to the quarters of Zulfiqar Khan, and ordering him to rule the Maratha nation with the guidance of Kam Bakhsh.[34] But the Marathas saw through the device of Aurangzeb, and none came to take up the cause of Shahu.[35] However, Ramchandrapant and Dhanaji Jadhav maintained contact with Shahu in the Mughal camp,[36] and tried to negotiate his release, so that he may be installed as the next *chhatrapati*, which led to serious differences between them and Tarabai.[37]

---

29 G T Kulkarni, *The Mughal-Maratha Relations*, pp. 246ff.

30 Bhimasena, *Dilkasha*, II, p. 155a.

31 Bhimasena, *Dilkasha*, II, p. 155b.

32 *Miscellaneous Sources of Indian History*, IV, no. 138, pp. 135-136.

33 Bhimasena, *Dilkasha*, II, p. 156b.

34 *Ma'asir-i-Alamgiri*, p. 304; Bhimasena, *Dilkasha*, II, pp. 154b-155a.

35 *Ma'asir-i-Alamgiri*, p. 304; *Shiva-charitra-pradipa*, p. 69. G S Sardesai, *New History of the Marathas*, I, p. 367; G T Kulkarni, *The Mughal-Maratha Relations*, p. 252.

36 J N Sarkar, *History of Aurangzib*, V, p. 158.

37 G S Sardesai, *New History of the Marathas*, I, p. 371.

In January 1707, the Marathas, under Dhanaji Jadhav and Santaji Mohite, were active in the Sholapur region. Zulfiqar Khan succeeded in forcing them to take up a defensive position in the fortress of Sangola. Tarabai sent an army to the help of Dhanaji Jadhav,[38] but there was no confrontation between the Mughals and the Marathas, and Zulfiqar Khan returned to Miraj.[39] Thus, almost till he breathed his last, on 21 February 1707 at Ahmadnagar,[40] the Marathas continued to trouble Aurangzeb, and he knew not even a moment of peace.

The death of Aurangzeb was followed by a struggle for succession among his sons. Prince Azam took command of the Mughal army in the Deccan, and proceeded towards the north to meet Prince Muazzam. On the advice of Zulfiqar Khan, he released Shahu from captivity in May 1707, permitted him to rule as his feudatory, and granted him the right to levy *chauth* and *sardeshmukhi* from the six *subas* of the Deccan, and from the provinces of Gondvana, Gujarat, and Thanjavur.[41] This was done with the sole intention of causing a rift among the Marathas, so that they would have no time and energy for harassing the Mughals. Initially, Shahu had not supporters among the Maratha officers and chiefs. But his gentle and sympathetic nature endeared him to the people as he passed

---

[38] *Akhbarat*, year 51, Ramzan 16, and Shawwal 29.

[39] G T Kulkarni, *The Mughal-Maratha Relations*, p. 254.

[40] *Ma'asir-i-Alamgiri*, p. 309. See G T Kulkarni, *The Mughal-Maratha Relations*, p. 259, and p. 262, n. 59. It is true, as Kulkarni alleges, that J N Sarkar, in his translation of the *Ma'asir-i-Alamgiri*, p. 309, gives the date of the death of Aurangzeb as 20 February 1707. Kulkarni poses as if it is he, who, for the first time, has corrected the date to 21 February 1707. But, in his *History of Aurangzib*, V, p. 14n, Sarkar himself very clearly states that, as the official record emphasizes that the death of Aurangzeb took place on a Friday, 'we must correct the text into Friday the 29th Zil. Q.= 21 Feb. 1707'.

[41] Elliot and Dowson, *History of India, as told by its Own Historians*, VII, p. 395; J C Grant Duff, *History of the Mahrattas*, I, p. 349; G S Sardesai, *Marathi Riyasat*, I, p. 743; R V Nadkarni, *The Rise and Fall of the Maratha Empire*, pp. 154-155.

through the Maratha land, and Mohan Singh Ambu Pandey,[42] Rustamrao Sujan Singh,[43] Parsoji Bhonsle,[44] Haibatrao Nimbalkar, Nemaji Shinde, and Chimnaji Damodar, joined his cause.[45] Thus, Shahu reached Ahmadnagar, which he decided to make the seat of his power, and where he wanted to make preparations for his impending struggle with Tarabai.[46]

Tarabai was aware of these developments, and she asked all the prominent Maratha officers and chiefs to swear their allegiance to Shivaji II. A number of them actually took the oath, but some officers, like Dhanaji Jadhav and Khandoji Ballal promised to do so only if Tarabai's contention, that the Shahu claiming to be the legitimate Maratha king was, in fact, an imposter, proved to be correct. Tarabai sent Parsoji Bhonsle's brother, Bapu Bhonsle,[47] while Dhanaji Jadhav sent Balaji Vishvanatha, who were both convinced was Shahu was not an imposter. Therefore, Dhanaji Jadhav remained indifferent during the battle of Khed, in which, Parashurampant Pratinidhi, fighting on behalf of Tarabai, was defeated and forced to flee towards Satara.[48] Consequent to this, Dhanaji Jadhav, and following him, Khandoji Ballal Chitnis and *Peshva* Nilkanth Pingle's brother, Bahiropant Pingle, openly came to the support of Shahu.[49] Shankaraji Malhar, the *sachiv*, was haunted by the thought that he had acted as a traitor to the rightful heir, Shahu, committed

---

42 Elliot and Dowson, *History of India, as told by its Own Historians*, VII, p. 395.

43 V K Rajwade, *Marathyanchya Itihasachi Sadhane*, XX, no. 60.

44 *Nagpurkar Bhonslyanchi Bakhar* (*The Chronicle of the Bhonsles of Nagpur*), p. 20.

45 G S Sardesai, *Marathi Riyasat*, I, p. 3. G S Sardesai, *New History of the Marathas*, II, p. 13.

46 R V Nadkarni, *The Rise and Fall of the Maratha Empire*, pp. 156-157.

47 *Nagpurkar Bhonslyanchi Bakhar* (*The Chronicle of the Bhonsles of Nagpur*), p. 20.

48 R V Nadkarni, The *Rise and Fall of the Maratha Empire*, pp. 157-158.

49 V K Rajwade, *Marathyanchya Itihasachi Sadhane*, XV, no. 360; G S Sardesai, *New History of the Marathas*, II, p. 15.

suicide,[50] and Shahu became master of all the territories to the north of the river Nira. After Chandanvandan submitted to him of its own accord, Shahu moved towards Satara. A Muslim officer, named Shaikh Mira, took Parashurampant Pratinidhi captive, and surrendered the fort to Shahu, who ascended the throne on 12 January 1708. Following the advice of some interested persons, like Khanderao Dabhade, Shahu adopted a conciliatory policy towards Tarabai. For the time being, he allowed her to live in peace, in the territories to the south of the river Krishna. He even offered to let Tarabai and Shivaji II to rule over the region to the south of Warna.[51] But his aunt was consolidating her position at Rangna, forcing Shahu to march against her in February 1708. The supporters of Tarabai ditched her,[52] and she took to flight. She corresponded with Dhanaji Jadhav and Khandoji Ballal, and urged them to either come over to her side, or to advise Shahu to lift the siege of Rangna. These officers, feeling that if Shahu and Tarabai remained embroiled in this internecine conflict, their services would be treasured by the king, and they would have a good opportunity to expand their own *jaghirs* at their expense, advised Shahu to lift the siege of Rangna. Therefore, in spite of the protests of Parsoji Bhonsle, Shahu retired to Panhala in June 1708. He planned to renew operations against Rangna after the monsoons. But in the meantime, Dhanaji Jadhav died, in June 1708 at Vadgaon, and his son, Chandrasen Jadhav, was appointed as *senapati*.[53] However, Shahu was not confident of his new *senapati*'s loyalty, and he gave up designs against Rangna. Tarabai captured Vishalgadh, and established the seat of her power at Kolhapur.[54]

Meanwhile, in 1707, Prince Muazzam emerged victorious in the struggle for the Mughals throne, and was crowned emperor

---

50 V K Rajwade, *Marathyanchya Itihasachi Sadhane*, XV, no. 289. G S Sardesai, *New History of the Marathas*, II, p. 16.

51 R V Nadkarni, *The Rise and Fall of the Maratha Empire*, pp. 158-159.

52 V K Rajwade, *Marathyanchya Itihasachi Sadhane*, III, nos. 64-67.

53 G S Sardesai, *New History of the Marathas*, II, p. 17.

54 R V Nadkarni, *The Rise and Fall of the Maratha Empire*, pp. 160-161.

as Bahadur Shah.[55] Shahu expressed his allegiance to him, and was confirmed in his possessions. He helped the new emperor in his campaign against Kam Bakhsh, and sought his help in settling his quarrel with Tarabai. But Bahadur Shah refused to be embroiled in the internal power struggle of the Marathas.[56] This led to renewal of hostilities between Shahu and Tarabai, which continued till the matter was settled once and for all through the treaty of Warna in 1731.[57]

Shahu appointed Balaji Vishvanatha, a Chitpavan brahmana who had served under Dhanaji Jadhav and had been in charge of the collection of *chauth* in Daulatabad, as his *senakarte*, 'organizer of armies', which made Chandrasen Jadhav, the *senapati*, jealous of him.[58] Things came to a head when Shahu sent Balaji Vishvanatha to report the movements of Chandrasen Jadhav, who engaged in a conflict with Damaji Thorat of Supa,[59] and whom Shahu suspected of harbouring sympathies for the cause of Tarabai and Shivaji II. Hostilities broke out between the two over a minor dispute, and Shahu openly supported Balaji Vishvanatha.[60] Chandrasen Jadhav openly insulted Shahu, who sent his *sarlaskar*, Haibatrao Nimbalkar, against him. Chandrasen Jadhav was defeated, and he, along with most of the soldiers of the Maratha army,[61] went over to Tarabai.[62] Shahu appointed Santaji Jadhav, the younger brother of Chandrasen Jadhav, as his *senapati*, in 1711.[63] But shortly afterwards, Haibatrao Nimbalkar, too, joined the faction of Tarabai, thus leaving Shahu bereft of the services of two of his topmost

---

55 William Irvine, *Later Mughuls*, I, pp. 22-32.

56 G S Sardesai, *New History of the Marathas*, II, pp. 20-21.

57 R V Nadkarni, *The Rise and Fall of the Maratha Empire*, pp. 161-162.

58 V K Rajwade, *Marathyanchya Itihasachi Sadhane*, II, p. 7.

59 According to J C Grant Duff (*History of the Mahrattas*, I, p. 363), however, Chandrasen Jadhav had been sent to collect *chauth* and *sardeshmukhi* from the Mughal territories.

60 *Life of Shahu Maharaja, the Elder*, p. 28.

61 V K Rajwade, *Marathyanchya Itihasachi Sadhane*, II, p. 10.

62 R V Nadkarni, *The Rise and Fall of the Maratha Empire*, pp. 163-165; G S Sardesai, *New History of the Marathas*, II, pp. 21-22.

63 R V Nadkarni, *The Rise and Fall of the Maratha Empire*, p. 166.

military officers. At this crucial juncture, Balaji Vishvanatha came to his help. He not only raised money to recruit an army,[64] but also brought about the downfall of Tarabai and Shivaji II with the help of Ramchandrapant and some dissatisfied Marathas from Kolhapur. Tarabai and Shivaji II were imprisoned, and Shambhuji was installed at Kolhapur, under the tutelarship of his mother, Rajasbai.[65] Chandrasen Jadhav sought shelter with Nizam-ul-mulk, the Mughal viceroy of the Deccan.[66] All these services of Balaji Vishvanatha must have pleased Shahu, and, when *Peshva* Bahiroji Pingle was defeated and taken captive by Kanhoji Angre in 1712, Balaji Vishvanatha was appointed *peshva* in 1713.[67] It was also decided that, thenceforth, for all pratical purposes, the duties of *senapati*, too, would be discharged by the *peshva* himself.[68]

Balaji Vishvanatha was able to affect conciliation with Kanhoji Angre,[69] and to suppress dissidents like Damaji Thorat and Udaji Chavan, thus securing the position of Shahu. The Marathas were now free to harass the Mughal territories, and Daud Khan Panni, the Mughal viceroy of the Deccan, was forced to allow Shahu to order his agents to collect *chauth* and *sardeshmukhi* from the six *subas* of the Deccan, as per the agreement between the Marathas and Bahadur Shah. But, in 1713, Nizam-ul-mulk, the new viceroy of the Deccan, stopped this payment on the grounds that the matter of the legitimate Maratha king was, as yet, unsettled. But shortly after, Nizam-ul-mulk was replaced by Sayyid Husain Ali Khan. In the meantime, Shahu had replaced *Senapati* Santaji Jadhav with Man Singh More, and then the latter, with Khanderao Dabhade.[70] The Mughal emperor was jealous of his own viceroy of the Deccan, and, encouraged by him, the Marathas, under *Senapati*

---

64 Sinha, *Rise of the Peshwas*, p. 10.

65 *Contra* G S Sardesai, *New History of the Marathas*, II, p. 23.

66 R V Nadkarni, *The Rise and Fall of the Maratha Empire*, p. 166.

67 V K Rajwade, *Marathyanchya Itihasachi Sadhane*, II, p. 17; G S Sardesai, *New History of the Marathas*, II, pp. 24ff.

68 R V Nadkarni, *The Rise and Fall of the Maratha Empire*, p. 167.

69 G S Sardesai, *New History of the Marathas*, II, pp. 25-27.

70 V K Rajwade, *Marathyanchya Itihasachi Sadhane*, II, p. 28; G S Sardesai, *New History of the Marathas*, II, pp. 37-38.

Khanderao Dabhade, harassed the Mughals everywhere.[71] When Sayyid Husain Ali Khan came to know of this, he entered into a treaty with the Marathas in February 1718, under which, he recognized the right of Shahu to receive payment of *chauth* and *sardeshmukhi* in the six *subas* of the Deccan, and recognized his authority over the territories conquered by the Marathas in Khandesh, Gondvana, Berar, and Karnataka.[72] But Farrukhsiyar refused to ratify the treaty,[73] and Mughal politics forced Sayyid Husain Ali Khan to leave for Delhi,[74] accompanied by Balaji Vishvanatha, Santaji Bhonsle, and Khanderao Dabhade heading 16,000 Maratha soldiers. In this conflict, Khanderao Dabhade played a significant rôle. The Sayyid brothers arrested the emperor, and seized power.[75] They raised Rafi-ud-Darajat as the new emperor, who ratified the treaty between Sayyid Husain Ali Khan and the Marathas, and issued *firmans* confirming it, on 13 and 24 March 1719.[76] Balaji Vishvanatha returned to Satara with these *firmans* and Shahu's mother, Yesubai, released from Mughal captivity at last, in May 1719.[77] The *peshva* was accorded a heroic welcome at Satara,[78] and, when he died on 02 April 1720 at Sasvad, his son, Bajirao I, succeeded him to the office on 17 April 1720.[79]

Following the murder of Sayyid Husain Ali Khan and the suicide of Sayyid Abdullah Khan, Nizam-ul-mulk, once again, became a prominent figure in Mughal politics. He opened correspondence with Shambhuji of Kolhapur, Chandrasen Jadhav, and some other Maratha chiefs, and tried to stop the

---

71 G S Sardesai, *New History of the Marathas*, II, p. 37.

72 V K Rajwade, *Marathyanchya Itihasachi Sadhane*, II, pp. 30-31; Scott, *History of the Deccan*, IV, p. 152; G S Sardesai, *New History of the Marathas*, II, pp. 38ff.

73 J C Grant Duff, *History of the Mahrattas*, I, pp. 337-338.

74 For details, see William Irvine, *Later Mughuls*, I, pp. 339-353.

75 G S Sardesai, *New History of the Marathas*, II, pp. 43-46.

76 A G Pawar, *Proceedings of the Indian Historical Records Commission*, XVII, pp. 209-213. See also *Life of Shahu Maharaja, the Elder*, p. 55.

77 G S Sardesai, *Selections from Peshwa Daftar*, XXX, pp. 255-265.

78 G S Sardesai, *New History of the Marathas*, II, pp. 47-48.

79 V K Rajwade, *Marathyanchya Itihasachi Sadhane*, II, p. 39n.

agents of Shahu from collecting *chauth* in the six *subas* of the Deccan.[80] But the Marathas repulsed the Mughal forces sent to implement these designs of Nizam-ul-mulk.[81] On 04 January 1721, Bajirao faced Nizam-ul-mulk himself at Chikhalthan near Baramati, and then led expeditions into Khandesh, Surat and Rajpipla, as far as the Godavari.[82] In October 1721, Nizam-ul-mulk had to leave for Delhi, where he was appointed *wazir* by the Mughal emperor on 13 February 1722.[83]

Bajirao took advantage of the absence of Nizam-ul-mulk from the Deccan, and, after a brief period of estrangement with Shahu,[84] exacted *chauth* from regions as far as Bundelkhand.[85] The position of Nizam-ul-mulk as *wazir* was fast becoming untenable at Delhi, and, without seeking the permission of the emperor, he left for the Deccan on the pretext that his presence was urgently needed there because of Maratha inroads into Malwa and Gujarat.[86] An angry emperor appointed Mubariz Khan as the viceroy of the Deccan, and the situation took such a turn that Nizam-ul-mulk had to seek the help of Shahu. Together, they defeated and killed Mubariz Khan, and Nizam-ul-mulk established himself at Haidarabad in 1725.[87]

In order to consolidate his position in the Deccan, Nizam-ul-mulk tried, with the help of Chandrasen Jadhav,[88] to stir up the rivalry between Shahu and Shambhuji of Kolhapur, who claimed authority over the territories between the rivers Krishna and Tungabhadra, and who regarded the two failed Karnataka

---

80 G S Sardesai, *New History of the Marathas*, II, pp. 73ff.

81 *Life of Shahu Maharaja, the Elder*, p. 42.

82 V K Rajwade, *Marathyanchya Itihasachi Sadhane*, II, p. 44; G S Sardesai, *New History of the Marathas*, II, p. 75.

83 G S Sardesai, *New History of the Marathas*, II, pp. 75-76; R V Nadkarni, *The Rise and Fall of the Maratha Empire*, pp. 173-174.

84 G S Sardesai, *New History of the Marathas*, II, pp. 94-95; R V Nadkarni, *The Rise and Fall of the Maratha Empire*, pp. 174-176.

85 V K Rajwade, *Marathyanchya Itihasachi Sadhane*, II, pp. 47-49.

86 G S Sardesai, *New History of the Marathas*, II, p. 77.

87 William Irvine, *Later Mughuls*, II, p. 146; V K Rajwade, *Marathyanchya Itihasachi Sadhane*, II, p. 49; G S Sardesai, *New History of the Marathas*, II, pp. 77ff.

88 G S Sardesai, *New History of the Marathas*, II, pp. 91ff.

expeditions of Shahu[89] as a challenge to him. A number of disgruntled Maratha chiefs, like Chandrasen Jadhav, Murarji Ghorpade, Udaji Chavan, Rambhaji Nimbalkar, and Trimbakrao Dabhade, closed ranks with Shambhuji and Nizam-ul-mulk.[90] Nizam-ul-mulk bribed the *pratinidhi* of Shahu, who advised the king not to send agents to collect *chauth* dues from Haidarabad. Nizam-ul-mulk then expressed his inability to pay *chauth* to Shahu, till the matter of the claims of Shambhuji of Kolhapur was settled.[91] In November 1726, he started military operations against Shahu, at a time when his *peshva* and *senapati* were both busy in the Karnataka campaign, and by February 1727, Nizam-ul-mulk and Shambhuji were camping at Poona.[92] But Bajirao returned from Karnataka, and forced, not only Nizam-ul-mulk to recognize Shahu as the legitimate Maratha king under the treaty of Mungi-Paithan (March 1728),[93] but also Shambhuji to accept Shahu as his sovereign under the treaty of Warna (April 1731).[94]

Khanderao Dabhade was a capable *senapati*, but he was unable to keep up with the fresh policy of the *peshva*, and became almost redundant. The *peshva* raised his own armies, and led his own military campaigns, dispensing with the services of the *senapati*. When Khanderao Dabhade died on 27 September 1729, Trimbakrao Dabhade was appointed to the office of *senapati* in January 1730,[95] and was confirmed in his ancestral *jaghir* in Gujarat, which had been granted by Shahu to Khanderao Dabhade for the maintenance of his troops, on 30 July 1727.[96] Bajirao was not in favour of the policy of the successors of Shivaji, under which various Maratha chiefs were allowed to collect *chauth* and *sardeshmukhi* from the entire province assigned to them. He proposed that he would give half

---

89 J C Grant Duff, *History of the Mahrattas*, I, p. 420.

90 R V Nadkarni, *The Rise and Fall of the Maratha Empire*, pp. 178ff.

91 V K Rajwade, *Marathyanchya Itihasachi Sadhane*, II, p. 55.

92 R V Nadkarni, *The Rise and Fall of the Maratha Empire*, p. 180.

93 G S Sardesai, *New History of the Marathas*, II, pp. 94ff.

94 G S Sardesai, *New History of the Marathas*, II, pp. 116ff; R V Nadkarni, *The Rise and Fall of the Maratha Empire*, p. 181.

95 G S Sardesai, *New History of the Marathas*, II, p. 122.

96 *Shahu Diaries*, 159.

of the revenue of yield from his *jaghir* of Malwa to the Dabhades, and that they should reciprocate in the like mannaer in respect of their *jaghir* of Gujarat. Trimbakrao Dabhade regarded this as an undue interference in the affairs of his *jaghir*, by the *peshva*.[97] He made common cause with Nizam-ul-mulk, who was already smarting after his defeat in the battle of Palkhed on 25 February 1728,[98] and with Udaji Pavar, and planned to make a concerted effort to destroy Bajirao. But before the armies of Trimbakrao Dabhade and Udaji Pavar could combine with the army of Nizam-ul-mulk, Bajirao fell on them, and defeated them at Dabhai in April 1731.[99] Trimbakrao Dabhade lost his life, and his brother, Yashvantrao Dabhade was named the next *senapati*,[100] but the Dabhades could never recover from this defeat at Dabhai,[101] and, thenceforth, the *peshva* took over the duties of the *senapati*.[102] The management of the affairs of Gujarat gradually passed into the hands of Pilaji Gaekvad and his descendants.

Nizam-ul-mulk finally realized the inadvisability of his confrontationalist policy towards the Marathas, and, in August 1731, it was agreed that he would have a free hand in the south, and Bajirao, in the north.[103] He even allowed the *peshva* to freely pass through his dominions towards Malwa. By 1739, Bajirao had established Maratha supremacy in Malwa, struck terror in the heart of the Mughal emperor at Delhi, defeated Nizam-ul-mulk in the battle of Bhopal, and, with the help of his brother, Chimnaji Appa, reduced the Siddis of Janjira, the Angres, and

---

97 G S Sardesai, *New History of the Marathas*, II, p. 123.

98 G S Sardesai, *Selections from Peshwa Daftar*, XXX, pp. 282-283.

99 V K Rajwade, *Marathyanchya Itihasachi Sadhane*, II, p. 61; G S Sardesai, *New History of the Marathas*, II, pp. 122ff.

100 G S Sardesai, *New History of the Marathas*, II, pp. 128-129; R V Nadkarni, *The Rise and Fall of the Maratha Empire*, p. 184.

101 C A Kinkaid and D B Parasnis, *A History of the Maratha People*, p. 231; G S Sardesai, *New History of the Marathas*, II, pp. 129-131.

102 R V Nadkarni, *The Rise and Fall of the Maratha Empire*, p. 183.

103 C A Kinkaid and D B Parasnis, *A History of the Maratha People*, p. 240.

the Portuguese, in the Konkan.[104] He breathed his last on 28 April 1740, at Raverkhedi,[105] while inpecting the *jaghirs* granted him by Nasir Jang, the son of Nizam-ud-din, as per one of the conditions of the treaty of Mungi-Paithan.[106]

Despite the attempts of Raghuji Bhonsle to have Babuji Nayak Joshi nominated as the next *peshva*,[107] Shahu appointed Nana Saheb, the 19 year old son of Bajirao, to that office, on 25 June 1740.[108] Nana Saheb, now known as Peshva Balajirao, consolidated the financial position of the Maratha empire, and got his own *jaghir* in Malwa confirmed by helping the Mughal emperor against Raghuji Bhonsle.[109] He sent a successful expedition in Karnataka under Sadashivrao Bhau, who exacted tributes from all the territories up to the river Tungabhadra.[110] In the course of this Karnataka expedition, Murarrao Ghorpade, a descendant of Santaji Ghorpade, requested Shahu that he be appointed *senapati* for his services at Trichinapoly, but the request was declined, as Shahu did not wish to deprive the Dabhades of that, now largely ceremonial, post.[111]

Shahu had no legitimate male heir, which led to intrigues between interested parties, each party wanting its own candidate

---

104 G S Sardesai, *New History of the Marathas*, II, pp. 135ff; R V Nadkarni, *The Rise and Fall of the Maratha Empire*, pp. 184-195.

105 G S Sardesai, *New History of the Marathas*, II, p. 181; V G Dighe, Peshva Baji Rao I (1720-1740), Chapter IV, in R C Majumdar and V G Dighe (ed), *The Maratha Supremacy* (*The History and Culture of the Indian People*, VIII), pp. 63-103, on p. 97.

106 R V Nadkarni, *The Rise and Fall of the Maratha Empire*, p. 196. He gives the date of the death of Bajirao as 25 April 1740.

107 G S Sardesai, *New History of the Marathas*, II, p. 190; R V Nadkarni, *The Rise and Fall of the Maratha Empire*, p. 197.

108 S V Puntambekar, Peshwa Balaji Rao (1740-1761), Chapter VI, in R C Majumdar and V G Dighe (ed), *The Maratha Supremacy* (*The History and Culture of the Indian People*, VIII), pp. 170-200, on p. 170.

109 J C Grant Duff, *History of the Mahrattas*, II, p. 15; G S Sardesai, *New History of the Marathas*, II, pp. 192ff; R V Nadkarni, *The Rise and Fall of the Maratha Empire*, pp. 198-200.

110 G S Sardesai, *New History of the Marathas*, II, pp. 251ff; R V Nadkarni, *The Rise and Fall of the Maratha Empire*, p. 202.

111 G S Sardesai, *New History of the Marathas*, II, p. 255.

to be nominated the successor. As Balajirao exercized a strong influence on the king, Raghuji Bhonsle and Rani Sakvarbai managed to convince the ailing Shahu of the *peshva*'s disloyalty, and had him removed from office for a short period of time.[112] But just before his death on 15 December 1749,[113] Shahu issued an order, making the office of *peshva* hereditary, and recognizing him as the head of both civil and military administration.[114] This signalled the end of the rôle of the *senapati* in Maratha history and polity.

Balajirao wanted Shambhuji of Kolhapur to succeed Shahu, as this would have meant the amalgamation of the Satara and Kolhapur houses. But Shahu appointed Ram Raja, the grandson of Tarabai, as his successor.[115] Tarabai tried to exercize total control over him, and, when she failed in her objective, she declared him illegitimate.[116] To put an end to this state of affairs, Balajirao assumed all political power after the conference at Sangola, and transferred all official work from Satara, to his own seat at Poona. All the other members of the *ashta-pradhana* council were divested of their powers. The *senapati*, Yashvantrao Dabhade, was given a cash allowance for his maintenance, and his *jaghir* of Gujarat was divided between Balajirao and the Gaekvads.[117] On his death, his son, Trimbakrao II Dabhade, became *senapati*, which was now a mere nominal position.[118] Tarabai took Ram Raja prisoner in November 1750,[119] and the Maratha king and his descendants languished in

---

112 G S Sardesai, *New History of the Marathas*, II, pp. 265-266; R V Nadkarni, *The Rise and Fall of the Maratha Empire*, pp. 202-203.

113 S V Puntambekar, Peshwa Balaji Rao (1740-1761), Chapter VI, in R C Majumdar and V G Dighe (ed), *The Maratha Supremacy* (*The History and Culture of the Indian People*, VIII), pp. 170-200, on p. 181. See G S Sardesai, *New History of the Marathas*, II, p. 273.

114 R V Nadkarni, *The Rise and Fall of the Maratha Empire*, p. 204.

115 He might have favoured Ram Raja, because Shambhuji was himself quite old at the time, and, he, too, had no male heir. G S Sardesai, *New History of the Marathas*, II, pp. 270ff.

116 G S Sardesai, *New History of the Marathas*, II, pp. 289-290.

117 G S Sardesai, *New History of the Marathas*, II, p. 292.

118 G S Sardesai, *New History of the Marathas*, II, p. 312.

119 G S Sardesai, *Selections from Peshwa Daftar*, VI, nos. 119, 124, 127, 139, 141, 147. See S V Puntambekar, Peshwa Balaji Rao

prison for a long time.[120] Tarabai harboured illwill against the *peshva*, but, later on, she reconciled with Balajirao, who kept a strict control over both her and Ram Raja.[121] The *peshva*, thus, became supreme in the Maratha state.

(1740-1761), Chapter VI, in R C Majumdar and V G Dighe (ed), *The Maratha Supremacy* (*The History and Culture of the Indian People*, VIII), pp. 170-200, on pp. 181-182.

120 It is said that the king and his descendants spent the next 68 years in prison. See C A Kinkaid and D B Parasnis, *A History of the Maratha People*, p. 301. Ram Raja was later released and crowned king on 23 March 1763 by Peshva Madhavrao I, but remained a political non-entity. G S Sardesai, *New History of the Marathas*, II, p. 298.

121 G S Sardesai, *New History of the Marathas*, II, pp. 296-298.

Chapter V

Conclusion

The rise of the Marathas around the middle of the seventeenth century AD, under their charismatic leader, Shivaji, was meteoric. They held their own against Bijapur and Golkunda; they succeeded in keeping the Mughals at bay to a large extent, and, by the second decade of the eighteenth century, the Mughal emperor had granted them the right to realize *chauth* and *sardeshmukhi* of the six provinces of southern India, thus recognizing their *de facto* supremacy in the Deccan.[1] Soon, the Maratha armies were active 'from Lahore to Murshidabad, from Delhi to Seringapatam'. But within less than two centuries of its establishment, the Maratha empire fell equally suddenly, after offering a brief resistance of just fifteen weeks.[2]

We have seen above that the sultanates of the Deccan—particularly Bijapur and Golkunda, and the Marathas, and the Mughals, were all vying for supremacy in southern India. In a political situation, where friction with neighbours was the normal state of things, land passed frequently from the hands of one master to those of the other, as a result of changes in political fortunes of these powers. But each new master usually left the tilling of the land to the 'old peasant', and the collection of revenue to the old intermediary. As a consequence, the offices of these intermediaries—the *deshmukhs* and the *deshpandes*,

---

1 S N Sen, *The Military System of the Marathas*, p. xiii.

2 Much has been written about the factors responsible for the fall of the Maratha empire—political, social, economic, and others. See J N Sarkar, *Shivaji and His Times*, pp. 373ff.

tended to become hereditary, and they started regarding the land under their charge as their personal fief or *vatan*. Gradually, this *vatan*, for them, became 'the only reality, the only object of a man's lifelong endeavour, the highest reward on earth',[3] with the abstract feelings of nationality, if at all present, occupying a secondary place. The 'feudal structure', thus, gained prominence. The term, 'feudal structure' usually refers to the mediaeval European form of government based on the relation between the vassal and his superior, wherein the former was awarded holding of lands on condition of homage and service. In the present context,[4] the term has been used in the sense of the granting of land (*jaghir*) to high officials in *lieu* of salaries, and hereditary appointments to such posts.

In its infancy, the Maratha state was a monarchy, governed by an enlightened aristocracy. Shivaji knew of the evils of the 'feudal structure', having observed its evil effects in the sultanates of Bijapur and Golkunda.[5] He tried his best to keep the Maratha state free of the evils of this 'feudal structure'. He was not in favour of granting land to his high officials in *lieu* of salary; also, he did not favour hereditary appointments.[6] In fact, his officers, including the ministers in the *ashta-pradhana* council, could not expect to even hold their office lifelong.[7] All the officers could be dismissed, transferred, or censured by the king.[8] Shivaji believed that granting of *jaghir* in *lieu* of salary to

---

3 J N Sarkar, *Shivaji and His Times*, pp. 377-378.

4 That is in the context, especially of the Marathas and the sultanates of the Deccan.

5 S N Sen, *Administrative System of the Marathas*, p. 36.

6 G S Sardesai, *New History of the Marathas*, I, p. 282; V G Dighe and S N Qanungo, Administrative and Military System of the Marathas, Chapter XVII, in R C Majumdar and V G Dighe (ed), *The Maratha Supremacy* (The History and Culture of the Indian People, VIII), p. 542.

7 S N Sen, *Administrative System of the Marathas*, p. 44; R V Nadkarni, *The Rise and Fall of the Maratha Empire*, p. 362.

8 S N Sen, *The Military System of the Marathas*, p. 11. As seen above, in Chapter II, Shivaji dismissed Netaji Palkar for his negligence during the siege of Panhala in 1666. On another occasion, he censured Prataprao Gujar for allowing Bahlol Khan to

officers, and hereditary appointments, were not compatible with the ideas of a strong monarchy that he envisaged. There is a view that the reversion to 'feudal structure' in the time of the successors of Shivaji led to the decline and fall of the Maratha empire.[9] Let us examine the validity of this theory, in the light of the decline in the status of the *senapati* in the post-Shivaji period, after lands came to be allotted to *senapatis* in *lieu* of salary, and the office became sort of herediaty.

Shivaji had put in place a very efficient system for administration of the Maratha state, which was based on the tried and tested system adopted by his mentor, Dadaji Konddev, for the management of Shahji's *jaghir* of Poona.[10] The system of Dadaji Konddev itself was copied from the administrative measures adopted by Malik Ambar and Todarmal.[11] The broad principles of Shivaji's administration may be summed up as follows :

1. Government servants were employed on the basis of merit, and the offices were not hereditary.[12]

---

repair to Tikota after the battle at Umbrani, in which the Marathas had gained the upper hand.

9 G S Sardesai, *New History of the Marathas*, II, pp. 54-59; S N Sen, *The Military System of the Marathas*, pp. 43-63; V G Dighe and S N Qanungo, Administrative and Military System of the Marathas, Chapter XVII, in R C Majumdar and V G Dighe (ed), *The Maratha Supremacy* (The History and Culture of the Indian People, VIII), pp. 550-553; R V Nadkarni, *The Rise and Fall of the Maratha Empire*, pp. 353ff; etc.

10 G S Sardesai, *New History of the Marathas*, I, pp. 97-100.

11 G S Sardesai, *New History of the Marathas*, I, p. 282.

12 M G Ranade (*Rise of the Maratha Power*, pp. 129-130) writes : 'None of the great men, who distinguished themselves in Shivaji's time, were able to hand over to their descendants large landed estates. Neither Moropant Pingle nor Abaji Sondev, nor Ragho Ballal or Datto Annaji or Niraji Raoji, among the Brahmans, nor the Malusares or Kanks, or Pratap Rao Gujar, Netaji Palkar, Hambirrao Mohite or the Maratha *Sardars*, were able to found ancient families such as those which Shahu's ministers in the early part of their eighteenth century succeeded in doing.'

2. All government servants were paid their salaries in cash, and land in the form of *jaghir* was not granted to them.[13]
3. All administrative work was divided among various departments, each with its well defined responsibilities.
4. Revenue was collected through a well supervised government agency, without taking the services of intermediaries.
5. Caste was not a consideration at the time of appointment to a government office.[14]

As noted earlier,[15] at the time of his coronation, Shivaji announced the formal creation of a council of eight ministers (called *ashta-pradhana*),[16] among whom all the departmental work was clearly divided. These ministers were :

1. *Peshva* (prime minister)—Moropant Trimbak/Trimal Pingle;
2. *Amatya* (revenue minister)—Ramchandra Nilkanth;
3. *Sachiv* (finance minister)—Annaji Datto;
4. *Mantri* (minister for interior)—Dattaji Trimbak;
5. *Senapati* (commander-in-chief)—Hambirrao Mohite;
6. *Sumant* (minister for external affairs)—Ramchandra Trimbak;
7. *Nyayadhish* (the chief judge)—Niraji Raoji; and
8. *Panditrao* (minister for religious affairs)—Raghunath Pandit.

The *peshva* had a supervisory rôle over the rest of the ministers. The institutions of civil administration were closely connected with military matters, and most of the principal ministers were

---

13 V G Dighe and S N Qanungo, Administrative and Military System of the Marathas, Chapter XVII, in R C Majumdar and V G Dighe (ed), *The Maratha Supremacy* (The History and Culture of the Indian People, VIII), p. 542.

14 *Cf* G S Sardesai, *New History of the Marathas*, I, p. 282.

15 Above, Chapter II.

16 See *Sabhasad-bakhar*, p. 82; *Chitnis-bakhar*, p. 162. G S Sardesai, Shivaji, Chapter IX, in R C Majumdar, J N Chaudhuri, and S Chaudhuri (ed), *The Mughul Empire* (The History and Culture of the Indian People, VII), p. 268. *Cf* G S Sardesai, *New History of the Marathas*, I, pp. 111-112; S N Sen, *Administrative System of the Marathas*, pp. 40-42.

expected to render military service when needed. This is clear from the *qanun zabta*, prepared in the first year of the coronation era of Shivaji, which lays down that all the ministers, except for the *nyayadhish* and the *panditrao*, were to render military service, in addition to their assigned work in civil administration.[17] But, be it noted, although, besides his *senapati*, Shivaji assigned military duties to five of his ministers, who were heads of various departments of civil administration, he never allowed the *senapati* to interfere in matters of civil administration.[18]

As the present work deals with the rôle of the *senapati* in the history and polity of the Marathas, a brief survey of the military set-up of the Marathas and the place of the *senapati* in it, may profitably be made in this context.

'The Maratha empire was primarily a military organization',[19] and the armed forces formed the basis of the king's might. The king was the supreme commander of the armed forces. Under him served the *senapati*, the commander-in-chief, who was earlier known as the *sarnobat*, from the Persian, *sar-i-naubat*.[20] We can form an idea of the importance of the armed forces and their commander-in-chief from the fact that the *senapati* of the cavalry got a place in the *ashta-pradhana* council, and he occupied the first place to the left of the king, while the *peshva* sat in the first place to the right of the king.[21]

---

17 The *qanun zabta*, mentioned in the *Sabhasad-bakhar*, p. 83, has been published by K N Sane, *Aitihasik Patren yadi Vagaire*, (1930 ed), pp. 57-361. See S N Sen, *Administrative System of the Marathas*, pp. 49-52. See also G S Sardesai, *New History of the Marathas*, I, p. 282. This was partly because some of the ministers were warlike men, who would have preferred military duties to the civil ones. *Cf* V K Rajwade, *Marathyanchya Itihasachi Sadhane*, VIII, pp. 8-10; G S Sardesai, *New History of the Marathas*, I, pp. 282-283.

18 S N Sen, *The Military System of the Marathas*, pp. 7, 11.

19 S N Sen, *The Military System of the Marathas*, p. vii.

20 J N Sarkar, *Shivaji and His Times*, p. 361.

21 M G Ranade, *Rise of the Maratha Power*, pp. 126-127; V G Dighe and S N Qanungo, Administrative and Military System of the Marathas, Chapter XVII, in R C Majumdar and V G Dighe (ed), *The Maratha Supremacy* (The History and Culture of the Indian People, VIII), pp. 541-542.

Sabhasad, who mentions the salary of some Maratha army personnel, makes no reference to the salary of the *senapati*.[22] But from other sources, it is known that the *senapati*, like *sachiv*, *mantri*, *sumant*, *nyayadhish*, and *panditrao*, was paid an annual salary of 10,000 of *huns*, while the *peshva* earned 15,000 of *huns*, and the *amatya*, 12,000 of *huns*.[23] The *qanun zabta*, drawn up in the first year of the coronation era, lays down that the robes of honour offered to the *senapati*, should not be inferior in any way to those of the crown-prince or the *peshva*.[24] From this, it may be inferred that, though his salary was lower than that of the *peshva*, his formal status was deemed equal to that of the crown-prince and the *peshva*.

It is quite clear from the *qanun zabta*, prepared in the first year of the coronation era of Shivaji, that, in the time of Shivaji, the *senapati* was in charge of military affairs,[25] although the *peshva*, Moropant Trimbak Pingle, is known to have taken part in battles.[26] *Peshvas* Balaji Vishvanatha and Bajirao I, under Shahu, also did the same.[27] In this respect, the position of the *peshva* has been compared to that of the *dalvai* in the Vijayanagara empire.[28] However, we have seen above that, besides the *senapati*, not only the *peshva*, but also the *amatya*, *sachiv*, *mantri*, and *sumant*, had to render military service. Up to the time of Shivaji II, the *peshvas* could neither be mistaken for the *senapati* or the *sarnobat*, nor could they set aside the authority of the *senapati* or the *sarnobat*. It has also been pointed

---

22 S N Sen, *The Military System of the Marathas*, p. 9.

23 G S Sardesai, *New History of the Marathas*, I, pp. 223-224, 280.

24 S N Sen, *The Military System of the Marathas*, pp. 9-10.

25 Regarding the duties of the *senapati*, the *Sabhasad-bakhar* (p. 77) says that he 'should maintain the army and make war and expeditions. He should preserve the (newly) acquired territories, render an account of (the spoils), and act according to the orders (of the king). He should make known (to the king) what the men of the army had to say. All military officers should go with him.' See S N Sen, *Shiva Chhatrapati*, p. 106.

26 Above, Chapter II.

27 Above, Chapter IV.

28 S N Sen, *The Military System of the Marathas*, p. 48 and n. It has been pointed out that both the terms, *peshva* and *dalvai*, mean the same, and had similar functions.

out above, that the *senapati*, under any circumstance, was not permitted to interfere in the civil administration.[29] In fact, *sarnobat* and *peshva*, as two distinct administrative functionaries, evolved between the fourteenth and the sixteenth centuries AD under the Bahmani *sultans* of the Deccan, and adopted by Shivaji. The rôles of the *senapati* or *sarnobat* and the *peshva* did not overlap, the former being involved in military affairs, and the latter in civil administration, under normal circumstances. Such was the standing of some generals, like Santaji Ghorpade and Dhanaji Jadhav, that no *peshva* could even think of challenging their rights.[30] It is another matter that these two generals often got embroiled in a bitter power struggle,[31] and this had an adverse effect on the fortunes of the Marathas.[32]

Cavalry and infantry occupied the most important place in Maratha army. The navy was constituted only after the conquest of Konkan by Shivaji, and employed mainly against the Siddis of Janjira.[33] The cavalry comprised of two types of soldiers—*bargir* and *shiladar*.[34] The former were provided horse and weapons by the state, while the latter had to arrange for them on their own.[35] The two classes of horsemen have been compared to the *maula* (regular) and *bhrita* (mercenary) of ancient India.[36] The *bargir*

---

29 It was the strict policy of Shivaji that no military officer or soldier should get involved in revenue collection. See S N Sen, *Administrative System of the Marathas*, p. 45.

30 S N Sen, *The Military System of the Marathas*, p. 48.

31 Such rivalries between Maratha officers were not uncommon, even in the time of Shivaji. The growing rivalry between the *peshva*, Moropant Trimbak Pingle, and the *sachiv*, Annaji Datto, was a cause of grave concern to the Maratha king in his last days. See G S Sardesai, *New History of the Marathas*, I, p. 266.

32 For details of the rivalry between Santaji Ghorpade and Dhanaji Jadhav, see above, Chapter III.

33 G S Sardesai, *New History of the Marathas*, I, pp. 289-291. See also S N Sen, *The Military System of the Marathas*, pp. 152ff.

34 *Shiladar* from the Persian, *silahdar*, 'equipment holder', that is one who arranges for his own horse and weapons. See S N Sen, *The Military System of the Marathas*, p. 5, n. 1.

35 S N Sen, *Administrative System of the Marathas*, p. 143.

36 *Arthasastra* (R Shamashastry's translation), pp. 571-572.

occupied a higher status than the *shiladar*,[37] and, according to Sabhasad, the *shiladar* served under the *bargir*.[38] Initially, Shivaji had to rely very heavily on the *shiladars*, and in the time of his *sarnobat*, Mankoji Dahatonde, about two-thirds of the three thousand strong cavalry of Shivaji comprised of *shiladars*.[39] But according to Sabhasad, in the year 1659, there were only 3,000 *shiladars* in the 10,000 strong Maratha cavalry.[40] This information of Sabhasad is corroborated by Khafi Khan, who tells us that Shivaji had procured about 10,000 or 12,000 Kachchh and Arab horses.[41] The Maratha cavalry was organized thus : 25 *bargirs* under one *havaldar*, five *havaldars* under one *jumladar*, 10 *jumladars* under one *hazari*, and five *hazaris* under one *panchhazari*, with the *sarnobat* or *senapati* as the commander-in-chief of the cavalry.[42] The organization of the *shiladars* was somewhat different, but they, too, were under the same *sarnobat* or *senapati* as the *bargirs*.[43] The organization of the Maratha infantry was thus : five *payaks* or foot soldiers under one *nayak*, five *nayaks* under one *havaldar*, two or three *havaldars* under one *jumladar*, 10 *jumladars* under one *hazari*,

---

37 J N Sarkar, *Shivaji and His Times*, p. 364. But *contra* G S Sardesai (*New History of the Marathas*, I, p. 286), who says that the *shiladar* was higher in status than the *bargir*.

38 *Sabhasad-bakhar*, pp. 28-29. See S N Sen, *Shiva Chhatrapati*, pp. 30-31; S N Sen, *Administrative System of the Marathas*, pp. 143-144; V G Dighe and S N Qanungo, Administrative and Military System of the Marathas, Chapter XVII, in R C Majumdar and V G Dighe (ed), *The Maratha Supremacy* (The History and Culture of the Indian People, VIII), p. 564.

39 S N Sen, *The Military System of the Marathas*, p. 8.

40 *Sabhasad-bakhar*, p. 11.

41 Elliot and Dowson, *History of India, as told by its Own Historians*, VII, p. 287.

42 See the *Sabhasad-bakhar* pp. 28-29. J N Sarkar, *Shivaji and His Times*, pp. 363-364; S N Sen, *Shiva Chhatrapati*, pp. 30-31; S N Sen, *Administrative System of the Marathas*, pp. 143-144.

43 J N Sarkar, *Shivaji and His Times*, p. 364. *Cf* S N Sen, *Shiva Chhatrapati*, pp. 30-31; S N Sen, *Administrative System of the Marathas*, pp. 143-144.

seven *hazaris* under one seven-*hazari*, with the *sarnobat* or *senapati* as the commander-in-chief of the infantry.[44]

The cavalry was paid better than the infantry. A cavalry *jumladar* received an annual salary of 500 of *huns*, as against the 100 of *huns* received by the infantry *jumladar* as his annual salary. A cavalry *hazari* was paid an annual salary of 1,000 of *huns*, as against the 500 of *huns* paid to the infantry *hazari* as his annual salary.[45] Even more glaring is the fact, noticed above, that it was the *sarnobat* or *senapati* of the cavalry, who was given a place in the *ashta-pradhana* council, in preference to the *sarnobat* or *senapati* of the infantry. This gives us an indication of the greater importance attached to the cavalry branch of the armed forces.

Well garrisoned forts formed the backbone of the Maratha defence. The significance of forts had been recognized even in ancient India, and *durga* (fort) was given a place in the seven constituents (*saptanga*) of the state.[46] Lokahitavadi says that Shivaji was famous for his forts.[47] Marathi sources reveal that, by the end of the reign of Shivaji, the Maratha state possessed not less than 240 forts.[48] In addition to the forts captured by him,

---

44 J N Sarkar, *Shivaji and His Times*, p. 364. *Cf* S N Sen, *Administrative System of the Marathas*, p. 143, who, however, differs in that he says that there were nine foot soldiers under a *nayak*; in J C Grant Duff, *History of the Mahrattas*, I, p. 181, and V G Dighe and S N Qanungo, Administrative and Military System of the Marathas, Chapter XVII, in R C Majumdar and V G Dighe (ed), *The Maratha Supremacy* (The History and Culture of the Indian People, VIII), p. 563, the number of foot soldiers under a *nayak* is given as ten. The *Chitnis-bakhar* gives a slightly different account of the organization of the Maratha army. See J N Sarkar, *Shivaji and His Times*, pp. 363n and 364n.

45 J N Sarkar, *Shivaji and His Times*, p. 364.

46 Beniprasad, *Theory of Government in Ancient India*, (2nd ed, Allahabad, 1974), p. 147.

47 Lokahitavadi, *Aitihasika Goshthi*, *vide* S N Sen, *Administrative System of the Marathas*, p. 28.

48 *Sabhasad-bakhar*, pp. 98-101; S N Sen, *Shiva Chhatrapati*, pp. 140-148; S N Sen, *Administrative System of the Marathas*, p. 28; G S Sardesai, *New History of the Marathas*, I, p. 281; V G Dighe and S N Qanungo, Administrative and Military System of the

Shivaji also commissioned the construction of over 110 new forts,[49] beginning, perhaps, with Rajgadh and Pratapgadh. Shivaji is known to have bestowed minute personal care upon the construction of these forts.[50] The Maratha forts were arranged in three distinct lines. The main forts were on the tops of the Sahyadri range; the second line of the forts was on the eastern spurs of the mountain range, and the third line, on the western spurs of the same range. There were also some forts, like Sindhudurg, Vijaydurg, Suvarnadurg, and Kolaba, along the sea coast.[51]

As seen above, Shivaji was vehemently opposed to the allotment of *jaghirs* in *lieu* of salary to government and military officials.[52] Civil and military officers were paid, partly in cash and partly in kind.[53] Grant of *jaghir* in *lieu* of salary implied alienating of government land,[54] which often led to divided loyalties among the subjects—loyalty towards the king and loyalty towards the landholder. No wonder, when his own son-

---

Marathas, Chapter XVII, in R C Majumdar and V G Dighe (ed), *The Maratha Supremacy* (The History and Culture of the Indian People, VIII), p. 566.

49 G S Sardesai, *New History of the Marathas*, I, p. 281.

50 See *Chitragupta-bakhar*, pp. 132-134, *vide* G S Sardesai, *New History of the Marathas*, I, pp. 285-286, and p. 286, n. 10, for the construction of Sindhudurg.

51 G S Sardesai, *New History of the Marathas*, I, p. 284.

52 G S Sardesai, *New History of the Marathas*, I, p. 282; S N Sen, *Administrative System of the Marathas*, p. 45; S N Sen, *The Military System of the Marathas*, p. 11. Shivaji is also known to have 'rigorously confiscated land gifts and inams for government service that had come down from previous regimes'. See G S Sardesai, *New History of the Marathas*, II, p. 56. Although Shivaji did not grant hereditary *jaghir* to his officers, including his generals, he did confer other marks of honour on some of them : the *sarnobats*, Kadtoji Gujar (Prataprao Gujar) and Hansaji Mohite (Hambirrao Mohite), were conferred high sounding titles; deserving officials were granted the right to carry the *aftabgir* and ride a *palki*. S N Sen, *The Military System of the Marathas*, pp. 12-13.

53 S N Sen, *Administrative System of the Marathas*, pp. 147-148.

54 *Cf* G S Sardesai, *New History of the Marathas*, II, p. 56.

in-law, Pilaji Shirke, asked for the grant of the *jaghir* of Dabhol for some valuable services rendered to him, Shivaji wrote him a polite letter, explaining his position thus : 'Our Maratha government does not allow grants of land to any body.'[55] He made some vague promise of conferring a *jaghir* on the son of his daughter and Pilaji Shirke, when he was born.

Interestingly, *Amatya* Ramchandra Nilkanth, elaborating on the evils of the grant of *jaghirs*, writes :

> 'The king is the supreme owner of all lands. To him the Zamindars do not render proper loyalty. Nor do they remain contented with what they possess. They are unjust to the cultivators of the soil. They erect independent fortifications, defy the master, grasp what does not belong to them, commit robberies outside. Once their position is fairly strengthened, they use it as a base for further expansion,.... If a foreign enemy invades a country, these landholders often openly join him, secretly convey to him important information. Thus, they become a fruitful source of weakness to the State. A jagirdar is rarely honest.'[56]

One wonders whether the *amatya* is describing the doings of Shivaji himself,[57] or he is predicting what officers like Santaji Ghorpade and Dhanaji Jadhav were to do during the reign of Rajaram[58] ? Not surprisingly, Shivaji did not permit the building of new fortresses by private individuals,[59] and even pulled down several old private fortifications, lest they pose a threat to his authority.[60]

---

55 See *Shiva-charitra-sahitya*, 3. 438.
56 G S Sardesai, *New History of the Marathas*, I, p. 281.
57 Above, Chapter II.
58 Above, Chapter III.
59 *Sabhasad-bakhar*, pp. 32-33; S N Sen, *Shiva Chhatrapati*, pp. 37-38.
60 G S Sardesai, *New History of the Marathas*, I, p. 283.

The departure from the policy of Shivaji regarding allotment of *jaghir* came about during the reign of Rajaram,[61] when Prahlad Niraji and Ramchandrapant tried to purchase the loyalty and support of the Maratha chiefs by creating *jaghirs* in their favour, mostly in the territories then in possession of the Mughals, or Bijapur or Golkunda; the Maratha chiefs had only to conquer their *jaghir*, before they could enjoy it.[62] Maratha *sardars*, who brought victory to their king, were also awarded *jaghirs*.[63] Partly, the departure from the policy of Shivaji regarding allotment of *jaghir*, during the reign of Rajaram, was also a result of the arrival of the Mughal emperor in the Deccan. Aurangzeb used grants of *jaghirs* as an inducement to lure Maratha chiefs to the Mughal camp.[64] Under such circumstances, it became difficult for the Maratha king to keep his *sardars* from shifting over their allegiance to the Mughal emperor. He had, perforce, to adopt the policy of encouraging the Maratha officials and chiefs to conquer the territories occupied by the Mughals,

---

61 Shambhuji, despite of his other shortcomings, cannot be blamed for reverting to the 'feudal structure'. He was embroiled in financial difficulties, but did not take the easy way out 'by creating fiefs in favour of his military officers'. See S N Sen, *The Military System of the Marathas*, p. 44. However, it may be pointed out here that, on the death of the *peshva*, Moropant Trimbak Pingle, in October 1680, Shambhuji appointed his son, Nilopant, to succeed his father as *peshva*. G S Sardesai, *New History of the Marathas*, I, p. 304. Although the office in question here is that of the *peshva*, and not of the *senapati*, this example shows that offices had started becoming hereditary, as early as the time of Shambhuji.

62 *Cf* R V Nadkarni, *The Rise and Fall of the Maratha Empire*, p. 353, who says, 'Hereditary fiefs were granted to the military leaders as an inducement to undertake the conquest of the Mughal territory.' Very often, the Maratha *sardars* had to resort to force even to collect their revenue dues. See G S Sardesai, *New History of the Marathas*, II, p. 56.

63 S N Sen, *The Military System of the Marathas*, p. 45.

64 The sultanates of Bijapur and Golkunda offered hereditary *jaghirs* in *lieu* of salary to their officers. In the administrative setup of the Mughals, too, the officers were allotted *jaghirs*, in keeping with their *mansab*, although such *jaghirs* were not hereditary. See S N Sen, *The Military System of the Marathas*, pp. 10-11.

which they were to be allowed to keep as their own *jaghirs*. Besides, there was great political turmoil in Maharashtra, right from the capture of Shambhuji in 1689 to the 'home coming' of Shahu in 1707, during which a number of Maratha *sardars* had raised their own forces, raided Mughal territories, carved out *jaghirs* for themselves, realized revenues from them, and consolidated their power. Thus, the Ghorpades firmly entrenched themselves in Karnataka to the south of the river Krishna; the Bhonsles, in Berar and Nagpur; the Nimbalkars, in Baglan; the Dabhades, in western Khandesh and parts of Gujarat.[65]

Shahu lacked the ability to curb these *sardars*. His *peshva*, Balaji Vishvanatha, in an attempt to preserve the authority of the king and avoid a rebellion by the *sardars*, worked out a compromise, and advised his king to acknowledge them as hereditary *jaghirdars*, on the condition that they render military service to the king, as and when required—an advice, which Shahu accepted.[66] The Maratha king was deemed entitled to *sardeshmukhi* and one-fourth of the *chauth*; around ninety percent of the remaining three-fourths of the *chauth*, designated *mokasa*, was granted to the *jaghirdar* as his share.[67] The *jaghirdar* enjoyed almost sovereign authority within his fief, the only check being the appointment of the civil establishment from the headquarters.[68] And gradually, these *jaghirs* became hereditary. The next *peshva*, Bajirao I, himself became the leading feudal lord, and carved out a *jaghir* for himself from the territories conquered by him on the west coast and in

---

65 G S Sardesai, *New History of the Marathas*, II, p. 55.

66 V G Dighe and S N Qanungo, Administrative and Military System of the Marathas, Chapter XVII, in R C Majumdar and V G Dighe (ed), *The Maratha Supremacy* (The History and Culture of the Indian People, VIII), pp. 550-551. The scheme might have been suggested to the *peshva* by the example of Kanhoji Angre, who offered allegiance to the Maratha king, on the condition that he be allowed to retain his fief and the command of the navy. See S N Sen, *The Military System of the Marathas*, p. 46.

67 S N Sen, *The Military System of the Marathas*, p. 46. See also G S Sardesai, *New History of the Marathas*, II, p. 56.

68 R V Nadkarni, *The Rise and Fall of the Maratha Empire*, pp. 353-354.

Hindustan.[69] The policy had mixed results.[70] 'In the long run it proved to be a ready instrument both for the rapid expansion and the equally rapid ruin of the Maratha Empire.'[71] The change brought about by Shivaji's successors ensured that, what they had initially granted to officers for meritorious service and for valour, gradually came to be demanded as a matter of right by the descendants of the grantees, irrespective of their competence.[72]

Shivaji was served by at least five[73] commanders-in-chief (*sarnobat*, later, *senapati*)—Tukoji Chor Maratha (about whom, next to nothing is known),[74] Mankoji Dahatonde (an equally ephemeral figure as his predecessor)[75], Netaji Palkar,[76] Kadtoji Gujar (who was given the title of *Prataprao* on his elevation to the position of *sarnobat*),[77] and Hansaji Mohite (who was given

---

69 V G Dighe and S N Qanungo, Administrative and Military System of the Marathas, Chapter XVII, in R C Majumdar and V G Dighe (ed), *The Maratha Supremacy* (The History and Culture of the Indian People, VIII), p. 551.

70 G S Sardesai, *New History of the Marathas*, I, pp. 353-354. Elsewhere, G S Sardesai observes : 'For the rapid expansion of the Maratha power no other arrangement could have served so well....But there is no doubt the system carried with it the seeds of decay....' See G S Sardesai, *New History of the Marathas*, II, pp. 56-57.

71 G S Sardesai, *New History of the Marathas*, I, p. 354; also, *New History of the Marathas*, II, pp. 56-57.

72 G S Sardesai, *New History of the Marathas*, II, pp. 58-59.

73 Maybe six. V G Dighe and S N Qanungo, Administrative and Military System of the Marathas, Chapter XVII, in R C Majumdar and V G Dighe (ed), *The Maratha Supremacy* (The History and Culture of the Indian People, VIII), p. 538, speak of one Noor Beg, who was appointed by Shivaji as *sarnobat* on the death of Dadaji Konddev in 1647.

74 Sabhasad (*Sabhasad-bakhar*, p. 8, *vide* S N Sen, *Administrative System of the Marathas*, p. 42) mentions Tukoji Chor Maratha as the first *sarnobat*, serving under Shivaji. But the circumstances of his replacement by Mankoji Dahatonde are not known. See also S N Sen, *The Military System of the Marathas*, p. 12.

75 *Sabhasad-bakhar*, p. 9.

76 *Sabhasad-bakhar*, p. 11; *91 Qalmi Bakhar*, pp. 76-77.

77 *Sabhasad-bakhar*, p. 59.

the title of *Hambirrao* on his elevation to the position of *sarnobat*).[78] Besides, there was Yesaji Kank, the *sarnobat* of the infantry,[79] who accompanied Shivaji to Agra, and also to Haidarabad.[80] During the reign of Shambhuji, Hambirrao Mohite continued to serve as *senapati*, right up to his death in a confrontation with Sharza Khan, near Wai, in December 1687. In the time of Rajaram, the command of the army was first put, probably, under Khandoji (or Mahadaji) Nayak Pansambal, and, on his death shortly after his appointment, it was entrusted to such able generals as Santaji Ghorpade and Dhanaji Jadhav.[81]

Shivaji did not believe in 'hereditary genius'.[82] But, gradually, even offices became hereditary, irrespective of the competence of the descendants to hold that office. None of Shivaji's five[83] *sarnobats* was succeeded to that office by any member of his family.[84] However, the office of the *senapati*, too, seems to have become sort of hereditary during the rule of the successors of Shivaji, when even *jaghirs* were conferred on the *senapatis*. After the death of *Senapati* Dhanaji Jadhav in June 1708, Shahu installed his son, Chandrasen Jadhav, as the *senapati*, and when the latter went over to the Nizam-ul-mulk, the position was given to Khanderao Dabhade.[85] Khanderao's

---

78 *Sabhasad-bakhar*, p. 79. It was Hambirrao Mohite, who was the *senapati* at the time of the coronation of Shivaji. See *Chitnis-bakhar*, p. 162.

79 *Sabhasad-bakhar*, p. 11; *91 Qalmi Bakhar*, pp. 76-77.

80 Above, Chapter II.

81 Above, Chapter III.

82 S N Sen, *The Military System of the Marathas*, p. 7. On the death of Tanaji Malasure during the capture of Singhgadh, his brother, Suryaji was appointed to succeed him, not because of his being a brother of Tanaji Malasure, but because of his merit. See S N Sen, *Administrative System of the Marathas*, pp. 44-45; *The Military System of the Marathas*, p. 12; G S Sardesai, *New History of the Marathas*, I, p. 199.

83 That is including Tukoji.

84 Above, Chapter II. See also G S Sardesai, *New History of the Marathas*, II, p. 58; S N Sen, *Administrative System of the Marathas*, p. 44.

85 For a short spell by Santaji Jadhav, the younger brother of Chandrasen Jadhav, and by Man Singh More, as *senapati* between

son was Trimbakrao, who was defeated and killed by Bajirao at Dabhai, in April 1731. Later on, Yashvantrao Dabhade was succeeded on the post of *senapati* by his son, Trimbakrao Dabhade II.[86] Yashvantrao Dabhade was appointed to the post of *senapati*, but, for all practical purposes, the duties of that office came to be discharged by the *peshva* himself.[87] On 15 December 1749, Shahu had to recognize the *peshva* as the head of all civil and military administration,[88] and this marked the end of the significance of the rôle of the *senapati* in Maratha history and polity. The Dabhade chiefs, however, continued to enjoy the *jaghirs* conferred on them from time to time. When Ramchandra Jadhav and Murarrao Ghorpade were offered the position of *senapati* on various occasions, the office had become a mere token of honour.[89]

The Maratha debacle in the battle of Panipat, in 1671, was followed by civil strife between Madhavrao I and Raghoba. Taking advantage of the disturbed political conditions, a number of Maratha chiefs, like Sindhia, Holkar, Gaikvad, and Pavar, affected greater independence in their *jaghirs*, with the result that the central Maratha authority was undermined, so much so, that the *peshva* could not even be sure of the military assistance of these chiefs in times of need.[90] The Maratha state, though it

---

Chandrasen Jadhav and Khanderao Dabhade, see R V Nadkarni, *The Rise and Fall of the Maratha Empire*, p. 166, and G S Sardesai, *New History of the Marathas*, II, pp. 37-38.

86 G S Sardesai, *New History of the Marathas*, II, p. 312.

87 Above, Chapter IV.

88 *Shahu-charitra*, pp. 134-135. See S V Puntambekar, Peshwa Balaji Rao (1740-1761), Chapter VI, in R C Majumdar and V G Dighe (ed), *The Maratha Supremacy* (*The History and Culture of the Indian People*, VIII), pp. 170-200, on p. 181; V G Dighe and S N Qanungo, Administrative and Military System of the Marathas, Chapter XVII, in R C Majumdar and V G Dighe (ed), *The Maratha Supremacy* (The History and Culture of the Indian People, VIII), p. 551. See also G S Sardesai, *New History of the Marathas*, II, p. 273; R V Nadkarni, *The Rise and Fall of the Maratha Empire*, p. 204.

89 S N Sen, *The Military System of the Marathas*, pp. 48-49.

90 V G Dighe and S N Qanungo, Administrative and Military System of the Marathas, Chapter XVII, in R C Majumdar and V G Dighe

covered 'more than half of Indian territory', was converted from an 'organic whole into an inorganic mass'.[91]

Shivaji appealed to the feelings of race and religion in the Maratha people. This, combined with his personal charisma, led the Marathas to submit to his leadership.[92] But the successors of Shivaji lost sight of the high ideals set by him.[93] The monarchical aristocracy established by Shivaji was soon replaced by a 'feudal' despotism. The army being an instrument of the state, its organization reflected the significant change brought about in the structure of the state by the successors of Shivaji. The army under the command of one supreme leader in the time of Shivaji, had changed its character by the time of the *peshvas*, and had devolved into a conglomeration of 'feudal' forces, led by various 'feudal' chiefs, 'who were not always inspired by common ideals or united by common interests',[94] and who were, not unoften, fighting against one another, and this had an adverse effect on the unity of command. The discipline of the army suffered.[95] The result of all this was the decline and fall of the Maratha empire.

(ed), *The Maratha Supremacy* (The History and Culture of the Indian People, VIII), p. 552.

91 M G Ranade, *Miscellaneous Writings*, p. 349.

92 S N Sen, *The Military System of the Marathas*, pp. 17ff.

93 R V Nadkarni, *The Rise and Fall of the Maratha Empire*, p. 357.

94 V G Dighe and S N Qanungo, Administrative and Military System of the Marathas, Chapter XVII, in R C Majumdar and V G Dighe (ed), *The Maratha Supremacy* (The History and Culture of the Indian People, VIII), p. 552; S N Sen, *The Military System of the Marathas*, p. xvi.

95 V G Dighe and S N Qanungo, Administrative and Military System of the Marathas, Chapter XVII, in R C Majumdar and V G Dighe (ed), *The Maratha Supremacy* (The History and Culture of the Indian People, VIII), pp. 567ff; R V Nadkarni, *The Rise and Fall of the Maratha Empire*, pp. 353-355.

Select Bibliography

Acworth, H A. *Ballads of the Marathas*. London, 1894.

Ajnapatra of Ramchandrapant Amatya. (Ed) G H Khare and S R Bhide. Poona, 1960.

Alamgirnama of Mirza Muhammad Kazim. (Ed) Khadim Husain and Abdul Hai. Calcutta, 1865-73.

Ali, Ahmad (ed). *Ma'asir-i-Alamgiri* of Saqi Musta'ad Khan. Calcutta, 1970-73.

Allan, J, T W Haig, and H H Dodwell. *The Cambridge Shorter History of India*. (Reprint) New Delhi, 1979.

Banerjee, A C. Peshwa Madhav Rao I. Chapter VII, in R C Majumdar and V G Dighe (ed), *The Maratha Supremacy* (The History and Culture of the Indian People, VIII), Bombay, 2001, pp. 201-224.

Behere, N K. *The Background of the Maratha Renaissance in the 17th Century*. Bangalore, 1946.

Bendre, V S. *Chhatrapati Sambhaji Maharaj*. Poona, 1960.

Brij Kishore. *Tara Bai and Her Times*. Bombay, 1963.

Burn, R (ed). *The Cambridge History of India*, IV. Cambridge, 1937.

Chaudhuri, J N. 'Aurangzeb (1658-1680)', Chapter VIII, in R C Majumdar, J N Chaudhuri, and S Chaudhuri (ed), *The Mughul Empire* (History and Culture of the Indian People, VII), Bombay, 1984, pp. 220-246.

Chaudhuri, J N. 'Aurangzeb (1681-1707)', Chapter X, in R C Majumdar, J N Chaudhuri, and S Chaudhuri (ed), *The Mughul Empire* (History and Culture of the Indian People, VII), Bombay, 1984, pp. 281-304.

Dalvi, G D. *Maratha Kulacha Itihas : Jadhav Gharanyachi Kaifiyat*, I. Bombay, 1912.

De, J C. Shivaji's Surat Expedition of 1664. *Indian Culture*, IV(4).

De, U N. *Some Aspects of Mediaeval Indian History*. New Delhi, 1971.

Diary and Consultation Books of Fort St George (1681-85). (Ed) A T Pringle, 5 vols. Madras, 1893-95.

Dighe, V G. Rise of the Peshwas—Balaji Vishwanath, Chapter III, in R C Majumdar and V G Dighe (ed), *The Maratha Supremacy* (The History and Culture of the Indian People, VIII), Bombay, 2001, pp. 43-62.

Dighe, V G. Peshwa Baji Rao I (1720-1740), Chapter IV, in R C Majumdar and V G Dighe (ed), *The Maratha Supremacy* (The History and Culture of the Indian People, VIII), Bombay, 2001, pp. 63-103.

Dighe, V G, and S N Qanungo. Administrative and Military System of the Marathas, Chapter XVI, in R C Majumdar and V G Dighe (ed), *The Maratha Supremacy* (The History and Culture of the Indian People, VIII), Bombay, 2001, pp. 535-577.

Duff, J C Grant. *A History of the Maharattas*, 3 vols; vol I. Calcutta, 1912. [The numbering of pages from 176 onwards is problematic in this edition.]

Edwardes, S M, and H L O Garret. *Mughal Rule in India*. Delhi, 1962.

Elliot, H M, and J Dowson (ed). *History of India, as told by its Own Historians*, 8 vols. (Reprint) Allahabad, (year of publication not mentioned).

Faruki, Zahiruddin. *Aurangzeb and His Times*. Delhi, 1972.

Fawcett, C (ed). *English Factories in India, New Series, 1670-1684*. Oxford, 1936-55.

Garret, H L O, and S M Edwardes. *Mughal Rule in India*. Delhi, 1962.

Ghosh, P.K., The Battle of Talikota – 1565, in K.K. Thaplyal and S.N. Misra (ed.) *Select Battles in Indian History,* I, Delhi, 2002, pp. 299-311.

Grewal, J S. *Muslim Rule in India*. Calcutta, 1970.

Jedhe-yanchi Shakavali. (Tr) J N Sarkar, in G S Sardesai (ed), *Shivaji Souvenir*, 1927.

Karvir Chhatrapati Gharanyacha Itihasachi Sadhane. (Ed) M V Gujar, 2 vols. Poona, 1962.

Keene, H G. *The Fall of the Moghul Empire*. (Reprint) Delhi, 1971.

Keluskar, and N S Takakhav. *Life of Shivaji Maharaj*. Manoranjan Press, 1921.

Kennedy, P. *History of the Great Moghuls*. (Reprint) Calcutta, 1968.
Khan, Y H. *Selected Documents of Aurangzeb's Reign, 1659-1706 AD*. Hyderabad, 1958.
Khare, G H. *Persian Sources of Indian History* (tr into Marathi), 3 vols. Pune, 1937.
Kinkaid, C A, and D B Parasnis, *A History of the Maratha People*, 3 vols. OUP, London, 1918-25.
Kinkaied, David. *Shivaji, the Founder of the Maratha Empire*. (Reprint) Delhi, 1984.
Kulkarnee, N H (ed). *Chhatrapati Shivaji : Architect of Freedom*. Delhi, 1975.
Kulkarni, A R. *Maharashtra in the Age of Shivaji*. Poona, 1969.
Kulkarni, G T. *The Mughal-Maratha Relations : Twenty Five Fateful Years (1682-1707)*. Pune, 1983.
Lal, K S. *Studies in Mediaeval Indian History*. Delhi, 1966.
Lane-Poole, Stanley. *Mediaeval India under Mohammadan Rule*. (Reprint) Delhi, 1963.
Lane-Poole, Stanley. *Aurangzeb and the Decay of the Mughul Empire*. Delhi, (year of publication not mentioned).
Ma'asir-i-Alamgiri of Saqi Musta'ad Khan. (Tr) J N Sarkar. Calcutta, 1871.
Mahaley, K L. *Shivaji, the Pragmatist*. Nagpur, 1969.
Maharashtra State Archive, Poona Residency Correspondence. (Ed) G S Sardesai and J N Sarkar, 14 vols. Salsette Chronicle.
Majumdar, R C, J N Chaudhuri, and S Chaudhuri (ed). *The Mughul Empire* (History and Culture of the Indian People, VII). Bombay, 1984.
Majumdar, R C, and V G Dighe (ed). *The Maratha Supremacy* (History and Culture of the Indian People, VIII). Bombay, 2001.
Manucci, Nicholo. *Storia do Mogor : 1653-1708*. (Tr and ed) William Irvine, 4 vols. London, 1907-1908.
Manucci, Nicholo. *Memoirs of the Mogul Court*. (Ed) S M Edwardes, (tr) William Irvine. London, 1957.
Marshall, D N. *Mughals in India, a Bibliographical Survey*. Bombay, 1967.
Marshall, D N, and V B D Taraporewala. *Mughal Bibliography* (Select Persian Sources for the Study of Mughals in India). Bombay, 1962.

Martin, François. *Memoires de François Martin*, tr as *Memories of François Martin*, by J N Sarkar, *Modern Review*, 1924.

Mawjee, P V, and D B Parasnis. *Sanad and Letters*. Bombay, 1913.

Morrison, B M. A History of Shivaji, an 18th Century French Account. *Journal of Indian History*, XLII, 1964, pp. 49-76.

Muntakhab-ul-Lubab-i-Muhammad Shahi of Khafi Khan. (Tr) J Dowson, in H M Elliot and J Dowson (ed), *History of India, as told by its Own Historians*, VII, pp. 207-533. (Reprint) Allahabad, (year of publication not mentioned).

Nadkarni, R V. *The Rise and Fall of the Maratha Empire*. Bombay, 1966.

91 Qalmi Bakhar. (Ed) V S Wakaskar. Baroda, 1930.

Nizami, K A. *Studies in Mediaeval Indian History and Culture*. Allahabad, 1966.

Orme, Robert. *Historical Fragments of the Mogul Empire*. Calcutta, 1905.

Qanungo, S N. Decline and Fall of the Maratha Power (1799-1818), Chapter XV, in R C Majumdar and V G Dighe (ed), *The Maratha Supremacy* (The History and Culture of the Indian People, VIII), Bombay, 2001, pp. 486-520.

Qanungo, S N, and V G Dighe. Administrative and Military System of the Marathas, Chapter XVI, in R C Majumdar and V G Dighe (ed), *The Maratha Supremacy* (The History and Culture of the Indian People, VIII), Bombay, 2001, pp. 535-577.

Paranjape, B G. *English Records on Shivaji (1659-1682)*, 2 vols. Poona, 1931.

Parasnis, D B, and P V Mawjee. *Sanads and Letters*. Bombay, 1913.

Pingulkar, V P. *A History of the Sawantwadi State*. Sawantwadi, 1911.

Puntambekar, S V. Peshwa Balaji Rao (1740-1761), Chapter VI, in R C Majumdar and V G Dighe (ed), *The Maratha Supremacy* (The History and Culture of the Indian People, VIII), Bombay, 2001, pp. 170-200.

Rajaramcharitam. (Ed) V S Bendre. Pune, 1931.

Rajwade, V K. *Marathyanchya Itihasachi Sadhane*, VIII, Kolhapur, 1903; XV, Dhulia, 1912; XVI, Bombay, 1912; XVII, Bombay, 1913.

Ranade, M G. *Rise of the Maratha Power*. Bombay, 1900.

Ranade, M G, Richard Temple, G S Sardesai, *et al. Shivaji and the Rise of the Maharattas*. Calcutta, 1953.

Rawlinson, H G. *Shivaji, the Maratha : His Life and Time*. Oxford, 1915.

Sambhaji Kalina Patra Sar Sangraha. (Ed) S N Joshi. Pune, 1949.

Sane, K N. *Aitihasik Patre yadi Vagaire*. Poona, 1930.

Sardesai, G S. *Marathi Riyasat* (Marathi), 8 vols. Bombay, 1915-25.

Sardesai, G S. *Ugraprakriti Sambhaji*. Bombay, 1935.

Sardesai, G S. *Sthirabuddhi Rajaram*. Bombay, 1936.

Sardesai, G S. *The Main Currents of Maratha History*. Bombay, 1949.

Sardesai, G S. *New History of the Marathas*, 3 vols. New Delhi, 1986.

Sardesai, G S. 'Shivaji', Chapter IX, in R C Majumdar, J N Chaudhuri, and S Chaudhuri (ed), *The Mughul Empire* (History and Culture of the Indian People, VII), pp. 247-280. Bombay, 1984.

Sarkar, J N. *India of Aurangzib*. Calcutta, 1901.

Sarkar, J N. *Studies in Mughal India*. (2nd ed) Calcutta, 1919.

Sarkar, J N. *Anecdotes of Aurangzib* (English tr of *Ahkam-i-Alamgiri*). (2nd ed) Calcutta, 1925.

Sarkar, J N. *Studies in Aurangzib's Reign*. Calcutta, 1933.

Sarkar, J N. *Shivaji and His Times*. (5th ed) Calcutta, 1952.

Sarkar, J N. *History of Aurangzib*, 5 vols. Calcutta, 1912-1925.

Sarkar, J N. *House of Shivaji* (Studies and Documents on Maratha History : Royal Period). New Delhi, 1978.

Sarkar, J N. *Short History of Aurangzib*. (3rd ed) New Delhi, 1979.

Sarkar, J N. *Fall of the Mughal Empire*, 4 vols. (4th ed) Hyderabad, 1988.

Sarkar, J N. The Last Campaign of Shivaji. *Indian Historical Quarterly*, IV(4).

Sarkar, Jagdish Narayan. *The Military Despatches of a Seventeenth Century Indian General*. Calcutta, 1969.

Sarkar, Jagdish Narayan. Mirza Raja Jai Singh and Shivaji. *Journal of Indian History*, XLII, 1964, pp. 251-264.

Sastri, K A N. *A History of South India*. (4th ed) OUP, Madras, 1975.

Sen, S N. *Siva Chhatrapati*, (tr of *Sabhasad Bakhar*, with extracts from Chitnis and *Shiva-digvijaya*), (Extracts and Documents Relating to Maratha History, I). Calcutta, 1920.

Sen, S N. *Administrative System of the Marathas*. (2nd ed) Calcutta, 1925.

Sen, S N. *Military System of the Marathas*. (2nd ed) Bombay, 1958.

Sen, S N. *Foreign Biographies of Shivaji* (Extracts and Documents Relating to Maratha History, II). London, (year of publication not mentioned).

Sen, S N (ed). *The Indian Travels of Thevenot and Careri*. New Delhi, 1949.

Sharma, S R. *Maratha History, Re-examined (1595-1707)*. Bombay, 1944.

Sharma, S R. *The Founding of the Maratha Empire*. (Reprint) Bombay, 1964.

Sharma, S R. *A Bibliography of Mughal India*. Bombay, (year of publication not mentioned).

Sharma, S R. *Religious Policy of Aurangzeb*. Calcutta, (year of publication not mentioned).

Shiva-bharata of Paramananda Kavindra. (Ed with Marathi tr) S M Divekar, 1927.

Shiva-charitra-pradipa. (Ed) D V Apte. Pune, 1925.

Shiva-charitra-sahitya. Various authors, 13 vols. Pune, 1926-65.

Shiva-chhatrapatichen-charitra of Krishna Anant Sabhasad. (Tr) S N Sen. 1925.

Sri Sampradyachi Kagadpatre. (Ed) S S Deo. Dhulia, 1915.

Sri Shiva-shahicha Lekhanalamkara. Joshi and Chandorkar. Poona, 1934.

Srinivasachari, C S. *A History of Gingee and its Rulers* (Annamalai University Historical Series, I). Annamalainagar, 1943.

Srivastava, A L. *The Mughul Empire* (4th ed). Agra, 1964.

Srivastava, Nidhi. *Santaji Ghorpade : Vyaktitva evam Krititva* (unpublished Ph D thesis, University of Lucknow, 2002).

Srivastava, Nidhi. *Jinji Durg ke Patan ki Tithi* (Hindi), in R C Tripathi, Agam Prasad, and Shalini Awasthi (ed), *Triratna—Heritage, Governance and Equity* (Hon'ble Shri T N Chaturvedi *Festschrift*), (Delhi, 2003), IV, pp. 1153-1160.

Srivastava, Nidhi. *Maratha Senapati Santaji Ghorpade : Katipaya Aitihasika Paksha* (Hindi), in S P Shukla, R S Bisht, M P Joshi, and Prashant Srivastava (ed), *History and Heritage* (in Honour of Professor Kiran Kumar Thaplyal), (Delhi, 2007), II, pp. 407-410.

Taraporewala, V B D, and D N Marshall. *Mughal Bibliography* (Select Persian Sources for the Study of Mughals in India). Bombay, 1962.

Tarikh-i-Dilkasha of Bhimsen Burhanpuri. (Tr) J N Sarkar. Bombay, 1972.

Tarikh-i-Firishta of Muhammad Qasim Firishta. (Tr) John Briggs. London, 1827-29.

Tripathi, R P. *Rise and Fall of the Mughal Empire*. Allahabad, 1956.

Waring, E S. *A History of the Mahrattas*. London. 1810.

Index